Adriana Duțescu

# Financial Accounting

An IFRS Perspective in Romania

Adriana Duțescu
Bucharest University of Economic
Studies
Bucharest, Romania

ISBN 978-3-030-29487-8    ISBN 978-3-030-29485-4  (eBook)
https://doi.org/10.1007/978-3-030-29485-4

© The Editor(s) (if applicable) and The Author(s), under exclusive license to Springer Nature Switzerland AG 2019
This work is subject to copyright. All rights are solely and exclusively licensed by the Publisher, whether the whole or part of the material is concerned, specifically the rights of translation, reprinting, reuse of illustrations, recitation, broadcasting, reproduction on microfilms or in any other physical way, and transmission or information storage and retrieval, electronic adaptation, computer software, or by similar or dissimilar methodology now known or hereafter developed.
The use of general descriptive names, registered names, trademarks, service marks, etc. in this publication does not imply, even in the absence of a specific statement, that such names are exempt from the relevant protective laws and regulations and therefore free for general use.
The publisher, the authors and the editors are safe to assume that the advice and information in this book are believed to be true and accurate at the date of publication. Neither the publisher nor the authors or the editors give a warranty, expressed or implied, with respect to the material contained herein or for any errors or omissions that may have been made. The publisher remains neutral with regard to jurisdictional claims in published maps and institutional affiliations.

This Palgrave Macmillan imprint is published by the registered company Springer Nature Switzerland AG
The registered company address is: Gewerbestrasse 11, 6330 Cham, Switzerland

# FOREWORD

I have been asked to provide a short introduction to "Financial Accounting-an IFRS perspective in Romania", coordinated by Professor Adriana Duțescu, the product of an enthusiastic team of academics from Romania.

I would like to stress that, in my opinion, this kind of academic endeavour is important because it offers a different perspective on financial reporting, in which material cultural differences are explained and exemplified, in a clear and concise manner. Throughout cultural diversity and specific national standards convergence efforts we shall better understand the complexity and potential of IFRS implementation.

As it has been stressed on several occasions, accounting should be the most straightforward of topics for policymakers to deal with. Accounting should keep capitalism honest, as Sir David Tweedie, my predecessor as Chairman of IASB used to say, and this expectation continues to put pressure on accounting standards and on their way of implementation.

There is criticism in terms of ambiguity and lack of precision of accounting information but one has to be aware that this is the "nature of the beast". Accounting is not an exact science; still, measurement techniques should aim to portray economic reality as closely as possible.

I am deeply convinced that IFRS Standards are an essential ingredient of trust in our market economy. Romania, an EU Member State since 2007, has changed its specific regulatory reporting framework in order to accommodate the implementation of IFRSs.

The advantages of increasing comparability and transparency and reducing the cost of capital are obvious. This is especially the case for emerging countries, despite the high implementation costs. In this context, I salute the effort of Romanian academics, which have highlighted, in an effective pedagogical manner, the major outcomes of IFRS implementation in Romania, offering examples, proposing solutions and allowing a broad field of debate for the ongoing controversies in the field.

I would like to invite you to read this book and provide your feedback on the specific areas of interest to the authors.

Enjoy the lecture!

London, UK

Hans Hoogervorst
Chairman IASB

# Preface

We, the authors, strongly believe that the quality of thinking provides an important competitive advantage in todays' data-driven, global environment. We are aware that not only the quantity but also the quality of knowledge and critical thinking make the difference. This book is dedicated to students enrolled in Economics and Business Programs, and to junior accountants in the beginning of their carrier. Other business professionals or individuals, seeking to improve their knowledge and expertise, might find this book useful and relevant. The value-added of the book is offered by the accounting knowledge reinterpretation, blended with best practices at global and local (national) level. All authors are Romanians, with solid academic background and some with international expertise. We choose to provide some examples and cases about Romania and the way it struggles with the accounting framework and techniques. One might consider this an extra bonus to readers, because Romania is an emerging market in Southeastern Europe, with an important growth potential and a good appetite for its business practices' harmonisation.

The current version of this book is based on the first Edition of *Financial Accounting*,[1] by Adriana Duțescu and Lavinia Olimid. Although we used the same strategy of combining the fundamentals of accounting knowledge with business cases and current challenges brought by Accounting Standards and Regulations, this new version is

[1] Duțescu. A, Olimid L, *Financial Accounting*, CECCAR Publishing House, 2004.

more complex and meaningful. Each chapter is developing principles, concepts, techniques and practical tools that accounting is using to support business decisions. The reader will find a comprehensive theoretical framework, that is enhanced by practical examples, solved exercises, chapter summary issues, quizzes and complex cases, in each of the eleven chapters of the textbook. Another important characteristic is that we prefer to use the International Financial Reporting Standards (IFRS) and their specific Conceptual Framework, as the "benchmark approach" but we also dedicate an important effort to highlight some particularities that the Romanian regulation and practice are providing. In our opinion this is an important endeavour, that demonstrates that there are still discrepancies and cultural challenges, despite the globalisation efforts.

Chapter 1 is introducing the business environment and the general impact of accounting standards and regulations on economic entities.

Chapter 2 is developing the accounting framework, based on IFRSs, the importance of the financial information to stakeholders and important definitions of fundamental concepts.

Chapter 3 is providing details on financial statements and their content, use, particularities and connections.

Chapter 4 is highlighting the accounting process and the transaction analysis flow, introducing the "T" account, the General Journal, the Ledger and the Trial Balance, as prerequisites of financial statements.

Chapter 5 is providing an integrated accounting approach on inventories, providing extensive examples and cases on valuation and measurement, business inventory cycle and special cases and procedures.

Chapter 6 is dedicated to non-current assets and their measurement, valuation, depreciation and amortisation, impairment, special cases and procedures.

Chapter 7 is on liabilities, receivables and other related items, highlighting best practices on trade payables and receivables, employees benefits and other related issues, Value-Added-Tax and other special issues.

Chapter 8 is focusing on equity and different events enabling the dynamics of different specific equity items.

Chapter 9 is dedicated to financial instruments and their complexity, importance, impact and challenge.

Chapter 10 is providing a summary of best practices of closing procedures, their impact on financial statements and fundamentals of financial analysis.

Chapter 11 is based on fundamentals of taxation and the connections and convergences with accounting.

We assume the limitations of the textbook and are grateful for comments and inputs from colleagues, students and other readers.

We would like to thank to the editors, for allowing us to make our endeavour public and their effective guiding throughout the entire process of publishing. The last but not the least we would like to thank your families for their ongoing support and endless patience.

Bucharest, Romania                                            Adriana Duțescu

# Contents

1 **Introduction** 1
Adriana Duțescu and Răzvan Hoinaru
1.1 *About Accounting: A Brief History* 1
1.2 *Business Entities* 3
1.3 *Availability of Accounting Information* 5
1.4 *Financial Accounting and Managerial Accounting* 6
1.5 *The Regulation of Accounting in Romania* 7
1.6 *The Relationship Between Accounting and Taxation* 7
1.7 *Conclusions* 8

2 **The Conceptual Framework** 11
Adriana Duțescu, Oana Stănilă, and Răzvan Hoinaru
2.1 *Introduction* 11
2.2 *Users of Financial Information* 13
2.3 *The Objective of Financial Statements* 15
2.4 *The Qualitative Characteristics of Financial Information* 16
2.5 *The Elements of Financial Statements* 19
2.6 *Conclusions* 25
*Reference* 28

## 3 The Financial Statements 29
Adriana Duțescu, Oana Stănilă, and Răzvan Hoinaru
3.1 Introduction 29
3.2 The Statement of the Financial Position (the Balance Sheet) 30
3.3 The Profit and Loss Account and Other Comprehensive Income (the Income Statement) 41
3.4 The Statement of Cash Flow 47
3.5 The Statement of Changes in Equity vs The Statement of Retained Earnings 52
3.6 Transparency in Financial Statements 54
3.7 Conclusions 56
Reference 62

## 4 Accounting Process and Transaction Analysis 63
Adriana Duțescu, Oana Stănilă, and Răzvan Hoinaru
4.1 Introduction 63
4.2 The Accounting Equation 64
4.3 Double Entry and the "T" Account 67
4.4 The Steps of the Transaction Analysis 72
4.5 The Ledger and the Trial Balance 78
4.6 The Balance Sheet and the Profit and Loss Account 81
4.7 Conclusions 86

## 5 Inventories 93
Elena Nechita and Adriana Duțescu
5.1 Definition 93
5.2 Valuation and Measurement 94
    5.2.1 Initial Valuation (Measurement) of Inventories 94
    5.2.2 Assigning Costs to Inventories 99
    5.2.3 Valuation of Inventories in the Balance Sheet 108
5.3 Acquisition, Production and Sale of Inventories 110
    5.3.1 Transactions Involving Purchased Inventories 111
    5.3.2 Transactions Involving Manufactured Goods 113
    5.3.3 Perpetual and Periodic Inventory 117
5.4 Conclusions 121

| | | | |
|---|---|---|---|
| 6 | **Non-current Assets** | | 131 |
| | Elena Nechita and Adriana Duțescu | | |
| | 6.1 | Introduction | 131 |
| | 6.2 | Tangible Non-current Assets | 132 |
| | 6.3 | Intangible Non-current Assets | 133 |
| | | 6.3.1 Definitions | 133 |
| | | 6.3.2 Recognition | 136 |
| | 6.4 | The Recognition and Valuation of Tangible and Intangible Non-current Assets | 140 |
| | | 6.4.1 Initial Recognition and Valuation | 140 |
| | | 6.4.2 Subsequent Expenditure | 144 |
| | | 6.4.3 Measurement at the Balance Sheet Date | 145 |
| | | 6.4.4 Measurement at Disposal, Exchange or Sale | 147 |
| | 6.5 | Acquired and Produced Non-current Assets | 147 |
| | | 6.5.1 Purchase of Non-current Assets | 147 |
| | | 6.5.2 Production of Non-current Assets | 148 |
| | 6.6 | Depreciation, Amortisation and Depletion of Tangible and Intangible Non-current Assets | 150 |
| | | 6.6.1 Depreciation of Tangible Assets | 151 |
| | | 6.6.2 Amortisation of Intangible Assets and Depletion | 161 |
| | 6.7 | Revaluation of Non-current Assets | 162 |
| | 6.8 | Impairment of Non-current Assets | 167 |
| | 6.9 | Sale/Disposal and Exchange of Assets | 168 |
| | 6.10 | Other Special Cases Related to Non-current Assets: IAS 20, IAS 40, IAS 36 | 170 |
| | | 6.10.1 Assets Obtained on a Grant (IAS 20 Government Grants) | 170 |
| | | 6.10.2 Investment Property (IAS 40) | 174 |
| | 6.11 | Conclusions | 178 |
| 7 | **Liabilities, Receivables and Other Related Items** | | 189 |
| | Adriana Duțescu and Lavinia Olimid | | |
| | 7.1 | Introduction | 189 |
| | 7.2 | Classification of Liabilities and Receivables | 190 |
| | 7.3 | Measurement and Valuation | 191 |
| | 7.4 | Current Liabilities and Receivables | 192 |

|  |  | 7.4.1 | Trade Liabilities and Receivables | 193 |
|---|---|---|---|---|
|  |  | 7.4.2 | Employees Benefits and Other Related Issues | 198 |
|  |  | 7.4.3 | Value Added Tax (VAT) | 201 |
|  |  | 7.4.4 | Other Current Liabilities and Receivables | 203 |
|  | 7.5 | Non-current Liabilities |  | 203 |
|  | 7.6 | Leasing |  | 205 |
|  | 7.7 | Provisions |  | 207 |
|  | 7.8 | Conclusions |  | 213 |

## 8 Equity 221
Adriana Duțescu

| 8.1 | Introduction | 221 |
|---|---|---|
| 8.2 | Share Capital | 222 |
|  | 8.2.1 Contribution to Capital | 223 |
|  | 8.2.2 Increase and Decrease of Capital | 225 |
| 8.3 | Legal Reserve and Other Reserves | 228 |
| 8.4 | Net Profit or Loss for the Year and Retained Earnings | 231 |
| 8.5 | Revaluation Reserve | 233 |
| 8.6 | Conclusions | 235 |

## 9 Financial Instruments 241
Adriana Duțescu

| 9.1 | Importance and Scope | 241 |
|---|---|---|
| 9.2 | Definitions | 242 |
| 9.3 | Classification of Financial Instruments | 246 |
| 9.4 | Recognition and Valuation | 246 |
| 9.5 | Impairment of Financial Assets | 251 |
| 9.6 | Hedge Accounting | 253 |
| 9.7 | Conclusions | 255 |
| References |  | 259 |

## 10 Closing Procedures, Financial Statements and Financial Analysis 261
Mădălina Dumitru and Adriana Duțescu

| 10.1 | Closing Procedures | 261 |
|---|---|---|
| 10.2 | Adjustments and Estimates | 263 |
|  | 10.2.1 Inventories Adjustments | 264 |

|  |  | 10.2.2 | Accruals and Prepayments | 265 |
|---|---|---|---|---|
|  |  | 10.2.3 | Bad Debts and Allowance for Receivables/ Debtors | 267 |
|  |  | 10.2.4 | Provisions | 268 |
|  |  | 10.2.5 | Exchange Differences | 269 |
|  | 10.3 | The Final Statements and Financial Analysis |  | 272 |
|  |  | 10.3.1 | Example of Ratio Analysis | 273 |
|  | 10.4 | Conclusions |  | 283 |
| 11 | **Fundamentals of Taxation** |  |  | 295 |
|  | Mirela Păunescu and Adriana Duțescu |  |  |  |
|  | 11.1 | Introduction |  | 295 |
|  | 11.2 | The Importance of Taxes for the Businesses |  | 296 |
|  | 11.3 | The Function and Purpose of Taxation |  | 297 |
|  | 11.4 | Categories of Taxes |  | 302 |
|  | 11.5 | Taxes in Romania |  | 304 |
|  | 11.6 | The Interaction of the Romanian Tax System with That of Other Tax Jurisdictions |  | 306 |
|  |  | 11.6.1 | The European Union Jurisdiction | 306 |
|  |  | 11.6.2 | Other Countries | 307 |
|  | 11.7 | Tax Avoidance and Tax Evasion |  | 307 |
|  | 11.8 | The Relationship Between Accounting and Taxation |  | 311 |
|  | 11.9 | Conclusions |  | 316 |
| **Appendix** |  |  |  | 321 |
| **Bibliography** |  |  |  | 337 |
| **Index** |  |  |  | 339 |

# List of Tables

| | | |
|---|---|---|
| Table 1.1 | Financial accounting vs. Managerial accounting | 6 |
| Table 2.1 | Different terms for the same concept | 13 |
| Table 3.1 | Links between financial statements | 31 |
| Table 3.2 | The Statement of the Financial Position as at December 31st, 201X (in lei) ABC S.A. | 33 |
| Table 3.3 | Example of Profit and Loss Account "by function" ("by destination") ABC S.A. Income Statement for the year ended December 31, 201X (in lei) | 43 |
| Table 3.4 | Example of Profit and Loss Account "by nature" ABC S.A. Income Statement for the year ended December 31, 201X (in lei) | 44 |
| Table 3.5 | Example of Cash Flow Statement (direct method) ABC S.A. Statement of Cash Flows for the year ended December 31, 201X (in lei) | 49 |
| Table 3.6 | Example of Cash Flow Statement (indirect method) ABC S.A. Statement of Cash Flows for the year ended December 31, 201X | 50 |
| Table 3.7 | Statement of Changes in Equity ABC S.A. for the year ended December 31, 20X1 | 54 |
| Table 3.8 | Relationships among financial statements | 55 |
| Table 4.1 | The "T" account | 68 |
| Table 4.2 | The balance-column account | 68 |
| Table 4.3 | Rules of accounts' functioning | 70 |
| Table 4.4 | Summary of accounts functioning | 71 |
| Table 4.5 | The Romanian format of the General Journal | 73 |

# LIST OF TABLES

| Table | Description | Page |
|---|---|---|
| Table 4.6 | Trial Balances format—one set of columns | 80 |
| Table 4.7 | Trial Balances format—three sets of columns | 81 |
| Table 4.8 | Trial Balances format—four sets of columns | 82 |
| Table 5.1 | Production of inventories—comparison Romanian vs. IFRS approach | 97 |
| Table 7.1 | Aging structure of trade receivables | 196 |
| Table 7.2 | Payroll extract—May 20X8 | 200 |
| Table 7.3 | Long-term bond | 205 |
| Table 7.4 | Financial leasing contract | 207 |
| Table 7.5 | Journal entries of the lessee, in a financial leasing contract | 208 |
| Table 7.6 | Journal entries for the lessor, in a financial leasing contract | 209 |
| Table 9.1 | Financial instruments—examples | 243 |
| Table 9.2 | Loan amortisation table | 251 |
| Table 10.1 | Anomalies established | 264 |
| Table 10.2 | Extract from the Financial Statements | 266 |
| Table 10.3 | Extract from the Trial Balance | 267 |
| Table 10.4 | Extract from the Statement of Financial Position | 268 |
| Table 10.5 | Extract from the Financial Statements | 268 |
| Table 10.6 | Extract from the Financial Statements | 269 |
| Table 10.7 | Extract from the Financial Statements | 271 |
| Table 10.8 | Extract from the Financial Statements | 272 |
| Table 10.9 | Extract from the Financial Statements | 272 |
| Table 10.10 | Income Statement for the year which ended on December 31st, 20X2 Peter (Television) plc | 274 |
| Table 10.11 | Statement of the Financial Position as of December 31st, 20X2 | 275 |
| Table 10.12 | Notes to the Financial Statements: Reconciliation of movements in equity | 276 |
| Table 10.13 | Workings for liquidity and working capital ratios | 277 |
| Table 10.14 | Workings for gearing (leverage) ratios | 279 |
| Table 10.15 | Workings for profitability ratios | 280 |
| Table 10.16 | Workings for efficiency (activity) ratios | 281 |
| Table 10.17 | Workings for market (investor) ratios | 282 |
| Table 11.1 | Main taxes in Romania | 304 |
| Table 11.2 | Example 1-assumption 1 | 309 |
| Table 11.3 | Example 1-assumption 2 | 310 |
| Table 11.4 | Example 1-comparison | 310 |
| Table 11.5 | Example 2 | 312 |
| Table 11.6 | Example 4 | 314 |

CHAPTER 1

# Introduction

### Adriana Duțescu and Răzvan Hoinaru

*Learning objectives:*

- *Understanding the importance of accounting in supporting management decisions*
- *Understanding the differences between financial and managerial accounting*
- *Understanding the connections between accounting and taxation*

## 1.1 ABOUT ACCOUNTING: A BRIEF HISTORY

Accounting and financial reporting are parts of the social sciences, meaning that they are socially constructed. Numbers may well look neutral, while accounts are structured in a rigid, but consistent in form; in fact, the reality might be a little different. There are many schools of thought in accounting that cast numbers in various lights. The best known ones are: positive accounting, Marxist accounting, Foucauldian, the critical school of accounting thought, etc.

On the other hand, the Mesopotamians, the Chinese, the Egyptians, the Venetians, and others had different accounting systems over time. The very basis of what we use nowadays dates back to 1494, when Luca Pacioli established the Golden Rules of Accounting (Assets = Equity + Liabilities). Later on, historians discovered a correlation in the Medici family wealth and proper use of accounting. However, when the golden rule was effectively out-smarted, the misuse of accounting technique revealed not only bad numbers, but also generated a decrease in wealth. This happened due to the capacity of accounting to better inform and its influence on decision-making process and end results.

Next, the mid-sixteenth century, particularly in Holland and the UK, came with a culture of accountability and a separation of different types of accounting. Factory owners and managers like Josiah Wedgwood had a deeper understanding of accounting than the bookkeepers themselves, who had very limited approaches to finance and production. It was during this time when a much clearer concept of a company's current assets was separated from an owner's equity, that a clearer concept of dividends and money effectively appeared. Shareholders were in a way, external to the company, despite having ownership of the company.

During the nineteenth century, professional guilds of accounting appeared and accounting started to be heavily regulated, not only by the professional associations, but also by the state (for example, Company Law in the UK). Nowadays, accounting is regulated by professional associations, states, supra-statist structures (i.e. the European Union [EU]), and international self-regulators like the International Accounting Standards Board (IASB), the Financial Accounting Standards Board (FASB) and Financial Accounting Foundation (FAF).

Various Parliaments and self-regulators around the world have been creating different sets of rules and new accounts, due to the economic needs of a society. Therefore, accounting is an economic technical discipline, but touches also on politics. Just ask yourself, 'Why does the USA have its own particular set of accounting practices named the "US Generally Accepted Accounting Principles (US GAAP)", while the EU uses the "International Financial Reporting Standards" (IFRS) as another set of standards?' Accordingly, accounting and financial reporting are a mix of economics, local culture and politics. This leads to two different types of financial reporting: "principles based", where guidelines are provided, and judgement is permitted during the preparation of the accounts, and "rules based", where clear guidelines and instructions are established.

Other main differences between accounting systems are due to the beneficiary: managers, creditors or investors. These users have different needs for data and information. In such a way, accounting systems or financial reporting systems are more conservative or leave more space for adjustments. The "productive" type of accounting focuses more on a historical cost accounting and Balance Sheet approach, while the "financialised" accounting is more centred on market valuations, modelling, forecasts and fair value accounting.

**Accounting** is an *information and measurement system that identifies, records and communicates relevant information about the activities of an organisation.*

The primary objective of accounting is to provide useful information for effective decisions, such as assessing opportunities, products, investments, social, and community responsibilities. Another important objective is related to stewardship, meaning that accounting reports what managers (stewards) have used/shall use, and the resources entrusted to them by the owners.

To achieve its objectives, accounting includes activities such as: identifying, measuring, reporting, and analysing business events and transactions (i.e. exchanges between entities). Accounting also involves interpreting information and designing information systems to provide useful reports that monitor and control an organisation's activities. The accounting department designs a system of internal controls for the organisation's use, in order to promote efficiency, and prevent the unauthorised use of the company's resources.

Accounting provides information only about transactions and events that can be expressed in money (i.e. currency units). The consequence is that important information, such as the capabilities of the management team or the imminence of a strike, although essential, cannot be translated into accounting language. Despite its limits, accounting offers information to interested parties about an organisation that is unique.

## 1.2 Business Entities

A very broad classification of organisations distinguishes them as "for profit" and "not-for-profit". In the United States, two-thirds of the active workforce is involved in "for-profit" or business enterprises. Business enterprises may be: **sole proprietorships** (sole trader), **partnerships** or **companies (corporations)**.

**A sole proprietorship** is an unincorporated business owned by one person who is often the manager as well. This small-sized business is not legally separated from its owner, and its duration expires when the owner either decides to terminate it or dies.

**A partnership** involves several people jointly owning and running a business. Some of those entities are large in size, i.e. international accounting firms, such as PricewaterhouseCoopers (PwC), Ernst & Young (EY), KPMG, Deloitte Touche Tohmatsu etc. A partnership is not legally separate from its owners, and each partner is responsible for the debts of the business (i.e. with unlimited liability). A partnership's life expires by choice or withdrawal of partners. A partner's shares cannot be sold without the agreement of the other partners. When this happens, a new partnership is formed. In the Anglo-Saxon world, partnerships were created to allow the provision of professional services by lawyers, doctors, architects, and accountants. In Romania, the best equivalent for partnerships is "societate civilă"/"societate în nume colectiv", which is mainly used by lawyers.

**A company** (also called a 'corporation') can emerge with the contribution of many individuals, each bringing in a fraction of the capital needed to operate the business, shares of capital are usually bought and sold frequently. These contributors are called shareholders, stockholders or owners. Although the shareholders own the company, it is often the case that they do not participate in daily management. The General Shareholders' Meeting (GSM) is generally called once a year, after the financial year has ended. It may approve or reject the financial statements prepared by management, extend or withdraw the mandate of managers and auditors, and debate other issues concerning the company's activity.

With very few exceptions, most companies are formed as **limited liability entities**, that is, the liability of the shareholders for the obligations assumed by the company is limited to the amount invested into the business. Creditors can claim the assets of the Company but cannot claim the personal assets of the shareholders. As opposed to a proprietorship or a partnership, a company's life is indefinite.

Companies may be **private** or **public**. A **private company** has few top members, most of which are directors. Generally, this is a company, where shares are not freely transferable. A shareholder wishing to sell his shares can do this only with the agreement of the other shareholders. The Romanian equivalent is the limited liability company (**'societate cu răspundere limitată [S.R.L.]'**).

A **public company** is usually bigger than a private company, and its shares are freely transferable. Most public companies are listed on the Stock Exchange. In the United Kingdom, the words 'public limited company' (PLC) are stated at the end of a company's name. In most European countries, 'public' is equivalent with 'owned by the state', which is not the case in the Anglo-Saxon world, whereby 'public' means 'open to everyone', and shares of public companies may be bought by individuals or companies, including state-owned companies. The Romanian equivalent of a public company is the share company ('**societate pe acţiuni [S.A.]**').

Romanian Company Law no. 31/1990 includes other less common types of companies: the unlimited company ('**societate în nume colectiv**') and two others: '**societate în comandită simplă**' and '**societate în comandită pe acţiuni**'.[1] The unlimited company is a legal entity where owners have unlimited responsibility for the company's obligations. The two other companies combine attributes of unlimited and limited companies. Members in charge of management have unlimited responsibility for the company's obligations, whereas other members' obligations are limited to the amount of capital contributed. The shares of the latter are not freely transferable in 'societatea în comandită simplă', but they can be exchanged without restrictions in 'societatea în comandită pe acţiuni'.

## 1.3 Availability of Accounting Information

In the Anglo-Saxon world the financial statements of sole traders and partnerships are completely private, and these entities are not obliged to publicly disclose their financial information to those other than the traders or partners concerned, unless they choose otherwise (i.e. to disclose them to a banker for the approval of loans). On the other hand in the same environment the financial statements of all companies (both private and public) should be published. There are national databases that contain the annual reports and financial information related to public companies in the specific jurisdiction (in Romanian: "de interes public"), allowing free access to all parties interested.

Romanian Company Law requires public and private companies to disclose their audited and approved financial statements. Financial statements are approved by the General Shareholders' Meeting, and after their approval, financial statements along with directors', auditors' and General Meeting reports should be filed with the tax authority. The deadlines are between 120 and 150 days after the financial year has

---

[1] These companies are not present in Anglo-Saxon company law, but can be found in French and German Company Law. They may be translated as "limited partnership" and "limited partnership by shares", although in Anglo-Saxon law, the word "partnership" is limited to entities providing professional services.

expired, depending on an enterprise's size, and its legal form. The public and listed company's annual reports are available in Romania for free, on the Bucharest Stock Exchange's website or on the company's specific websites. Also, the Ministry of Finance of Romania's website provides a minimum set of financial information for all legal entities within the national jurisdiction.

## 1.4 Financial Accounting and Managerial Accounting

**Financial accounting** provides information mainly to decision makers not involved in the day-to-day operations of an enterprise. Financial accounting is concerned with the production of general financial statements for users, such as investors, lenders, government agencies, employees, suppliers, customers, and the general public. Financial statements should fairly present (give a true and fair view of) an enterprise's financial position, performance, and cash flows for the past year. A complete set of financial statements includes: the Balance Sheet (the Statement of the Financial Position), the Profit and Loss Account (Income Statement), the Statement of Changes in Equity, the Cash-Flow Statement, and accounting policies and explanatory notes. The responsibility for issuing the financial statements belongs to management.

**Managerial accounting** is an integral part of management activity and provides information that is used by management to formulate strategies, to plan, coordinate and control the activity, make decisions,

Table 1.1 Financial accounting vs. Managerial accounting

| Financial accounting | Managerial accounting |
|---|---|
| • regulated; | • not regulated; |
| • mainly concerned with past performance; | • mainly concerned with predictions, includes future expectations of the management team; |
| • historical financial statements (past events) are disclosed year-end | • a budget system may be based on historical information, but also on predictions; |
| • prudence is enforced: provides for all potential losses, but records revenues only when they are earned | • relevance is enforced: revaluations, changes of depreciation rates (i.e. flexibility in working with historical records) |

*Source* The authors

optimise the use of resources, and safeguard assets. For example, by reporting variances from planned costs, managerial accounting enables managers to control costs, and take corrective action.

Table 1.1 shows the main differences between financial and managerial accounting:

## 1.5   The Regulation of Accounting in Romania

The accounting regulator in Romania is the Ministry of Finance. In the rule-setting process, professional accounting bodies have an advisory role, but their influence is limited. Two main laws underlie the regulation of accounting in Romania:

- Company Law no. 31/1990 as subsequently amended, and
- Accounting Law no. 82/1991 as subsequently amended.

The main regulation at present in financial reporting and accounting is the Ministry of Finance Order (OMFP) no. 1.802/2014, which is amended by OMFP no. 166/2017.

Companies that control other companies (subsidiaries) are required to prepare consolidated group accounts, if they meet a certain size criteria or if the group includes one or more listed companies.

The national securities regulator, the Authority of Financial Supervision (in Romanian: "Autoritatea de Supraveghere Financiară") requires businesses with publicly-traded securities to periodically disclose the annual report, along with an audit review report, and on a continuous basis, information related to its operations, and material changes of its financial positions and performances.

## 1.6   The Relationship Between Accounting and Taxation

Financial reporting and tax reporting fulfil different information needs. The tax policy of a government has declared aims and objectives, such as the growth of certain industries and areas or of heavy taxation for others. The following example illustrates the need for separate accounting and tax reporting.

Suppose a government aims at increasing capital expenditure in the economy. One way of securing this objective is to shorten the useful lives of non-current assets and, consequently their depreciation expense, allowed for the calculation of income tax, to change (increased). From an accounting standpoint, the useful life of a non-current asset is plainly the period of time over which the asset is expected to be used by the business. The consequence of the tax allowance on useful life is the deduction of a higher depreciation amount from the taxable profit, that is, a lower taxable profit, less tax paid, and more cash in the business.

On the other hand, to use a lower useful life for accounting purposes is equivalent to misleading users of financial statements with respect to the company's non-current assets. In Romania, the tax code is based on the Law nr. 227/2015, updated by the Government Decree no. 25/2017. In this tax code, one can find rules related to direct and indirect taxes, the persons liable for these taxes, and exemptions from those taxes. More information on taxation is provided in Chapter 11 of the book.

## 1.7 Conclusions

The following table is intended to conclude the chapter.

**Chapter summary questions:**

| | |
|---|---|
| What is the purpose of accounting? | The purpose of accounting is to provide useful and timely information to different stakeholders about the true and fair view of the economic entity. |
| What types of economic organisations do you know about? | The Anglo-Saxon approach classifies economic entities into:<br>• Sole proprietorship<br>• Partnership<br>• Limited liability<br>• Corporation.<br>The Romanian approach classifies economic entities into:<br>• Unlimited entities<br>• Limited liability entities<br>• Share companies. |

| How does financial accounting differ from managerial accounting? | Financial accounting is about the past performance of the entity and is dedicated to all stakeholders; it is based on principles, standards, rules. Managerial accounting is about "ground" information that is related to cost, product/activity performances, and predicts the future through budgets and other performance management tools. The main (and probably the only) user is the management. |

## Quizzes (select one answer)

1. Accounting is about:
   a. The business environment and opportunities
   b. Managers and employees
   c. Customers and suppliers
   d. The business and its performances
2. A corporation is an entity that:
   a. Has only one owner
   b. Has unlimited liabilities
   c. Has shareholders who are not liable to business liabilities
   d. Has shareholders who are responsible for business liabilities
3. Financial accounting refers to:
   a. Financial statements
   b. Budgets and costs
   c. Forecasts
   d. Flexible business scenarios
4. Managerial accounting refers to:
   a. Financial statements
   b. Rules and regulations
   c. Budgets and forecasts
   d. Accounting policies and explanatory notes
5. Tax accounting is about:
   a. Expenses and revenues in the Profit and Loss Account
   b. Assets and liabilities
   c. Owner's equity
   d. Expenses and revenues permitted for tax purposes

6. The financial statements are dedicated:
   a. Only to governmental agencies
   b. Only to clients and suppliers
   c. Only to managers
   d. To all stakeholders

**Exercises**

**Exercise 1**: Let's suppose you are the manager of an IT Company and you have to expand the business abroad. Identify the relevant accounting information that is crucial to your decision. How is this information helpful and why?

**Exercise 2**: Discuss the differences and connections between financial accounting and managerial accounting. Provide examples of information that relates both to financial and managerial accounting.

**Exercise 3**: Ana wishes to open a Romanian restaurant but needs a 10,000 lei bank loan. The bank had asked for the future three years' Profit and Loss Account and the Cash-Flow Statement for the restaurant. Ana has no accounting knowledge and does not understand the need for that financial information. She has asked for your help and guidance in understanding this and to proceed accordingly to the bank's requirements. Comment and discuss.

**Exercise 4**: ABC Company has an accounting profit of 100,000 lei, but the taxable profit computed by the Company's accountant is 120,000 lei. One shareholder has asked ABC Company for further details and an explanation to justify this difference. You had been assigned to take care of this matter and to present your analysis to the Management Board. Provide a brief report.

**Exercise 5**: You and your two friends are willing to fund a consultancy business to provide financial services to clients. What would be your option in terms of the legal format of your entity? What format would you prefer and why?

CHAPTER 2

# The Conceptual Framework

*Adriana Duțescu, Oana Stănilă, and Răzvan Hoinaru*

*Learning objectives:*

- *Understanding and applying accounting language*
- *Understanding and applying main accounting concepts and principles*
- *Understanding the concept of financial statements and their objectives*
- *Understanding the recognition and evaluation principles*

## 2.1 INTRODUCTION

The process of globalisation gives businesses and individuals from different countries the opportunity to invest internationally and to interact with each other more easily than in the past. An increasing number of companies have international operations. This trend towards global businesses raises many accounting problems, as each country has its own set of accepted accounting principles. Consider the case of a Swedish company that has subsidiaries in the United States, India and Romania. Each subsidiary has to prepare financial statements that are compliant with the national/local accounting standards but at the same time they need to produce a second set of financial statements according to the Swedish accounting regulations, thus enabling the parent company to produce group accounts. Now, if the Swedish group wishes to gain access to financial markets in United States, it has to file accounts with the local securities regulator group that comply with US GAAP standards.[1] However, the redundancies of the process are obvious.

Previously, accounting organisations around the world responded to this problem by establishing an independent private sector body in 1973, the International Accounting Standards Committee (IASC), through an agreement between the professional accounting bodies across ten Western countries. Its objectives were to formulate accounting standards and promote their worldwide acceptance, to improve and harmonise regulations, as well as accounting standards and procedures used by businesses and other organisations during their financial reporting. The International Accounting Standard Board (IASB) developed 41 International Accounting Standards (IASs), 17 International Financial Reporting Standards (IFRSs), and several interpretations of the standards, through a transparent process that involved providers, users of financial statements, the national standards setting bodies, and other interested groups. Its *Framework for preparation and presentation of financial statements*[2] plays the role of a conceptual framework. IASC ceased its operations in 2001, when a reformed body, the IASB, was created.[3]

IASB has a wider funding basis than IASC, which includes major accounting firms, private financial institutions and industrial companies throughout the world, central and development banks, and other international organisations and professional associations. The reformed body has 14 members (12 of whom are full-time), all of whom with diverse professional backgrounds. IASB's mission is more explicit as it seeks to develop, "in the public interest, **a single set** of high quality, global accounting standards that require transparent and comparable information in general purpose financial statements."

At present, about 144 jurisdictions require the use of international standards for all domestic listed companies. The European Union (EU) requires the use of IFRSs for the financial statements prepared by listed

---

[1] Generally Accepted Accounting Principles, a generic term for accounting standards in the US.

[2] In Romanian. *Cadrul general de întocmire și prezentare a situațiilor financiare.*

[3] IASB is the standard-setting body organised as a not-for-profit corporation, which is incorporated in the United States of America. IFRS Foundation has nineteen Trustees who provide oversight, arrange financial support, and appoint members of IASB and related councils and committees.

**Table 2.1** Different terms for the same concept

| UK | US | IASB |
| --- | --- | --- |
| Stock | Inventory | Inventory |
| Shares | Stock | Shares |
| Own shares | Treasury stock | Treasury shares |
| Debtors | Receivables | Receivables |
| Creditors | Payables | Payables |
| Finance lease | Capital lease | Finance lease |
| Turnover | Sales (or revenue) | Sales (or revenue) |
| Fixed assets | Non-current assets | Non-current assets |
| Profit and loss account | Income statement | Income statement |
| Net profit | Net income | Net profit |
| Preference shares | Preferred stock | Preference shares |
| Ordinary shares | Common stock | Ordinary shares |
| Nominal value | Par value | Par value |
| Share premium | Paid-in surplus | Share premium |
| Retained profit | Retained earnings | Accumulated profits |

*Source* Alexander and Nobes (2001)

groups starting on, or after, January 1st, 2005, a decision that involves approximately 6000 companies.

One final general point refers to the language of international standards. IASB has published texts of all IASs/IFRSs, including exposure drafts, into English. Approved translations of the standards are available in more than twenty languages, including Romanian. Some researchers suggest that the international regulator uses "a mixture of UK and US terms" as shown in Table 2.1.

In this book, we shall also use these concepts interchangeably depending on the regional context.

## 2.2 Users of Financial Information

Financial statements are prepared for the purpose of providing useful information to a large range of rational decision-makers: investors, employees, lenders, suppliers and other trade creditors, customers, governments and their agencies, and the public. Financial information is thus meant for decision-makers who have different interests. In its Framework, IASB points out seven groups who work with financial information, and what they are looking for in a business' financial statements:

- investors
- employees
- lenders
- suppliers
- customers
- governments
- the public

**Investors** want information concerning their investment's risks and rewards. Information about future cash flows associated with an investment is vital, but not always available. A company's financial position and performance are the best substitutes and can be found in the annual financial statements. Would it be possible to mislead investors through the financial statements? The answer is "yes", as some companies can manipulate the profit figure using alternative accounting policies and methods to suit management's interests (i.e. the choice of inventory's valuation and depreciation methods). This is why financial statements are checked by independent auditors. At the same time, financial analysts perform adjustments to data contained in the financial statements to enable comparisons between companies.

**Employees** and their organisations are interested in assessing employment stability and whether a fair share of the value added of the company has been allocated to them.

**Lenders** are interested in whether the repayment of the loans has taken place and if it is granted, as well as the associated interest costs, and if the payments will be made on time.

**Suppliers** need information concerning the short-term liquidity of their debtors, while **customers** take a long-term view of an enterprise.

**Government** agencies do rely on specific reporting aggregate data from the financial statements of individual businesses to obtain sector or macroeconomic indicators.

**The public** needs information regarding the impact of an enterprise's activity on the local economy and environment.

Financial statements cannot meet all the information needs of the users, but it is assumed that if they meet an investors' needs, then most of the other needs are met. The preparation and presentation of financial statements is the responsibility of management. Its own information needs are satisfied through different reports, which are prepared more frequently, and are more detailed than the financial statements.

## 2.3 The Objective of Financial Statements

As pointed out before, information on future cash flows generated by an enterprise, in terms of their amount, certainty and timing, is vital, but often unavailable. Users make their own predictions by adjusting data disclosed in the financial statements over a period of time, using other available means of information (i.e. mass-media disclosures, journal articles, social media etc.). Therefore, the **objective of financial statements** is to provide decision-makers with useful information about the performance and changes of the financial position of an enterprise.

The **financial position** of an enterprise is characterised by several aspects: the resources controlled, the financial structure, liquidity, and solvency. The relevant information on these topics is primarily found in the **Balance Sheet** ("bilanț" in Romanian), with details presented in the explanatory notes. The Balance Sheet lists, in quantitative terms, all assets owned and controlled by an enterprise, and all liabilities owed, along with shareholder's interest (equity) in the business at a particular time. It is a snapshot of the financial position of the business at a certain point. If it is to describe the balance sheet through a metaphor, an interesting one would be "the selfie of the company".

Companies operating in different industries control different resources and have different financial structures. The resources of a mining company consist mostly of equipment, while the most important resources of a retailer are inventories. A mining company relies more heavily on bank loans, while a retailer uses payment facilities from its suppliers.

Liquidity measures how quickly an enterprise's economic resources can be converted into cash to meet its current obligations towards suppliers, employees or government. Solvency takes a longer view. It answers questions such as: "Can the company meet its long-term liabilities when they are due?" Solvency is thus the ability to meet all obligations, regardless their maturity.

Information on **performance** reflects the enterprise's ability to obtain profit; in other words, to obtain revenues that exceed the incurred expenses. Information about performance is contained mainly in the **Profit and Loss Account** ("Contul de Profit și Pierdere" in Romanian) or the Income Statement and associated explanatory notes. The Profit and Loss Account is a record of revenues generated, and expenses incurred by the business in a given period, known as the financial year.

The **Statement of Changes in Equity** brings in additional information about other events impacting the performance of the enterprise, such as equity gains and losses that do not pass through the Profit and Loss Account. After all, the change in equity between two separate moments in time shows the increase or decrease of wealth during that period.[4]

Information regarding **changes in the financial position** discloses the enterprise's ability to generate cash—the ultimate condition to continue the activity in the future—and the use of this cash for operating, investing and financing activities. Information on this topic is typically found in the **Statement of Cash Flows** ("Situaţia Fluxurilor de Numerar" in Romanian) and in the explanatory notes to this statement. More detailed information on Financial Statements is provided in Chapter 3.

## 2.4 The Qualitative Characteristics of Financial Information

Most conceptual frameworks are broadly about the nature of the desirable characteristics of financial information, but there is no consistency in the terminology used to describe it. We shall refer again to IASB's Framework, which sets out the main financial information characteristics, that financial statements should have:

- **relevance**
- **faithful representation**
- comparability
- verifiability
- understandability
- timeliness

Information within the financial statements has **relevance** when it has the ability to influence the economic decisions of its users. Relevant information has both predictive and confirmatory value, as it affects future decisions, and helps assess the accuracy of past decisions. Users need information regarding resources that will be quickly converted into cash, in order to compare it to an enterprise's short-term obligations and assess its liquidity. A potential investor will analyse liquidity over a period

---

[4] Assuming that no contributions or withdrawals of capital were made and no dividends were paid.

of time, compare it to other companies that operate in the same sector and assess the capabilities of the enterprise's management to meet the short-term obligations.

Those who prepare financial statements decide what information is relevant based on its *materiality* or importance. If information is omitted or misstated, economic decisions will be influenced, and the respective information will be considered material information. Each material item requires a separate presentation in the financial statements, whereas non-material amounts should be combined with amounts of a similar nature and role, and be globally presented. To illustrate materiality, consider that an enterprise issues letters of guarantees to third parties (i.e. subsidiaries) to enable them to obtain bank loans. Such commitments are not included in the Balance Sheet as they are not liabilities of that entity. Nevertheless, in this off-balance sheet example, any risk should be disclosed in a note in the financial statements, as users need to evaluate the worst-case scenario, that is, the financial burden of the enterprise if the third parties fail to repay their loans. From the multitude of letters of guarantees issued, only the most important are described in detail; the rest are usually aggregated and presented under a heading such as "other credit guarantees".

Information should **faithfully represent** the transactions or other events that it depicts. Secondly, information should be in accordance with the substance and economic reality of transactions, and not merely with their legal form. For most transactions, the legal form and the economic substance are identical. Complex transactions, however, may be arranged in such a way that these two aspects become distinct. The selling of land with a repurchase option may sometimes be disguising a secured loan whereby the repurchase price is not a market one but builds up on the original sale price.

Next, financial information should be *neutral*, that is it should not lead users to subjective, biased decisions. A company may be eager to conclude a merger and could decide to delay the disclosure of information of significant costs, until after the merger is complete. Shareholders are thus led to believe that they are making the right choice and no side effects will occur.

**Comparability** is an important feature of financial information, providing a basis for benchmark analysis. Comparability requires the same reporting framework, similar main concepts, and methods (techniques) that are embedded in the production of the financial information, ensuring that all comparative financial information is consistently disclosed.

**Verifiability** means that independent analysts can reach the same conclusion, but not necessarily the same consensus, based on their analysis of an annual report (set of financial statements).

It is assumed that financial information with such qualities gives what is commonly known as a "true and fair view" of the performance and changes in an entity's financial position. Information in the financial statements should be in a form which is **understandable** to users who have sufficient knowledge and diligence. Financial statements of listed companies sometimes comprise of tens of pages of tables and explanations. To understand them, users need accounting and financial analysis skills. On the other hand, there is a need for clarity and conciseness of financial information.

There are some underlying assumptions one has to make when assessing the quality of financial information: that the entity is under "going-concern" and that the "accrual basis of accounting" is used.

**Going-concern** is another important assumption, upon which the financial information is produced and disclosed. It refers to the ability of the company to continue its business as usual to stay operational. If there is any doubt that the company is able to continue its business in a going-concern manner, then it should disclose this information.

**Accrual basis of accounting** presumes that revenues are disclosed when earned and expenses when incurred irrespective of any related cash-flows. For example, if electricity is consumed during the month of May 20X0 and paid in June 20X0, under the accrual basis, the expense should be disclosed in the month of May 20X0.

IASB's Framework adds two constraints to relevant and reliable information: **timeliness** and **the balance between costs and benefits**. The passing of time damages relevance, while early reporting without sorting out all aspects of a certain transaction or event impairs reliability. Certain influences that are presented on the Balance Sheet at a particular date are easier to measure afterwards, i.e. the full effects of discontinuing a certain activity. Hence, it is considered that an entity should annually disclose its financial statements or, if the disclosure is performed in a different timeframe, the reason of the exception should be specified.[5]

Information in financial statements comes at a cost. When deciding the content of financial statements, an enterprise should consider

---

[5] IAS 1, par. 36.

a balance between costs and benefits. Certain companies publish environmental data on a voluntary basis, thus incurring an additional cost. Lately (2013 EU Directive), all EU Member States, Romania included, introduced an obligation for listed and public companies to disclose non-financial information (i.e. information on Corporate Social Responsibility, environmental protection, the impact on the local communities etc.) under the basis of the IFRS. There are important benefits associated with these disclosures, such as a better public image that may lower other costs (i.e. cost of capital).

## 2.5 The Elements of Financial Statements

### a. Definitions

The elements of financial statements relate to the financial position and performance of an entity. Three elements are linked to the financial position of an enterprise: assets, liabilities, and equity. There is an accounting equation (equilibrium) that is the core of the accounting analysis, and that depicts all specific effects of any transaction or event in the financial statements of a business:

**ASSETS = EQUITY + LIABILITIES**

This equilibrium was first emphasised by Luca Pacioli in 1494, who is considered to be the "father" of modern accounting. In other words, transactions that influence businesses have this dual aspect that includes an asset (what is it?), and its source of financing (where does it come from?) as a liability or equity. Further details about this are found in Chapters 3 and 4 of this book.

The definitions of elements of the financial statements include the following:

- **An asset** is a resource controlled by an enterprise. The resource should come from a past transaction or event and is accompanied by an expectation of an inflow of future economic benefits. All three aspects—control, origin and expectation—are necessary to define an asset.
  Assume that a company has purchased industrial equipment for its shoe-making factory. The item meets the definition of an asset because: (1) it is controlled by the company who will use 100% of it in production; (2) a transaction between the company and the

equipment's seller has already taken place; and (3) the company expects to sell the shoes that the equipment will produce. It is a rather different situation when the company's business purchases equipment and then leases it to shoe manufacturers. The issue here is who controls the equipment; that is, which party gets the rewards and bears the risks of ownership associated with this equipment. If a shoe manufacturer controls it, then, from the leasing company's standpoint, the equipment does not fulfil the definition of an asset regardless of the fact that its legal title remains with the leasing company.[6]

- **A liability** is a present obligation of an enterprise. The obligation should originate in a past transaction or event and entail the expectation of an outflow of economic benefits. Again, to define a liability, the same three features are required: existence, origin and expectation.

  Suppose that a company has purchased a pair of parts needed to overhaul a chemical equipment. The three above-mentioned features are present: the company has a present obligation to the supplier, a transaction has taken place, and an outflow of cash will soon follow. Now, assume that the company is required to overhaul its equipment every five years, and the last major repair dates back two years ago. Does the company have a liability at the time of the Balance Sheet date? No, because it may choose to dispose of the equipment and avoid the obligation to provide for those future overhaul costs.

- **Equity** is the owner's residual claim to the assets or the residual interest in the assets of an enterprise after deducting all its liabilities. Equity is sometimes called *net assets*, because it is a net result of liabilities subtracted from assets, or what remains after all liabilities are settled.

## EQUITY = ASSETS − LIABILITIES

The next two elements of the financial statements are coupled with an enterprise's performance. Conceptual frameworks define **revenues (income)** and **expenses** by referring to assets, liabilities and equity, elements already explained.

---

[6] See Chapter 7 for details on leasing agreements.

- **Income (revenues) represents** increases in economic benefits that augment equity, and are not contributions from owners. If we refer to the algebraic formula above, equity expands when assets increase, or liabilities decrease as part of the enterprise's operations or from other events. Income occurs simultaneously with either the increase of assets, such as cash or debtors, in the case of a sale, or with the decrease of a liability, if there is a sale discount.
  Income from the ordinary activities of a company is called **revenue**, whereas income that occurs from other events is known as **gains**. For a car manufacturer, the sale of spare parts is described as revenue, but the profitable sale of an outdated assembly line is disclosed as a gain. As commonly assumed, revenue and related expenses are generally not offset in the Profit and Loss Account: the revenue from sales (the sale price of the spare parts) and the related expenses (the cost of the spare parts sold) are separately disclosed. Nevertheless, within the Anglo-Saxon world of accounting, the gain from the sale of an assembly line (its sale price) is reported as the net of the associated expense (the carrying amount[7] of the assembly line) so that only the profit (or loss) made on this transaction is visible in the Profit and Loss Account.
- **Expenses** are decreases in economic benefits that reduce equity and are not distributions to owners. Equity declines when assets decrease, or liabilities increase as a result of flowing production activities, development of the business or from other events. Expenses occur concurrently with decreases of assets when materials are used in production. Expenses also occur when liabilities increase due to the purchase of various services (e.g. electricity or salaries), and because of tax obligations.
  Although losses are expenses that may arise from the ordinary activities of an enterprise, it is also through other events that they may the incurred. For the same car manufacturer above the cost of the spare parts sold is an expense, while the stock of spare parts destroyed by a fire is reported as a loss.

As a consequence of these definitions, profit can be calculated in two ways:

---

[7] See Chapter 6 for further explanation.

$$\text{PROFIT} = \text{EQUITY}_1 - \text{EQUITY}_0$$

where 0 and 1 are two consecutive moments in time.

Or:

$$\text{PROFIT} = \text{REVENUES} - \text{EXPENSES},$$

b. **Recognition criteria**

An item may meet the definition of an element in the financial statements but may not be recognised as such; that is, its amount is not incorporated in the financial statements. Problems occur when there is a weak or remote expectation of the inflow/outflow of future economic benefits or when the measurement used is not just difficult, but also not trustworthy.

IASB's Framework sets forth two cumulative criteria that govern the recognition of an item which meets the definition of an element:

- It is probable[8] that the associated inflow/outflow of economic benefits will take place;
- The item's cost or value can be measured reliably.

A delivery van purchased by a farm will easily fulfil these criteria: it will carry farm products to customers, and its cost is mentioned in the invoice. The research activity of a chemical laboratory may satisfy the second recognition criterion, but a long time may pass before this knowledge will be converted into economic benefits. Until these become probable, no asset is to be recognised in the Balance Sheet from such activities.

Similarly, the recognition of a trade creditor is not problematic: it is certain that cash will leave the enterprise and the amount will be written down in the purchased product's invoice. However, imagine that a company is undergoing litigation with a customer, and has received legal advice that the probability of an unfavourable outcome is unmaterial. This company does not recognise a liability in the Balance Sheet, because the first recognition criterion has not been met.

---

[8] It is likely; it may be expected to happen (Oxford Dictionary).

c. **Measurement**
The elements of financial statements are valued using a number of measurement bases that can be classified into two groups: historical (historical cost) and current (current cost, realisable value and present value) methods.

**Historical cost** is the most used valuation base, and at the same time, the most criticised. It represents the amount of cash paid to acquire an asset at the time of its acquisition; for a liability, it is generally the fair value of the consideration received in exchange for incurring the liability. Its main disadvantage is the fact that it measures assets and liabilities prior to the date of the financial statements, which is then irrelevant to the current value. Historical costs have the advantage that they can be understood and used with a minimum of effort.

**Example 1**: An amount of 1 million lei is due for a plot of land and is payable over three instalments to the former owner. The land has a historical cost of 1 million lei and if not decided otherwise, will be the value disclosed on the annual Balance Sheet for this asset; at the same time, the amount of 1 million lei will represent the liability to be paid to the former owner.

**The current cost** of an asset is the amount that will be paid to acquire a similar asset; for a liability, it is the amount needed to settle the obligation at present. It is a forward-looking measurement base but finding a current value is a judgemental approach and it also involves the choice between the replacement of the physical asset and that of the service that it provides.

**The realisable value** is the amount that an enterprise will obtain in exchange of an asset if it was sold through a normal course of business. The **settlement value** of a liability is the amount that will be paid if the obligation was settled in the normal course of business. It is important to note that valuation takes place during an ordinary means of business and not through a forced sale or settlement. The realisable value has the advantage of being easily understood by users; indeed, some less knowledgeable users tend to interpret Balance Sheet values as market values. Yet, using this value for all assets and liabilities and in all circumstances, would violate the going-concern assumption.

**Example 2**: ABC Company owns, by the end of 20X7, 10,000 lb of raw coffee beans at US$110/lb; the market price at the same date is US$104/lb (this is considered a good approximation for the net realisable value). If ABC Company used the principle of disclosing its inventory at the lower of carrying amount and net realisable value, then the raw coffee beans will be disclosed at the end of 20X7 at US$1,040,000 (10,000 lb * US$104/lb).

The **present value** is based on discounted cash inflows that are generated by an asset and on discounted cash outflows that are needed to settle a liability during the normal course of business. A mathematical expression would be $PV = \sum \frac{CF_t}{(1+i)^t}$, where CF is future cash-flows, $i$ is the discount rate, and $t$ the period of time.[9]

**Example 3**: What is the present value of a two years' liability, with a 10% annual interest that is capitalised and 121 lei as a future payment, by the end of year two?

**Solution**: The present value of the liability is 100 lei; 100 lei = 121/$(1+0.1)^2$.

Uncertainty is the main problem of this measurement base, and it relates to the amount of cash flows and their timing; the choice of the discount rate could also raise questions.

**The fair value** represents the amount for which an asset could be exchanged between knowledgeable, willing parties at an arm's length transaction known as the **IFRS 13 Fair Value Measurement** definition. The fair value is generally understood as the asset's market value, as determined by qualified evaluators.

**Example 4**: A company used the revaluation method for its buildings: at December 31st, 20X5, the fair value of the headquarters building was 100 million lei and at December 31st, 20X7, the fair value of the same building was 95 million lei. Therefore, at the Balance Sheet date, the building will be disclosed at its fair value, respectively 100 million in 20X5 and 95 million lei in 20X7.

We shall discuss measurement issues throughout this text book and observe how several bases are used for the same element. Stocks (inventories) may be measured at a historical cost or at a net realisable value, whichever is lower. An enterprise has the choice to value land, buildings or equipment items at historical cost or fair value, and use this base for related calculations. Lastly, recoverable value enters into the analysis when testing non-current assets for impairment.

---

[9] A variation has been used since biblical times when land was valued by means of earnings multiple though undiscounted as interest was forbidden among Israelites.

## 2.6 Conclusions

The following summary questions are intended to provide important conclusions of this chapter.

### Chapter summary questions:

| | |
|---|---|
| Who are the users of the financial/accounting information? | The users of the financial/accounting information are: investors, creditors/lenders, customers, employees, government and the general public. |
| What is the objective of financial statements? | The objective of financial statements is to provide useful information to decision-makers, related to the financial position, performances and cash-flows of the company. |
| What qualitative characteristics should financial information have? | The expected qualitative characteristics of the financial information are: relevance, faithful representation, comparability, timeliness, understandability. |
| What does the "going-concern" mean? | The going-concern concept refers to the ability of the company to continue its business as usual to stay operational. No exceptional events are expected to occur in the near future. |
| Define assets, liabilities, equity, revenues and expenses | **Assets** are resources controlled by the business, coming from a past transaction or event, and expected to generate inflow of future economic benefits. |
| | **Liabilities** are present obligations from a past transaction or event, and are expected to generate an outflow of economic benefits. |
| | **Equity** is a residual interest in a company's net assets; it is the difference between assets and liabilities, and refers to owners equity. |
| | **Income and gains** are increases of economic results of the business/increases in profits. |
| | **Expenses and losses** are decreases of economic results of the business/decreases in profits. |
| What is the accounting equation? What does it mean? | The accounting equation is:<br>**Assets = Equity + Liabilities**<br>It means that every transaction or event affecting the entity should be represented through this equation. |

## Quizzes (select only one answer)

1. Historical cost means:
   a. Last year's price of the good
   b. The price paid on the asset when acquired or the production cost incurred to produce it
   c. Last month's market price of the good
   d. Last year's replacement cost for the good
2. Fair value is:
   a. The replacement cost of the good
   b. The residual value of the good
   c. The market price of the good
   d. The present value of the good
3. A car should be disclosed in the Balance Sheet of the user as a/an:
   a. Liability
   b. Asset
   c. Expense
   d. Revenue
4. A loan to be paid in three years should be disclosed as a:
   a. Revenue
   b. Asset
   c. Liability
   d. Equity
5. A present value method is used to measure:
   a. A long-term liability
   b. The profit
   c. The loss
   d. Cash-flow
6. If assets are 100,000 lei and liabilities are 110,000 lei then equity amounts to:
   a. +10,000 lei
   b. −10,000 lei
   c. +90,000 lei
   d. −90,000 lei
7. When revenues are 30,000 lei and expenses are 25,000 lei, and in the previous year, a 10,000 lei loss was incurred, the effect in the current annual balance sheet for equity is:
   a. +5000 lei
   b. −5000 lei

c. +10,000 lei
   d. −10,000 lei
8. A plot of land with a historical cost of 1 million lei and a fair value of 1.1 million lei, for which the revaluation method is appropriate, will be disclosed in the annual Balance Sheet at:
   a. 1 million lei
   b. 1.1 million lei
   c. 0.1 million lei
   d. 0.9 million lei
9. If a company will liquidate its operations next year, it means that:
   a. It is under "going-concern"
   b. It is not under "going-concern"
   c. It is operating as business as usual
   d. It is not relevant to stakeholders
10. Using the same accounting methods and techniques means that the financial information is:
    a. Relevant
    b. Comparable
    c. Neutral
    d. Unbiased

## Exercises

**Exercise 1**: ABC Company has a cash amount of 15,000 lei, inventories of 5000 lei, receivables of 2000 lei, bank loans of 9000 lei, and debts to suppliers of 2000 lei. Apply the accounting equation to determine the level of equity.

**Exercise 2**: What is the present value of a two year's liability, with a 5% annual interest, and an amount of 5450 lei to be paid at maturity?

**Exercise 3**: The management of the ABC Corporation is analysing the impact of specific valuation methods of their equipment, in the financial statements. It is estimated that the market price of the equipment will drop in the following years, due to technological progress. Explain the pros and cons of specific valuation methods (historical cost and revaluation method).

**Exercise 4**: Company XYZ has used the historical cost method for its buildings and is considering the change to revaluation method for these assets. What should the company do in order to ensure the comparability of the financial information?

## REFERENCE

Alexander, D., Nobes C., Financial Accounting: An International Introduction, *Pearson Education Limited*, first edition, Harlow, Great Britan, 2001.

CHAPTER 3

# The Financial Statements

*Adriana Duțescu, Oana Stănilă, and Răzvan Hoinaru*

*Learning objectives:*

- *Understanding and assessing each component of the financial statements: Balance Sheet (the Statement of the Financial Position), Profit and Loss Account (Income Statement), Cash-Flow Statement, Statement of Changes in Equity, and accounting policies and explanatory notes*
- *Assessing relationships among financial statements components*
- *Evaluating the financial position, the operating performance and the cash-flow position, based on financial statements*

## 3.1 Introduction

Financial accounting provides information mainly to decision-makers who are not involved in the day-to-day operations of an organization. The information is distributed primarily through financial statements. Financial statements describe the condition of an enterprise, the events that have occurred during the year and should give a "true and fair view" of an enterprise's financial position, performance and changes in its financial position.

In addition to the accounting concepts and policies outlined in the previous chapter, **IAS 1—Presentation of Financial Statements** focuses on the structure and content of the Balance Sheet and the Profit and Loss Account. It recommends several formats for these two statements and requires that a Statement of Changes in Equity and a Cash-Flow

Statement (fully settled by **IAS 7—Statement of Cash Flows**) should accompany the Balance Sheet and the Profit and Loss Account.

A complete set of financial statements includes (according to the IASB's conceptual framework) the following statements:

- **The Statement of the Financial Position (the Balance Sheet)** that lists, in different currencies, all assets and liabilities of an enterprise, along with the shareholders' interest (equity) in a business at a particular date;
- **The Statement of Profit and Loss and Other Comprehensive Income** (also called **Income Statement**) is a record of revenues generated and expenses incurred over a given period. The statement shows the performances or non-performance of a business in terms of profit (revenues exceed expenses) or losses (expenses exceed revenues), but also gains and losses generated by business events;
- **The Statement of Cash Flows** discloses the cash flows of a business (inflows and outflows), generated from an enterprise's operating, investing and financing activities. This statement supplements the accrual-based information disclosed in the profit and loss account with the enterprise's capacity to generate cash;
- **The Statement of Changes in Equity** shows the causes and effects of equity modifications within the current period, in order to help owners and potential investors to better assess the risks and rewards of their investments;
- **Accounting policies and explanatory notes** disclose information about the basis of preparation of the financial statements, accounting policies used and information which is not presented elsewhere in the financial statements, but are necessary for a true and fair presentation.

Table 3.1 shows the connections between financial statements.

## 3.2 The Statement of the Financial Position (the Balance Sheet)

The **Statement of the Financial Position**, also called the **Balance Sheet,** is a statement of assets, liabilities and owner's equity of a business at a particular date, usually at the last day of a given financial year. It is a statement outlining what a business owns (or is owed), and controls given at a particular period of time (i.e. during the financial year), and their sources of finance. When preparing a Balance Sheet, the accountant has to be

Table 3.1  Links between financial statements

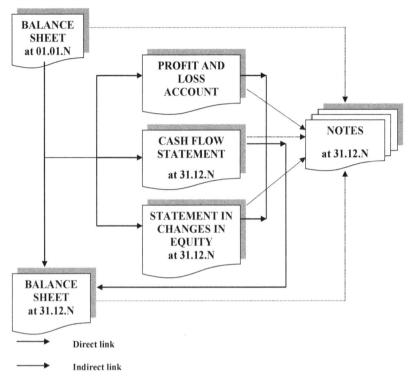

*Source* Duțescu (2002)

aware that the items listed in this financial statement are not necessarily at fair value, but some of the assets are carried at the historical cost, while long-term liabilities for example are held at a net present value.

A Balance Sheet is a mirror of the following accounting equation:

**ASSETS = EQUITY + LIABILITIES**

or

**ASSETS − LIABILITIES = EQUITY**

## Formats of presentation

The Balance Sheet format of disclosure can be a "list", starting with assets, continuing with liabilities and ending with equity, or a "table" format, showing on one side assets, on the opposite liabilities and equity.

The international pattern is in favor of the "list" format, the **IAS 1 Presentation of financial statements** emphasizing some minimum levels of needed information.

Regardless of the format of the Balance Sheet's presentation, comparative information should always be presented; depending on national or regional requirements, the current year is compared with the previous year or with the last two years. In Europe, assets are disclosed in their increasing liquidity order and liabilities in their decreasing maturity order, while in the USA the opposite rule functions.

The explanatory notes and accounting policies should include details concerning the specific accounting policies used for the line-items presented in the balance sheet and sub-classifications to provide details of their movement.

This Balance Sheet format makes a distinction between **current** and **non-current assets** and **current and non-current liabilities**. Basically, current assets consist of inventories, receivables and cash or other assets that an enterprise will use in the normal course of its operating cycle. Similarly, current liabilities are those that an enterprise expects to settle within twelve months of the Balance Sheet date or in the normal course of its operating cycle, if longer. The stocks of a China manufacturer and the stocks of a wine producer are both current assets, even though the stocks of the latter sometimes require more than twelve months to be ready for sale. All other assets and liabilities are classified as non-current.

A different Balance Sheet format is used in Romania by companies that apply the specific Accounting Regulations. This format emphasizes the investor's interest in an enterprise and is described by the second form of the fundamental accounting equation:

## ASSETS – LIABILITIES = EQUITY

The Romanian format of the Balance Sheet, as enforced by the legislation is (Table 3.2):

As discussed before, the assets are divided, for Balance Sheet purposes, into:

a) non-current assets (i.e. property, plant and equipment, also called tangible or fixed assets, intangible assets, financial assets, etc.); and
b) current assets.

**Table 3.2** The Statement of the Financial Position as at December 31st, 201X (in lei) ABC S.A.

|  | 201X–1 | 201X |
|---|---|---|
| **Assets** |  |  |
| **Non-current assets** |  |  |
| Intangible assets | x | x |
| Tangible assets | x | x |
| Financial non-current assets | x | x |
| **Current assets** |  |  |
| Stocks (inventories) | x | x |
| Trade and other debtors | x | x |
| Short-term investment | x | x |
| Cash and bank deposits | x | x |
| Prepayments | x | x |
| **Total assets** | X̲ | X̲ |
| Liabilities to be paid within 1 year | x | x |
| Net current assets (net current liabilities) | x | x |
| Total assets minus current liabilities | x | x |
| Liabilities due in more than 1 year | x | x |
| Provisions | x | x |
| Advanced revenues and deferred revenues | x | x |
| **Equity and Liabilities** | x | x |
| Capital and reserves | x | x |
| Issued capital | x | x |
| Reserves | x | x |
| Accumulated profits | x | x |
| **Total Equity and Liabilities** | X | X |

*Source* Duțescu (2002)

To be classified as an asset, an item must satisfy the following conditions:

a) it is probable that future economic benefits will flow into the entity;
b) its cost can be reliably measured.

A **non-current asset** is an asset acquired for continuing use within a business, that is either earning income or insuring profits from its use. The **IAS 16—Property, Plant and Equipment** defines a non-current asset as: "held for use in the production or supply of goods and services, for rental to others, or for administrative purposes; and are expected to be used during more than one period" (IAS 16, par. 6).

Non-current assets can be classified into: a) intangible assets, b) tangible assets, and c) financial assets and investments.

**Intangible assets** are assets which do not have a physical form, they cannot be touched, and have no physical substance. **Intangible assets** also provide benefits to the firm over a long-term basis. Trademarks, copyrights, franchise rights, patents and goodwill are examples of intangible assets. The cost principle governs accounting for intangibles, just as it does for tangible assets. For example, the amount paid to an inventor for the patent rights to a new product is recorded as an intangible asset. Similarly, the amount paid to a franchisor of a fast-food restaurant for the exclusive rights to operate in a certain geographic area is recorded as an intangible asset. Like tangible assets, intangibles are generating expenses with amortisation, to show their use over time.

**Tangible assets** are assets with physical shape; it has a "physical" existence, it can be touched, therefore, it is "tangible". The category of **property, plant and equipment** consists of various tangible, productive assets used in the main operation of a business. Land, buildings, equipment, machinery, furniture and fixtures, trucks and tools are all examples of assets held for use during the operation of a business, rather than for resale.

The distinction between inventory and equipment depends on the company's intent when acquiring the asset. For example, Lenovo classifies a computer system as inventory because it manufactures it in order to sell it. However, this same computer used by an accounting firm would be classified as equipment because the intention is to use it during the long-term period in the business.

**Financial assets** and other investments are securities of other companies to be kept for more than one year, receivables with more than one year's maturity, or investment properties: i.e. investments in subsidiaries, in associates, in joint-ventures, land and building as investment properties etc.

For example, company D may invest in company I by purchasing some of I's shares. If this investment is performed with the purpose to hold the securities for more than one year, company D would classify them as a non-current asset of D's (financial assets).

Non-current assets can be held and used by a business for a number of years but they lose their value over time. Every tangible or intangible asset has a limited life, except land. For example, equipment may be used over a couple of years, therefore the accountants may use an allocation scheme to spread a portion of the total cost of the equipment to each period of use, through a process known as **"depreciation"**. For intangible assets, this is called **"amortisation"** (Chapter 6 provides more details on the topics of depreciation and amortisation). A specific accumulated depreciation account is used to account for the depreciation, recorded for each of these assets over their lifespan.

Securities that are not expected to be sold within the next year are classified as financial investments. In many cases, the financial investment is in the common stock (shares) of another company. Sometimes companies invest in another company either to exercise some influence or to control the operation of that company. Other types of assets classified as investments include land, buildings and equipment held for capital appreciation rather than for use and are called Investment properties (see, for more details, **IAS 40—Investment Property**). Another possible category of assets is "biological assets", represented by living land and animals **(IAS 41-Agriculture)**.

**Current assets** are the items owned by a business with the intention of turning them into cash in a short period (usually within one year) and cash and cash equivalents that are owned by a business.

Current asset categories are: (a) inventories; (b) receivables; (c) cash and cash equivalents.

**Inventory** is an asset held for use or resale during the normal course of business operations. The distinction between inventory and non-current assets is the intention of the owner. For example, for a company that produces computers, some of the computers are non-current assets because they are used in various activities of a business, for longer than one year, to support some on the entity's functions (i.e. HR, Finance computers etc.). Most of the computers produced by this company are however inventories because the company intends to sell them.

A retail firm's inventory will generally consist only of merchandise purchased that have not been sold yet; in the Balance Sheet, these assets are disclosed as "Merchandise" Inventory.

A manufacturing entity will have three different types of inventory: raw materials, work in progress and finished goods. Direct materials or raw materials are inputs of a production process, that transforms these into finished goods, using labour and other "ingredients". The non-finished products are called "work-in-progress". Inventory that has completed the production process and is available for sale is called "finished goods".

**Account receivables** (or **Clients**) are claims on what the entity is entitled to receive from its clients, in the form of cash or other assets. This concept refers to a business' right to receive something from its clients, in exchange of goods and services that has been sold. There are some other receivables within the Balance Sheet of an entity, for example, shareholders' receivables, meaning the amount to be received from shareholders as capital contribution or because of cash or services advanced to them. Other receivables, refers to claims related to other business parties, such as suppliers that are paid in advance or employees who are paid in advance etc. A "promissory note" is a written promise to repay a definite sum of money on demand or on an agreed date into the future. Promissory notes normally require a payment of interest to use someone else's money. The party that agrees to repay money is the issuer of the note, and the party that receives money in the future is the debtor, the one whom has to pay. A company that holds a promissory note received from another company has an asset, called "notes receivable". The company that has to pay a promissory note to another company as a liability is called a "note payable". Over the life of the note, the debtor incurs interest expense on its note payable and the issuer earns interest revenue on its note receivable.

Can you think of a situation in which a company's operating cycle is longer than one year? A construction company is a good example. A construction company essentially builds an item of inventory, such as an office building, according to the customer' specifications. The entire process, including constructing the building and collecting the sales amount from the customer, may take three years to complete. According to the definition of the current assets, because the inventory will be sold, and the accounts receivable will be collected within the operating cycle, they will still qualify as current assets.

In addition to cash, accounts receivable and inventory, the two other most common types of current assets are **marketable securities** and **prepaid expenses**. Excess cash is often invested into stocks and bonds of other companies. If the investments are made for a short-term, they are classified as current and are called either "short-term investments" or marketable securities.

**Short-term investments** are stocks and shares of other businesses that are currently owned by a separate business, but with the intention of selling them in the near future (less than 12 months).

**Prepayments** are included in the current assets category and refer to amounts of money already paid by a business for benefits which have not yet been enjoyed, but which will be accrued within the next accounting period.

Alternatively, some investments are made for the purpose of exercising influence over another company and thus are made for the long-term. These investments are classified as "noncurrent assets".

Various prepayments, such as office supplies, rent and insurance are classified as prepaid expenses and thus are current assets. These assets qualify as current because are typically consumed within one year.

**Cash and cash equivalents** are the most liquid assets and in the US GAAP's Balance Sheet format are the first items that appear in the assets part. **Cash equivalents** are not cash but can be converted into cash so easily that they are considered similar to cash. Examples of items normally classified as cash equivalents are commercial papers issued by corporations, treasury bills issued by the government and money market funds offered by financial institutions. The classification of cash equivalents is limited to investments that are readily convertible to known amounts of cash and that have an original maturity of three months or less.

The "source of financing" part of a Balance Sheet contains a "liability" category and an "equity" category.

A **liability** is an obligation to transfer assets or to provide services in the future. The obligation may arise from a transaction with an outside party. For example, a business incurs a liability when it buys equipment, or when it borrows money. Also, the obligation may arise in the absence of individual transactions. For example, interest expense accrues with the passage of time; until this interest is paid, it is a liability. Income tax, a liability of companies, accrues as income is earned.

Liabilities are classified as current and non-current liabilities, based upon their maturity.

**Current liabilities** are debts of a business that must be paid within a fairly short period of time; if not, they will be liquidated in less than 12 months.

**Non-current liabilities** are debts which are not payable within the "short-term" (will not be liquidated shortly), but over more than one year.

A **current liability** is an obligation that will be satisfied within the next operating cycle or within one year if the cycle is shorter than one year. For example, the classification of a note payable in the Balance Sheet depends on its maturity date. If the note will be paid within the next year, it is classified as current; otherwise, it is classified as a long-term liability. On the other hand, because of their nature, accounts payable, wages payable and income tax payable are all short-term or current liabilities.

**Accounts payable** (also called **Suppliers** or **Trade payable**) represent amounts owed for the purchased inventory, works or services. Often, accounts payable is the first account listed in the current liability category because it requires the payment of cash before other current liabilities.

**Taxes payable** show the amount that the entity owes for the income taxes. It is shown separately from other obligations because of its specific nature. The liability for income taxes is shown separately from other tax liabilities, such as property taxes.

**Accrued liabilities** represent the amounts that have been owed to outside parties and which have not yet been paid by the entity. Interest earned by a lender, but not yet paid by the entity, is a liability also referred to as an "accrued debt". Another example are the wages and salaries owed to employees for the work they have performed, but for which no payment has occurred yet. The term accrued liabilities, although frequently used as a Balance Sheet category, is not as descriptive as the names used in the detailed records for specific accrued liabilities, such as interest payable, salary and wage payable.

**Unearned revenues** (**deferred revenues**) represent the liability that arises because the entity has received advance payment for a service it has agreed to provide in the future. An example is deferred subscription revenues, which represent magazine subscription payments received in advance, for which the publishing company agrees to deliver issues of its magazine during the future period.

**Current Maturities of Long-Term Debt** is another account that appears in the current liability category of the Balance Sheet. On other companies' Balance Sheets, this item may appear as Long-Term Debt, or Current Portion. This account should appear when a firm has a liability and must make periodic payments. For example, assume that on January 1, 20X7, your firm obtained a 10,000 lei loan from the bank. The terms of the loan require you to make payments in the amount of 1000 lei per year for 10 years, payable each January 1, beginning January 1, 20X8. In this case the 1000 lei shall be disclosed on an annual basis as a current liability until the period of time is completed.

**Long-term liabilities** are obligations that will be settled in more than one year. All liabilities that are not appropriately classified as current liabilities are reported as long-term liabilities. Typical long-term liabilities are: bonds payable, long-term notes payable, pension liabilities, deferred long-term revenues (advances from customers), long-term capital lease obligations, and long-term deferred taxes.

**A bond** is a security or financial instrument that allows firms to borrow money and repay the loan over a long period of time. The bonds are sold or issued to investors who want to invest and to have a return on their investment. The borrower (issuing firm) promises to pay interest on specified dates, usually annually or semi-annually. The borrower also promises to repay the principal on a specified date, called the due date or maturity date. Generally, bonds are issued in denominations of "X" currency amount (i.e. 10 lei/bond). The denomination of the bonds is usually referred to as the "face value" or "par value". This is the amount that the firm must pay at the maturity date of the bond.

**Pension liabilities**. Many large firms establish pension plans to provide retirement amounts to employees after the end of their active life.

**Stockholders' Equity** (**owners' equity** or **shareholders' equity**) represents the owner's claims on the net assets of a business. These claims arise from two sources: contributed capital and earned capital. **Contributed capital** appears in the Balance Sheet in the form of capital stock (share capital) and earned capital takes the form of Retained earnings and Profit (or Loss) of the year. **Capital stock** indicates the owner's investment in a business. **Retained earnings** represents the accumulated earnings, or net income, from past years.

Most companies have a single class of capital stock called common stock. This is the most basic form of ownership in a business. All other claims against a company, such as those of creditors and preferred stockholders, take priority. **Preferred stock** (preferred shares) is a form of capital stock that, as the name implies, carries with it certain preferences. For example, a company must pay dividends on a preferred stock before it makes any distribution of dividends on common stock. In the event of liquidation, preferred stockholders have priority over common stockholders in the distribution of the entity's assets.

**The liquidity** is an important concept and deals with the ability of a company to pay its current debts as they become due, using current assets. Bankers and other creditors are particularly interested in the liquidity of businesses to which they have lent money. A comparison of current assets and current liabilities is a starting point in assessing the ability of a company to meet its obligations. The **working capital** ("capital circulant" in Romanian), one important outcome of the Balance Sheet, is one of the ways the liquidity of a business might be disclosed as the difference between current assets and current liabilities at a point in time. The management of **working capital** is an important task for any business. A company must continually strive for a balance in managing its working capital. For example, a low working capital, or negative working capital, may signal the inability to pay creditors on a timely basis. On the other hand, an overabundance of working capital could indicate that a company is not investing enough of its available funds in productive resources, such as new machinery and equipment. Liquidity is also assessed as a **current ratio**, as a percentage of current assets to current liabilities (Current Assets/Current Liabilities) and reflects the percentage of current assets covering short-term liabilities. It should be over 1 or higher than 100% for an entity to be considered liquid.

Another important aspect derived from the Balance Sheet is the **solvency** level. Solvency means the capacity of the entities to pay their long-term debts and can be computed in various ways: Debts/Equity or Debts/Total Assets or Long-term Debts/(Long term Debts + Equity). Companies with higher levels of debt are considered to have a higher financial risk but this is not necessarily a bad outcome, if the level assumed by a company is reached and is beyond the safety limits.

The following example will recap the main issues on the Balance Sheet format:

**Example 1**: Prepare a Balance Sheet for Dip Co. as at December 31, 20X1, given the information below (in lei):

| | |
|---|---|
| Accounts payable | 1560 |
| Capital | 61,880 |
| Warehouse | 65,000 |
| Accrued costs of rent | 780 |
| Trade receivable | 650 |
| Dividends pied | 5200 |
| Prepayment | 390 |
| Machines | 10,400 |
| Bank overdraft | 2600 |
| Profit for the year | 10,400 |
| Motor vehicles | 11,700 |
| Taxes payable | 4550 |
| Inventories | 20,800 |
| Long term loan | 32,500 |
| Cash | 130 |

## Solution:

| Assets | Lei | O.E. + Liabilities | Lei |
|---|---|---|---|
| Non-current assets: | **87,100** | Owner's Equity | **67,080** |
| Warehouse | 65,000 | Capital | 61,880 |
| Machines | 10,400 | Profit | 10,400 |
| Motor vehicles | 11,700 | Dividends pied | (5200) |
| Current assets: | **21,970** | Non-current liabilities | **32,500** |
| Inventories | 20,800 | | |
| Trade receivable | 650 | Long term loan | 32,500 |
| Prepayment | 390 | Current liabilities | **9490** |
| Cash | 130 | Bank overdraft | 2600 |
| | lei **109,070** | Account payable | 1560 |
| | | Taxes payable | 4550 |
| | | Accrued costs | 780 |
| | | | lei **109,070** |

## 3.3 The Profit and Loss Account and Other Comprehensive Income (the Income Statement)

The **Profit and Loss Account** and **other comprehensive income** or **the Income Statement** shows details of how the profit (or loss) of a period has been generated. Also, the **Profit and Loss Account** has to match the revenues earned with the costs (expenses) incurred to earning the revenues. The difference between the revenues and expenses is identified as the net income (profit) or the net loss. This is called the matching convention and "pairs" revenues with the appropriate expenses, or outputs with inputs.

**Revenues (income)** represents an increase of the entity's economic benefits. Most of entity's revenues are earned by selling goods and services during the ordinary activities of a business, which are classified as "operating revenues", as well as from other events that are not "operating transactions". This would include for example, interest revenues from a bank deposit or gains for foreign exchange conversion rate, also called "financial revenues".

**Expenses** are decreases of an entity's economic benefits and might be in connection to a company's operations, therefore called **"operating**

expenses" (i.e. salary expenses, utility expenses, depreciation expenses etc.) or are generated by financial activities, called "**financial expenses**" (i.e. interest expenses, losses for foreign exchange conversion rate etc.).

**Other comprehensive incomes** are those items of revenues, expenses, gains, and losses that are excluded from the net profit computation. This means that they are instead listed after net income on the **Profit and Loss Account** (i.e. gains on non-current assets revaluation, gains/losses for foreign exchange operations etc.).

**Formats of presentation for the Profit and Loss Account** go by two main presentation formats: the "by nature format" and the "by destination" format.

**The Profit and Loss Account** reports revenues and gains earned and the expenses and losses incurred by an enterprise over an accounting period and the resulting net profit or loss as:

- **net profit** is recorded when revenues exceed expenses;
- **net loss** (or simply loss) is recorded when expenses exceed revenues.

The equation disclosed within this statement is:

**NET PROFIT OR LOSS FOR THE YEAR = REVENUES − EXPENSES**

The profit or loss for the year is the single common item for the Balance Sheet and Profit and Loss Account. Both profit or loss appear on the face of the Balance Sheet, under the heading "Profit or loss of the year" or may be included in "Accumulated profits (losses)", "Retained earnings (Uncovered losses)" or "Profit (loss) carried forward".

To demonstrate this, let's go back to the fundamental accounting equation:

$$\text{ASSETS} = \text{EQUITY} + \text{LIABILITIES}$$
$$\text{ASSETS} = \text{CAPITAL} + \text{PROFIT/LOSS} + \text{LIABILITIES}$$
$$\text{ASSETS} = \text{CAPITAL} + (\text{REVENUES} - \text{EXPENSES}) + \text{LIABILITIES}$$

Directive 2013/34/EU of the European Parliament and IAS 1 allow for different presentation formats of the Profit and Loss Account since each has different merits for an enterprise. The options are: the function of expense ("by function") format and the nature of expense ("by nature") format. The "by function" format is also referred to as the "cost of sales" method.

**Table 3.3** Example of Profit and Loss Account "by function" ("by destination") ABC S.A. Income Statement for the year ended December 31, 201X (in lei)

|  | 201X-1 | 201X |
|---|---|---|
| Revenue | x | x |
| Cost of sales | (x) | (x) |
| **Gross profit** | **X** | **X** |
| Other operating income | x | x |
| Distribution costs | (x) | (x) |
| Administrative expenses | (x) | (x) |
| **Profit from operations** | **X** | **X** |
| Net interest costs | (x) | (x) |
| **Profit before tax** | **X** | **X** |
| Income tax expenses | (x) | (x) |
| **Net profit for period** | **X** | **X** |

Source Duţescu (2002)

Financial analysts find the requirements in IAS 1 to be very useful to disclose information on the nature of expenses when a "by function" format is used. Enterprises classifying expenses by function should disclose additional information, including depreciation and amortisation or expenses and staff costs. This would enable analysts to determine the value added and other ratios from the financial statements (Table 3.3).

The "by nature" format also provides information from which value added can be determined. In this format all revenues and expenses are classified and aggregated based on their nature (Table 3.4).

In both presentation formats, revenues and expenses are divided into two segments: the "Operating Profit or Loss" and the "Financial Profit of Loss", the result of the year (either Profit or Loss) being the addition to the two.

The **Net revenue** amounts represents the total sales revenue, net of VAT, and other sales taxes. **Gross margin** is the difference between sales revenue and cost of goods sold.

The **Cost of goods sold** is the purchase cost of merchandise sold in the retail business or the production cost of goods sold for finished goods that is based upon: the cost of raw materials in the finished goods + the cost of labour required to make the goods + the amount of overhead costs for production in a manufacturing business.

**Table 3.4** Example of Profit and Loss Account "by nature" ABC S.A. Income Statement for the year ended December 31, 201X (in lei)

|  | 201X-1 | 201X |
|---|---|---|
| Revenue | x | x |
| Other operating income | x | x |
| Changes in stocks of finished goods and work in progress | x | x |
| Raw materials and consumables used | x | x |
| Staff costs | x | x |
| Depreciation and amortisation expense | x | x |
| Other operating expenses | x | x |
| **Operating Profit (Loss)** | X | X |
| Net interest costs | x | x |
| **Profit before tax** | X | X |
| Income tax expenses | x | x |
| **Net profit for the year** | X | X |

*Source* Duțescu (2002)

Other revenues may be earned in other circumstances than the sale of goods and services, as for example:

- dividends or interest received/to be received from investments;
- profits on the sale of non-current assets;
- bad debts written off in a previous accounting period which were unexpectedly paid in the current period.

Other business expenses will appear as follows:

- **Selling and distribution expenses** in relation to selling and delivering goods to customers, as for example:
  – salaries of sales management
  – salaries and commissions of salespeople
  – marketing costs (i.e. advertising, sales expenses etc.)
  – maintenance costs and delivery costs
  – discounts offered to customers for early payment of their debts
  – bad debts written off

- **Administration expenses** are the expenses in connection to the management and administration of a business:
  - salaries of management and office staff
  - rent of headquarters or property taxes
  - insurance
  - telephone and postage
  - printing and stationery
  - heating and lighting
- **Finance expenses** might be:
  - interest on a loan
  - bank overdraft interest

Other important financial information in the **Profit and Loss Account** refers to:

- **Earnings Before Interest Taxation, Depreciation and Amortisation (EBITDA)**, refers to the operating profit or loss of a business, before subtracting depreciation and amortisation expenses. It is considered one of the most important financial pieces of information in connection to measuring the operating effectiveness and efficiency of a business;
- **Earnings Before Interest and Taxation (EBIT)**, refers to the operating profit or loss of a business, after subtracting depreciation and amortisation expenses. It is considered to be the net operating result (either operating profit or loss) of a business;
- **Earnings Before Taxation (EBT)**, refers to the net profit of loss of a business before tax. It is the algebraic sum of the operating result (profit or loss from operations) and the financial result (profit or loss from financial activities);
- **Earnings After Taxation (EAT)**, refers to the net profit or loss of a business after tax. It represents the amount that might be distributed through dividends that are reinvested into the company, or are just kept in the Retained Earnings until a decision is reached.

## Example 2:
On January 1, 20X7, J.A. Ltd started a business trading as a grocery shop and using a rented truck which he drove around.

1. J.A. Ltd rented the truck at a cost of $1500 for five months. The running expenses for the truck were $300 per month.
2. J.A. Ltd hired a part-time worker at a cost of $150 per month.
3. J.A. Ltd borrowed $3000 from the bank, at an interest of $30 per month.
4. For the four months until 31 May 20X7, the total sales made consisted of cash sales of $15,500 and credit sales of $1500.
5. From January 1st, 20X7 to May 31st, 20X7 the purchases from the producers were $7000 and had sold every item. He also made a payment for purchases on credit of $1000 to the producer.
6. J.A. Ltd's office telephone and postage expenses for the total five months up to May 31st, 20X7 was $250.

Required: Prepare the income statement for the period.
**Solution**:

| | |
|---|---|
| Sales ($15,500 + $1500) | $17,000 |
| (−) Cost of sales | $7000 |
| Gross profit | $10,000 |
| Expenses: | |
| Wages (5 months * $150) | $750 |
| Truck rental | $1500 |
| Truck expenses | $1500 |
| Telephone and postage | $250 |
| Interest charges (5 * 30) | $150 |
| | $4150 |
| Net profit ($10,000 − $4150) | $5850 |

**Conclusion:**
The relationship between the Profit and Loss Account and the Balance Sheet are:

- The net profit is transferred to the Balance Sheet of a business, as part of the owner's equity;
- The cost of sales is $7000, even though $1000 of the costs have not yet been paid for. The $1000 owed to the producer will be shown in the Balance Sheet as an account payable.

$$\text{Gross profit margin} = \frac{\$10,000}{\$17,000} * 100\% = 58.8\%$$

## 3.4 The Statement of Cash Flow

The purpose of the **Statement of Cash Flow** (or the **Cash-Flow Statement**) is to summarise the cash effects of a company's operating, investing and financing activities over a period of time. Because it summarises flows for a period of time whereby the Statement of Cash Flow is similar to the Income Statement, it is a dynamic statement. However, it differs from the Income Statement in two important respects. First, the Income Statement reports on the operating and financing activities during the period. The Statement of Cash Flow is broader and reports on financing and investing activities, as well as operating activities. Second, an Income Statement is prepared on an accrual basis. This means that revenues are recognised when they are earned and when expenses are incurred, regardless of when cash has been received or paid. Alternatively, a Statement of Cash Flows reflects the cash effects from buying and selling products and services.

The main formulas used in this statement are the following:

**CASH AT 31.12.N = CASH AT 01.01.N + / − CASH FLOW OF THE YEAR**

**CASH FLOW OF THE YEAR = CASH INFLOWS − CASH OUTFLOWS**

The Statement of Cash Flow (also called "the Statement of Changes in Financial Position") discloses cash inflows and outflows, as opposed to the Profit and Loss Account, which discloses revenues and expenses.

A cash inflow consists of cash flowing in or out of a company. Therefore, an over-the-counter sale for cash is regarded as cash inflow, while a sale on credit is not (the receipt of money from the trade debtor is a cash inflow). Borrowing more money from the bank and issuing shares for cash are also cash inflows.

$$Cash - flow = Cash\ ins - Cash - outs$$

or

$$Cash - flow = Receipts - Payments$$

The Statement of Cash Flows is organised into three main areas:

1. **Cash flows from operating activities** are inflows and outflows of cash related to the daily operations of a firm. This is key information for users that shows the ability of an enterprise to generate enough cash to continue its existing operations, pay off dividends and make new investments;

2. **Cash flows from investing activities** are cash flows related to investments and long-term assets, whether they are purchased or sold. For example, cash payments to acquire property, plant and equipment, or cash proceeds from sales of tangible and intangible assets;
3. **Cash flows from financing** consist of all the cash flows relating to long-term debts and share capital. For example, cash payments to shareholders as dividends, cash contributions from owners to increase capital, repayment of bank loans and the related interest.

There are two ways to present a Statement of Cash Flow: the **direct method** and the **indirect method**. The two methods differ in their operating cash flow section, which is based on adjustments to Income Statements and Balance Sheet items.

Users have no difficulty understanding the **direct method** because it shows all cash inflows and cash outflows (receipts and payments) that contribute to operating, investing and financing activities. An outline of the cash flow statement using this method of presentation is shown in Table 3.5.

**Illustration**:

Statement of Cash Flows
ABC S.A., for the year ending December 31, 201X (lei)

| Operating activities: | |
|---|---|
| Cash received from customers | 800,000 |
| Cash received for interest | 20,000 |
| Cash paid for salaries | (200,000) |
| Cash paid for rent | (120,000) |
| Cash paid for other activities | (300,000) |
| Cash from operating activities | 200,000 |
| *Investing activities:* | |
| Purchase of building | (300,000) |
| *Financing activities:* | |
| Payment of dividends | (30,000) |
| *Decrease in cash* | (130,000) |
| *Cash as of January 1* | 450,000 |
| **Cash as of December 31** | **320,000** |

**Table 3.5** Example of Cash Flow Statement (direct method) ABC S.A. Statement of Cash Flows for the year ended December 31, 201X (in lei)

|  | 201X–1 | 201X |
| --- | --- | --- |
| **Cash Flows from Operating Activities:** |  |  |
| Cash receipts from customers | x | x |
| Cash paid to suppliers and employees | (x) | (x) |
| Income tax paid | (x) | (x) |
| Proceeds from extraordinary items | x | x |
| **Net Cash Flows from Operating Activities** | X | X |
| Cash Flows from investing activities: |  |  |
| Cash paid for the acquisition of equipment | (x) | (x) |
| Cash received from the sale of a building | x | X |
| **Net Cash Flows from Investing Activities** | X | X |
| **Cash Flows from Financing Activities:** |  |  |
| Cash receipts from share capital | x | X |
| Cash receipts from a bank loan | x | X |
| Repayment of a bank loan | (x) | (x) |
| **Net Cash Flows from Financing Activities** | X | X |
| Total Net Cash Flow | X | X |
| **Cash and cash equivalents at the beginning of year** | X | X |
| **Cash and cash equivalents at the end of year** | X | X |

*Source* Duțescu (2002)

While users need more accounting knowledge to grasp the particularities of the ***indirect method***, companies prefer it since it draws on already disclosed information (from the Balance Sheet and the Income Statement) that is adjusted for cash flow purposes. Since it provides new information, **IAS 7—Statement of Cash Flows** encourages companies to use the indirect method.

The essence of the indirect method is to adjust the net profit/loss before taxation with non-monetary expenses and revenues, with the variation of the working capital (variation of stocks + variation of current receivables − variation of current liabilities), as well as other items which have an effect on investing and financing cash flows (i.e. gains and losses from sales of fixed assets, foreign exchange gains or losses etc.). Only the operating segment is different from the direct method of disclosure; the investing and financing cash-flows are similar (Table 3.6).

**Table 3.6** Example of Cash Flow Statement (indirect method) ABC S.A. Statement of Cash Flows for the year ended December 31, 201X

|  | 201X-1 | 201X |
|---|---|---|
| Net Profit | x | x |
| Add: non-cash expenses (depreciation, provisions etc.) | x | x |
| Subtract non-cash revenues (provisions) |  |  |
| Changes in working capital: | x | x |
| (±) Variation of stocks | x | x |
| (±) Variation of receivables | x | x |
| (±) Variation of liabilities | x | x |
| ± Financial expenses/revenues | x | x |
| ± Investing losses/gains | x | x |
| **Net Cash Flows from Operating Activities** | **X** | **X** |
| **Cash Flows from Investing Activities** |  |  |
| Cash paid for the acquisition of equipment | (x) | (x) |
| Cash received from the sale of a building | x | x |
| **Net Cash Flows from Investing Activities** | **X** | **X** |
| **Cash Flows from Financing Activities** |  |  |
| Cash receipts from share capital | x | x |
| Cash receipt from a bank loan | x | x |
| Repayment of a bank loan | (x) | (x) |
| **Net Cash Flows from Financing Activities** | **X** | **X** |
| Total net cash flow | X | X |
| Cash and cash equivalents at the beginning of the year | X | X |
| **Cash and cash equivalents at the end of the year** | **X** | **X** |

*Source* Duțescu (2002)

## Illustration:

Based on the Income Statement and the Balance Sheet of ABAC S.A. (in thousands of lei), the following case provides the Statement of Cash Flow, using the indirect method:

ABC S.A.

Income statement for the year ended December 31, 201X (lei)

| Sales | 167,000 |
|---|---|
| Less cost of sales | 112,000 |
| Gross margin | 55,000 |
| Operating expenses | (30,000) |
| Interest expenses | (2000) |
| Depreciation of fixed assets | (4000) |
| **Net Profit for the year** | **19,000** |

*Note* The company has not paid dividends in 201X–1

## ABC S.A.
## Balance Sheet as at December 31 201X (lei)

|  | 201X-1 |  | 201X |
|---|---|---|---|
| Non-current assets at cost | 78,000 |  | 100,000 |
| Less accumulated depreciation | 36,000 |  | 40,000 |
| Net book value of fixed assets |  | 42,000 | 60,000 |
| Inventories |  | 5000 | 6000 |
| Account receivables |  | 2000 | 4000 |
| Cash |  | 2500 | 0 |
| Current assets |  | 9500 | 10,000 |
| Total Assets |  | 51,500 | 70,000 |
| Share capital |  | 5000 | 5000 |
| Accumulated profits |  | 13,500 | 32,500 |
| Total Equity |  | 18,500 | 37,500 |
| Long-term loans |  | 30,500 | 29,500 |
| Account payables |  | 2500 | 2500 |
| Bank overdraft |  | 0 | 500 |
| Total Liabilities |  | 33,000 | 32,500 |
| Total Equity and Liabilities |  | 51,500 | 70,000 |

## ABC S.A.
## Statement of Cash Flows (indirect method) for the year December 31, 201X (lei)

|  |  | 201X |
|---|---|---|
| Net Profit |  | 19,000 |
| Add: non-cash items |  | 4000 |
| Depreciation Expense |  |  |
| Changes in working capital |  |  |
| (-) Increase in inventories (6000 – 5000) | (1000) |  |
| (-) Increase in account receivables (4000 – 2000) | (2000) | (2500) |
| (+) Bank overdraft | 500 |  |
| (+) Interest expense |  |  |
| Net Cash Flows from Operating Activities |  | 20,500 |
| Cash Flows from Investing Activities: |  |  |
| Cash paid for the acquisition of equipment |  | (22,000) |
| (100,000 – 78,000) |  |  |
| Net Cash Flows from Investing Activities |  | (22,000) |
| Cash Flows from Financing Activities: |  |  |
| Decrease in long-term loans (29,500–30,500) |  | (1000) |
| Net Cash Flows from Financing Activities |  | (1000) |
| Total Net Cash Flow |  | (2500) |
| Cash and cash equivalents at the beginning of the year |  | 2500 |
| Cash and cash equivalents at the end of the year |  | 0 |

*Note* Variation of trade creditors is nil (2500 – 2500)

ABC's total cash flow is a negative, meaning that the outflows of cash were exceeding the inflows of cash. The company's statement of cash flow informs users that the cash inflow from operating activity has been used for investing in non-current assets and repaying long-term loans.

The Cash Flow Statement is particularly important as companies sometimes manipulate profits, using accounting policies that suit management's interests at a point in time. For example, the choice of the depreciation method leads to different accounting profit figures. Therefore, one might think that company A is doing better off than company B because its net profit is higher. The Statement of Cash Flows shows a different reality as company B generates a higher total cash figure for the year and positive cash flows from operating activities.

When analyzing a Cash-Flow Statement, the reader should bear in mind the following:

1. a positive operating cash flow is an absolute "must" to remain in business. Cash is needed to meet day-to-day obligations, invest in fixed assets, and pay interest and dividends;
2. a negative cash flow from investing activities is also a common situation, whereby during the reporting period, a company has purchased non-current assets or has made financial investments. These are expected to bring back future dividends, interest or future cash flows from operating activities;
3. a negative cash flow from financing activities occurs frequently because companies finance their growth from profits made, but also by either issuing more shares or borrowing more. Attracting additional finance comes at a cost and puts pressure on the company: on the one hand, more shareholders means more future cash outflows in the form of dividends, while on the other hand, the company will pay more interest in the future.

## 3.5 The Statement of Changes in Equity vs The Statement of Retained Earnings

The **Statement of Changes in Equity**, reports on changes in the wealth of an enterprise over a reporting period and discloses a reconciliation between the beginning balance of equity and the ending balance of each disclosed item. There are two reasons for such changes: (1) transactions with owners and (2) the activities of an enterprise. Transactions with owners consist of capital contributions and distributions to owners during the relevant period. The profit or loss for a period is the main cause for changes in equity from an enterprise's activities. Other causes could be the revaluation of non-current assets and foreign exchange differences. According to **IAS 1—Presentation of Financial Statements**, companies choose the appropriate format that best explains particular modifications within each item of equity.

This Statement highlights:

a) the net profit or loss over a period;
b) items of other comprehensive income that do not directly affect the net profit or loss of a business, but impact the equity, such as revaluation reserves or changes in accounting policies;
c) a reconciliation between the beginning of the balance of equity and the ending balance of each disclosed item.

Examples of items to be disclosed in this statement are: the net profit or loss attributable to shareholders, increase and decrease of capital, share premium and reserves, treasury shares purchased or sold (Chapter 8 offers details about this concept), distributed dividends, changes in accounting policies, correction of errors, effects of changes of the fair-value of some assets etc.

The following example presents a possible disclosure format for the Statement of Changes in Equity (Table 3.7).

As mentioned at the beginning of this chapter, apart from the Balance Sheet, the Profit and Loss Account, the Statement of Cash Flows and the Statement of Changes in Equity, the financial statements also include **accounting policies and explanatory notes**.

In many jurisdictions, including Romania, financial statements are disseminated and accompanied by a management report. This report reviews the factors that have influenced an enterprise's performance during the reporting period and describes funding, risk management and dividend policies. The report also incorporates other useful information

**Table 3.7** Statement of Changes in Equity ABC S.A. for the year ended December 31, 20X1

| Items | Opening balance | Increases[a] | Decreases[a] | Closing balance |
|---|---|---|---|---|
| Share capital | X | X | X | X |
| Share premium | X | X | X | X |
| Legal reserve | X | X | X | X |
| Revaluation reserves | X | X | X | X |
| Other reserves | X | X | X | X |
| Accumulated profits | X | X | X | X |
| Profit or loss for the year | | X | X | X |
| Total | X | X | X | X |

[a]Companies should disclose the nature of the events that have generated all the variations
*Source* Duțescu (2002)

for assessing the performance of an enterprise, information that is not presented elsewhere in the financial statements.

Financial statements are the responsibility of management. An independent auditor's report assures shareholders and other users that financial statements are not biased and are presented fairly that give a true and fair view of an enterprise's financial position, performance and changes in the financial position.

Let's remember the connections among financial statements (Table 3.8).

## 3.6 Transparency in Financial Statements

The provision of transparent and useful information on market participants and their transactions is essential for an effective and efficient market and is one of the most important preconditions for imposing market discipline. Left to themselves, markets may not generate sufficient levels of disclosure. Market forces normally balance the marginal benefits and the marginal costs of additional information disclosures, but the end result may not be what the market participants really need.

The public disclosure of information is predicated on the existence of relevant accounting standards and adequate disclosure methodologies. Public disclosure normally involves publication of relevant qualitative and quantitative information in annual financial statements, which are often

**Table 3.8** Relationships among financial statements

| INCOME STATEMENT FOR N | | | STATEMENT OF CHANGES' EQUITY FOR N | | |
|---|---|---|---|---|---|
| Revenues | lei | xxx | Changes in capital stock accounts | lei | xxx |
| Expenses | | xxx | Beginning balance, retained earnings | | 25,316 |
| Net income | lei | 5,948 | Add: Net income | | 5,948 |
| | | | Ending balance, retained earnings | lei | 31,264 |

| BALANCE SHEET | N-1 | N |
|---|---|---|
| Cash | lei 20,778 | lei 35,406 |
| All other assets | xxx | xxx |
| Total assets | lei xxx | lei xxx |
| Liabilities | lei xxx | lei xxx |
| Capital stock | xxx | xxx |
| Retained earnings | 25,316 | 31,264 |
| Total liabilities and stockholders' equity | lei xxx | lei xxx |

| STATEMENT OF CASH FLOW FOR N | | |
|---|---|---|
| Cash flows from operating activities | | |
|   Net income | lei | 5,948 |
|   Adjustments | | xxx |
| Net cash from operating activities | lei | xxx |
| Net cash used for investing activities | lei | xxx |
| Net cash used for financing activities | lei | xxx |
| Increase in cash | lei | 14,628 |
| Cash balance, beginning of year | lei | 20,778 |
| Cash balance, end of year | lei | 35,406 |

*Source* The authors

supplemented by interim financial statements and other relevant information. The provision of information involves costs; so, when determining disclosure requirements, its usefulness for the public must be evaluated against the anticipated cost incurred by an enterprise.

The timing of disclosure is also important. Disclosure of negative information to an unsophisticated public may damage the image of the enterprise in question. When the information is of inadequate quality and/or the users are not deemed capable to properly interpret the information, public disclosure requirements should be carefully phased and progressively tightened. In the long run, an extensive disclosure regime is beneficial, even if some problems are experienced in the short-term given that the cost of being transparent is high.

Transparency refers to the principle of creating an environment where information on existing conditions, decisions and actions are made accessible, visible and understandable to all market participants.

Accountability refers to the need for the market participants, including the authorities, to justify their actions and policies, and accept responsibility for their decisions and results. Transparency is necessary for the concept of accountability to take hold amongst the three major groups of market participants: borrowers and lenders, issuers and investors, as well as national authorities and international financial institutions.

Transparency and accountability have become strongly debated topics in discussions of economic policies over the past decade. Policymakers have become accustomed to secrecy. The changed world economy and financial flows, which brought about increased internationalisation and interdependence, have put the issue of openness at the forefront of economic policymaking. There is a growing recognition of national governments, including central banks, that transparency improves predictability and hence, the efficiency of policy decisions.

In the context of public disclosure, financial statements should be easy to interpret. While more information is better than less, the provision of information is costly. Therefore, the net benefits of providing more transparency should be carefully evaluated.

The adoption of IFRS is a necessary measure to facilitate transparency and proper interpretation of financial statements.

## 3.7 Conclusions

The following summary questions are intended to conclude this chapter:

**Chapter summary questions:**

| | |
|---|---|
| Which of the following are financial statements? | Financial statements are:<br>• The Statement of the Financial Position (Balance Sheet)<br>• The Statement of Profit and Loss and Other Comprehensive Income (Income Statement)<br>• The Statement of Cash Flows<br>• The Statement of Changes in Equity<br>• Additionaly entities disclose explanatory notes and accounting policies. |
| What is a Balance Sheet and what equation does it go by? | A Balance Sheet shows a company's net assets (net worth), as stated in the fundamental equation of accounting:<br>Assets = Equity + Liabilities<br>Assets − Liabilities = Equity<br>A Balance Sheet indicates a company's liquidity (the capacity to pay the short-term debts) and solvency (the capacity to pay all obligations). |

# 3 THE FINANCIAL STATEMENTS

| | |
|---|---|
| How are assets and liabilities classified on in a Balance Sheet? | Both assets and liabilities are classified based on "current" vs "non-current"; "current" means less than 12 month and "non-current" means more than 12 months. |
| What is the Profit and Loss Account and Other Comprehensive Income? | The Profit and Loss Account and Other Comprehensive Income shows a company's profitability, as well as the difference between revenues and expenses. When revenues are higher than expenses there is a profit, while the opposite means a loss. |
| What are the presentation formats for a Profit and Loss Account? | A Profit and Loss Account can be disclosed using a "by nature" format (expenses and revenues are classified based on their nature) or using a "by destination" format (expenses and revenues are classified based on their destination). |
| What is the Statement of Cash Flows? | The Statement of Cash Flows shows all sources of cash and all payments in cash for the financial year. This statement classifies cash flows as operating, investing and financial cash-flows. |
| What are the presentation formats available for the Statement of Cash Flows? | The presentation formats for the Statement of Cash Flows are the direct method and the indirect method. |
| What is the Statement of Changes in Equity? | The Statement of Changes in Equity shows all variations in equity positions, i.e. the capital of a business, reserves, retained earnings etc. |
| How are financial statements connected to each other? | The Balance Sheet is connected to the Statement of Profit and Loss through the net profit (loss) of the year, which is also an item of equity |
| | The Balance Sheet is connected with the statement of cash flows via cash and cash equivalents from the beginning of the year until the end of the year (same figures in both statements). The Statement of Cash Flows is connected with the Statement of Profit and Loss via the net profit before tax, when the indirect method is used to present the Statement of Cash Flow. |
| What does liquidity and solvency mean? What does profitability mean? | For a company to be liquid, it means that it has enough cash from its current assets to pay its current liabilities |
| | For a company to be solvent, it means that an entity is able to pay its long-term liabilities. |

**Quizzes (only one correct answer)**

1. Which one of the following is a non-current liability?
   a. A bank loan repayable within 2 years
   b. A mortgage repayable within 2 months
   c. A trade payable
   d. Other payables due in 6 months
2. Which of the following expenses are included in the cost of sales?
   a. Cost of raw materials
   b. Loan interest
   c. Salespeople's salaries
   d. Management salaries
3. Knowing that the sales are 100,000 lei, the cost of sales are 60,000 lei, and other expenses are 20,000 lei, which of the following statements is true?
   a. The gross profit margin is 60%
   b. The gross profit margin is 40%
   c. The gross profit margin is 20%
   d. The gross profit margin is 80%
4. Which one of the following is an asset?
   a. A bank loan
   b. A van
   c. An account payable
   d. The owner's capital
5. Which one of the following is a liability?
   a. Cash at bank
   b. An account receivable
   c. An account payable
   d. A trademark
6. Which one of the following is an owner's equity?
   a. Wage payable
   b. A truck
   c. Cost of goods sold
   d. Retained earnings
7. A Balance Sheet shows:
   a. The financial position of an entity
   b. The cash flow of a period
   c. The performance of an entity
   d. The changes in equity

8. What is the cash flow from operating activities, knowing that: the net income is $200, the annual depreciation of fixed assets is $125, accounts receivables were $586 last year and $673 for the current year, inventories were $610 last year and $657 this year, accounts payable were $332 last year and $389 this year, and the current year's gain on sale of equipment was $20:
   a. $228
   b. $382
   c. $402
   d. $248
9. On which Balance Sheet category do Profit or Loss belong?
   a. Assets
   b. Liabilities
   c. Shareholders' equity
   d. None of the above
10. The following data is provided for last year: the net income was $30,000, current assets (other than cash) increased by $12,000, and current liabilities increased by $8000. Under the indirect method, the cash flows from operating activities should be:
    a. $34,000
    b. $10,000
    c. $30,000
    d. $26,000

## Exercises

**Exercise 1:** Identify each of the following as an (A) asset, (B) liability, (C) revenue or (D) expense:

—-Accounts payable
—-Lease expense
—-Equipment
—-Prepaid insurance
—-Service revenue
—-Notes payable
—-Cash
—-Unearned service revenue
—-Building

**Exercise 2:** The lettered items below represent a classification scheme for the Balance Sheet, and the numbered elements are items of it. In the blank next to each item, write the letter indicating which category it belongs to.

a. Current assets
b. Investments
c. Property, plant and equipment
d. Intangible assets

e. Current liabilities
f. Long-term liabilities
g. Stockholders' equity
h. Not in the Balance Sheet

___1. Patent
___2. Building held for sale
___3. Prepaid rent
___4. Wages payable
___5. Note payable in five years
___6. Building used in operations
___7. Inventory

___8. Prepaid insurance
___9. Utility expense
___10. Accounts receivable
___11. Interest expense
___12. Revenue received in advance
___13. Short-term investments
___14. Retained earnings

**Exercise 3:** Prepare the Income statement and the Balance sheet for the ABAC Co., for the year ending December 31, 201X, based on the following: Capital $1025, notes payable $500, wage expense $925, accounts receivable $475, dividends $125, interest revenue $2200, cash $225, building $2000, accounts payable $100, utilities expenses $150, beginning of retained earnings $75, and rent expenses $250.

**Exercise 4:** Based on the list below, prepare the Balance Sheet and determine the Retained Earnings:

| Accounts payable | 7600 | Dividends payable | 6000 |
| Accounts receivable | 5500 | Patents | 10,000 |
| Automobiles | 9200 | Heat, light and water expense | 2400 |
| Buildings | 150,000 | Income tax payable | 2500 |
| Capital | 65,000 | Interest revenue | 3000 |
| Cash | 10,500 | Prepaid expenses | 800 |
| Fees expense | 2600 | Bonds loans | 21,300 |
| Sales revenue | 31,500 | Legal reserves | 4200 |
| Depreciation of buildings | (35,000) | Retained earnings | ? |

**Exercise 5:** Classify the following information into a Balance Sheet and determine the missing value of the elements (amounts are in $):

| | | | |
|---|---|---|---|
| Office equipment | 19,800 | Bond loans | ? |
| Depreciation of office equipment | 3100 | Expenses with salaries | 9000 |
| Salaries payable | 6900 | Patents | 5700 |
| Share capital | 14,400 | Prepayments from clients | 2000 |
| Prepaid expenses | 2700 | Expenses with utilities | 4800 |
| Dividends payable | 7500 | Legal reserves | 3600 |
| Land | 17,300 | Consumables | 900 |
| Bank account | 19,500 | Notes payable | 2500 |
| Revenues from services | 26,000 | Retained earnings | ? |

**Exercise 6:** The owner of the business ABAC S.A. does not understand how the company can be $17,600 ahead of last year in terms of cash and cash equivalents, and yet show an $11,000 loss for the year. Can you help him?

### ABAC S.A. – Profit and Loss Account

| | 20X8 ($) | 20X7 ($) |
|---|---|---|
| Revenues | 191,400 | 182,600 |
| Operating expenses | (202,400): | (146,300): |
| • Depreciation | 26,400 | 26,400 |
| • Fuel | 77,000 | 46,200 |
| • Salaries | 44,000 | 35,200 |
| • Taxes and licenses,, | 22,000 | 17,600 |
| • Repairs | 30,800 | 19,800 |
| • Miscellaneous | 2200 | 1100 |
| Profit (Loss) | (11,000) | 36,300 |

### ABC CO – Balance Sheet

| | 20X8 ($) | 20X7 ($) |
|---|---|---|
| Non-current assets......... | 198,000 | 224,400 |
| Accounts receivable....... | 8800 | 26,400 |
| Cash....................... | 22,000 | 4400 |
| Total of assets.......... | 228,800 | 255,200 |
| Accounts payable........... | 30,800 | 22,000 |
| Accrued salaries............. | 8800 | 5500 |
| Other accruals................ | 3300 | 1100 |
| Long-term debt.......... | 100,100 | 129,800 |
| Total liabilities......... | 143,000 | 158,400 |
| Capital of business......... | 85,800 | 96,800 |
| Total liabilities and capital | 228,800 | 255,200 |

### Case study

A British fashion retailer Next is among the biggest in the world, with about 700 shops globally, and $4.1 billion in revenue as of 2017. For a while they were making headlines as their sales forecasts was not very accurate, and instead, too optimistic. Interestingly enough is that this company has a Loss Prevention Manager. No business wants to make losses, as its primary purpose is to make sales. While the fashion industry at times can be difficult as trends change rapidly and customers adapt quickly.

In 2012, Next was the official clothing supplier to the 2012 London Olympics. Their 2012 Annual Report is very interesting from an accounting point of view. Their pre-tax profit was close to £570 million. Even so, when looking at their assets, Next holds large inventories of clothes. The inventories' value in the Balance Sheet was about £372 million while the cost of the goods sold was about £1320. In January 2012, their inventories fell in value, and made a loss close to £80 million. This loss occurred as the costs were higher than the net realisable value.

Provide a brief analysis of Next's 2012 inventory evolution, and their impact in the annual financial statements.

(*Sources* Next Annual report 2012, UK Reuters 2017, Digital Commerce 2017, Statistica.com).

### REFERENCE

Duțescu, A., Ghid pentru întelegerea si aplicarea Standardelor Internationale de Contabilitate, *CECCAR Publishing House*, Bucuresti, 2002, ISBN 973-85640-8-5.

CHAPTER 4

# Accounting Process and Transaction Analysis

*Adriana Duțescu, Oana Stănilă, and Răzvan Hoinaru*

*Learning objectives:*

- *Understanding the usefulness of double-entry accounting*
- *Using the accounting equation to analyse business transactions*
- *Understanding the "T" account and the rules of functioning*
- *Recording business transactions using the step approach*
- *Analysing business transactions and using the output for decision making*
- *Understanding the trial balance and its usefulness*

## 4.1 Introduction

This chapter is dedicated to accounting techniques, from the initial data (inputs) to journal entries and financial statements. The whole process, which is composed of transactions and other events at one end and financial statements at the other end, is called the **accounting process**. The accounting process consists of the identification and analysis of transactions and other events as well as classifying and summarizing their effects and reporting this information in financial statements or other reports.

These reports are used for internal purposes and are designed to mirror the business transactions, events and the effects of operations and financial events and to convert them into accounting jargon, in order to provide information for both internal reporting and external statements.

Reports may be used by stakeholders, for example potential investors, who may intend on investing in the company and are interested to find information about assets (cash, equipment), debts, profits and dividends paid.

The following concepts and techniques are detailed further on:

- The accounting equation;
- Double-entry accounting and the "T" account;
- The steps of the transaction analysis;
- The closing procedures and the trial balance;
- Preparing the Balance Sheet and the Income Statement.

## 4.2 The Accounting Equation

The relationship between the three basic accounting items, assets, liabilities and equity, is expressed in the accounting equation, shown as follows:

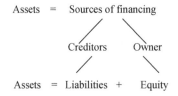

The equation shows that assets are equal to their source of financing. In fact, it measures the economic resources and the sources of financing a business. The sources of financing are divided into liabilities and owner's equity. From this it can be derived another important relationship, called ***net assets*** or ***net worth***:

$$Assets = Liabilities + Equity$$

or

$$Equity = Assets - Liabilities$$

or

$$\text{Net assets (net liabilities)} = Assets - Liabilities$$

To recap, we can say that **assets** are the economic resources of a business, that are expected to bring future benefits. Assets represent what the business owns or controls, such as cash, inventories, equipment, buildings, land etc.

**Liabilities** are debts owed to other entities, called creditors. The creditors have a claim on the company's assets until the payment is made.
**Owner's equity** or **Capital** represents the owner's claim to the company's assets from the initial investment into the business's capital.

### The effect of transactions on accounting equation

In accounting terms, a transaction is defined as an event which affects the financial position or the performance of a business. Buying and selling goods and receiving or paying money are examples of transactions. There are two main types of transactions, in connection to cash and goods and services sold/purchased:

- *cash transactions*: where money is received in exchange for goods or services
- *non-cash transactions*: where goods or services are supplied or received on agreement that payment will be made at a maturity date.

The transaction is the basic operating event of the business. For example, cash is used to purchase goods, these goods are then sold and the cash received from clients is used then to purchase more goods which, in turn, are sold, etc. This cycle of cash → goods → cash is called the *operating cycle*.

To show how transactions are recorded in terms of the accounting equation, consider the following examples:

### Example 1:

*Transaction (a)*: The owner Ion Popescu (I.P.) invested **30,000** lei in the business I.P. S.R.L.

The effect on the accounting equation is an increase in assets and increase in equity.

**Analysis**: Mr. I.P. opened a bank account for his business of **30,000** lei. This transaction increased the asset "Cash" (or "Bank Account") and at the same time increased the equity by the same amount. The equation for the business would appear as follows:

| Assets | = | Liabilities | + | Equity |
|---|---|---|---|---|
| Cash | = | | | Capital |
| (a) **+30,000** | | | | **+30,000** |

Total Assets: 30,000 lei = Total Liabilities + Equity: 30,000 lei

*Transaction (b)*: The business purchased office equipment for 2500 lei on account.

The effect on the accounting equation is an increase in assets and increase in liabilities.

**Analysis**: The company purchased office equipment for 2500 lei on account. This transaction caused the asset "Office equipment" (the specific asset) to increase, and the liability "Accounts Payable" (the debt to the supplier of the equipment) to increase by the same amount. The accounting equation is:

| Assets | | | = | Liabilities | + | Equity |
|---|---|---|---|---|---|---|
| Cash | + | Office Equip. | = | Accounts Payable | | Capital |
| Bal. lei 30,000 | | | | | | 30,000 lei |
| (b) | | +2500 | | +2500 | | |
| Bal. 30,000 lei | + | 2500 lei | = | 2500 lei | + | 30,000 lei |

Total Assets 32,500 lei = Total Liabilities + Equity 32,500 lei

*Transaction (c)*: The company purchased office supplies of 350 lei paying cash.

The effect on the accounting equation is a decrease in assets and increase in other assets.

**Analysis**: The company purchased office supplies in the amount of 350 lei for cash. This transaction caused the asset "Cash" to decrease by 350 lei and the asset "Office Supplies" to increase by the same amount. The effect on the equation is as follows:

| Assets | | | | | = | Liabilities | + | Equity |
|---|---|---|---|---|---|---|---|---|
| Cash | + | Office Supp. | + | Office Equip. | = | Accounts Payable | | Capital |
| Bal. 30,000 | | | | 2500 | | 2500 | | 30,000 |
| (c) −350 | | +350 | | | | | | |
| Bal. 29,650 | + | 350 | + | 2500 | = | 2500 | + | 30,000 |

Total Assets 32,500 lei = Total Liabilities + Equity 32,500 lei

*Transaction (d)*: The company partially paid the supplier of the office equipment, an amount of 500 lei.

The effect on the accounting equation is a decrease in assets and decrease in liabilities.

**Analysis**: The company paid 500 lei to the supplier of the office equipment. Earlier the purchase of the office equipment on account was recorded.

This payment caused both the asset "Cash" and the liability "Accounts Payable" to decrease by 500 lei. The effect in the equation is as follows:

| Assets | | | | | = | Liabilities | + | Equity |
|---|---|---|---|---|---|---|---|---|
| Cash | + | Office Supp. | + | Office Equip. | = | Accounts Payable | | Capital |
| Bal. 29,650 | | 350 | | 2500 | | 2500 | | 30,000 |
| (d) −500 | | | | | | −500 | | |
| Bal. 29,150 | + | 350 | + | 2500 | = | 2000 | + | 30,000 |
| Total Assets 32,000 lei = Total Liabilities + Equity 32,000 lei | | | | | | | | |

*Transaction (e)*: The company purchased office supplies on account of 400 lei.

The effect on the accounting equation is an increase in assets and increase in liabilities.

**Analysis**: The owner purchased office supplies on account for 400 lei. This transaction caused an increase in the asset "Office Supplies" by 400 lei and an increase in the liability "Accounts Payable" by the same amount. The effect of this transaction is as follows:

| Assets | | | | | = | Liabilities | + | Equity |
|---|---|---|---|---|---|---|---|---|
| Cash | + | Office Supp. | + | Office Equip. | = | Accounts Payable | | Capital |
| Bal. 29,150 | | 350 | | 2500 | | 2000 | | 30,000 |
| (e) | | +400 | | | | +400 | | |
| Bal. 29,150 | + | 750 | + | 2500 | = | 2400 | + | 30,000 |
| Total Assets 32,400 lei = Total Liabilities + Equity 32,400 lei | | | | | | | | |

## 4.3 Double Entry and the "T" Account

Every transaction impacts at least two items from the accounting equation. This forms the basis of **double-entry accounting**, introduced by Luca Pacioli in 1494. The reason that double-entry accounting has been in existence for over 500 years is because it ensures accuracy and good representation of the business development and its operations.

A company opens **an account** for each asset, liability, equity and for each expense and revenue that is impacting its business. **The "Ledger"** (in Romanian. "Cartea Mare") contains all the accounts used during a financial year. An account has two parts, which separate increases from decreases of the item described. The simplest account form has the shape

**Table 4.1** The "T" account

| The "T" account ||
|---|---|
| DEBIT | CREDIT |
|  |  |
|  |  |
|  |  |

*Source* The authors

**Table 4.2** The balance-column account

| The balance-column account ||||
|---|---|---|---|
| Corresponding account | DEBIT | CREDIT | BALANCE |
|  |  |  |  |
|  |  |  |  |

*Source* The authors

of the letter "T", with **debit** on the left side and **credit** on the right side. Another format is a "balanced column" one and has debit and credit columns for recording entries and a third column for showing the balance of the account after each entry. Tables 4.1 and 4.2 illustrations provide a graphical example of the two formats.

The list of all possible synthetic T accounts and their symbols is called "the chart of accounts" (planul de conturi). An example is provided in Appendix.

Some countries have compulsory charts of accounts (as for example Romania), whereas other countries are more flexible, in the sense that companies have more liberty in designing their own chart of accounts (e.g. UK, USA).

Each account is characterised by the following details:

- The **name of the account** is given by the name of the appropriate asset, liability, equity, expense or revenue (e.g. "Cash", "Capital", "Salary expense" etc.);
- The **code or the symbol of the account** is a number attached to each account, facilitating the use of software (for example, in the Romanian chart of accounts the following symbols are used: 512 "Bank account", 101 "Capital" and 641 "Salary Expense").

- The **description of the transaction** may be replaced with the name and/or symbol of the corresponding account, i.e. for the debit account, the name of the credit account;
- The left-hand side is called, by convention, the **debit side** of the account;
- The right-hand side is called, by convention, the **credit side** of the account;
- The total of the amounts posted on the debit side is called the **total debit amount** (TDA). It comprises, for example, the opening balance (OB) of asset accounts and the current debit amount (CDA), i.e. the debit movement during the period;
- The total of the amounts posted on the credit side is called the **total credit amount** (TCA). It comprises, for example, the opening balance (OB) of equity and liability accounts and the current credit amount (CCA), i.e. the credit movement during the period;
- The difference between the total debit amount and the total credit amount is called the **closing balance** (CB). When the total debit amount exceeds the total credit amount, the account has a **debit closing balance**. A **credit closing balance** occurs in the opposite case. The closing balance at the end of an accounting period becomes the opening balance (OB) at the beginning of the next period. An account having the same total debit amount with the total credit amount is called a **"balanced account"** (zero ending balance).

## Double-entry accounting

Double-entry accounting assumes that each transaction has a double effect, at least on two accounts: one effect will be recorded as a debit in one account and the other effect will be recorded as a credit in another account. It follows that the total debit must equal the total credit for each transaction. To demonstrate the rules as to when to debit and when to credit an account, we shall come back to the fundamental accounting equation:

$$\text{ASSETS} = \text{EQUITY} + \text{LIABILITIES}$$

We have linked assets to inflows of economic benefits and liabilities to outflows of economic benefits. Therefore, one can classify accounts into **"active accounts"**, and **"passive accounts"**. What is the difference in functioning?

Assume that increases in assets are posted to the DEBIT side of asset accounts. As an asset is the opposite of a liability, it follows that increases in liability and equity accounts should be posted to the CREDIT side of these accounts. This works similarly for decreases in assets, liabilities and equity accounts, which should logically be posted on the opposite side of the respective accounts. Therefore, decreases in assets are posted to the CREDIT side of asset accounts, while decreases in equity and liability should be posted to the DEBIT side of equity and liability accounts.

We have also noted that an expense decreases equity, while revenue increases equity. Therefore, expense accounts should behave in an opposite way to equity accounts, that is, similarly to asset accounts. Revenue accounts follow the same pattern as equity accounts.

Accounts have a closing balance where the increases in such accounts are recorded. Asset accounts have debit opening and closing balances. For example, when the Raw Materials account shows a debit opening balance, it means that materials are still in the company (in the warehouse) at the beginning of the accounting period (purchases or production may have exceeded consumption or sale during the past accounting period). The other possibility is a nil (zero) balance. Likewise, its closing debit balance means that materials are still in the warehouse, at the end of the accounting period.

Liability and equity accounts may have also opening and closing credit balances. For example, the credit opening balance of the "Account Payable" account reflects the fact that the current accounting period starts with a liability from the past accounting period (obligations incurred may have exceeded payments during the past accounting period). Similarly, the closing credit balance of this account reflects an outstanding liability at the end of the accounting period. Expense and revenue accounts normally have nil opening and closing balances.

The rules of debit and credit may be summarized as in Table 4.3.

Table 4.3 Rules of accounts' functioning

| Type of account | Nature of account | To record increase | To record decrease |
| --- | --- | --- | --- |
| Asset | Active | Debit | Credit |
| Liability | Passive | Credit | Debit |
| Equity | Passive | Credit | Debit |
| Revenue | Passive | Credit | Debit |
| Expense | Active | Debit | Credit |

*Source* The authors

**Table 4.4** Summary of accounts functioning

| \<The "T" account\> | |
|---|---|
| DEBIT | CREDIT |
| *Opening balance of asset accounts* | *Opening balance of liability and equity accounts* |
| Increase in asset accounts | Decrease in asset accounts |
| Increase in expense accounts | Decrease in expense accounts |
| Decrease in equity accounts | Increase in equity accounts |
| Decrease in liability accounts | Increase in liability accounts |
| Decrease in revenue accounts | Increase in revenue accounts |
| *Closing balance of asset accounts* | *Closing balance of equity and liability accounts* |

*Source* The authors

To illustrate these rules simply, each type of account is shown below in T-accounts:

| Assets | = | Liabilities | + | Owner's Equity | + | Revenue | − | Expense |
|---|---|---|---|---|---|---|---|---|
| Debit to increase + ↑ | Credit to decrease − ↓ | Debit to decrease − ↓ | Credit to increase + ↑ | Debit to decrease − ↓ | Credit to increase + ↑ | Debit to decrease − ↓ | Credit to increase + ↑ | Debit to increase + ↑ | Credit to decrease − ↓ |

The same functioning rules but in a different perspective are shown in Table 4.4.

The same rules are expressed in the following succession of "T"-accounts:

| All asset accounts | | All equity accounts | | All liability accounts | |
|---|---|---|---|---|---|
| Opening debit balance | Decreases | Decreases | Opening credit balance | Decreases | Opening credit balance |
| | Closing debit balance | Closing credit balance | | Closing credit balance | |
| Increases | | | Increases | | Increases |
| | | | | | |
| | | | | | |

| All expense accounts | | All revenue accounts | |
|---|---|---|---|
| Increases | Decreases | Decreases | Increases |
|  |  |  |  |

Each **active account** is characterised by the following equation (assuming debit to the left of "=" and credit to its right):

| | DEBIT = | CREDIT | |
|---|---|---|---|
| Opening debit balance | + Current debit amount | = Current credit amount | + Closing debit balance |

Each **passive account** has a similar equation:

| | DEBIT = | CREDIT | |
|---|---|---|---|
| Current debit amount | + Closing credit balance | = Opening credit balance | + Current credit amount |

Besides **active** and **passive accounts** there are also **bifunctional accounts**, that might have either a debit closing balance or a credit closing balance. A classic example of a bifunctional account is the Profit and Loss Account which records revenues in its credit side and expenses in its debit side. Therefore, when revenues are higher than a credit closing balance, the profit is disclosed and when expenses are higher, there is a debit closing balance, a loss.

## 4.4   The Steps of the Transaction Analysis

Accountants record transactions and other events on the basis of source documents (in Romanian "documente primare"), such as sale invoices, checks, receipts, bills, payrolls, bank statements etc. Source documents are very important as they grant objectivity and verifiability to accounting information. Every transaction (or event) shall be assessed and analysed, following the subsequent steps presented.

**Step one** of the transaction analysis looks at the source documents that underlie a transaction. For example, the analysis of an invoice may show a credit purchase or a credit sale. Once the **nature** of a transaction is established, its effects on the financial position and performance are ascertained, as step number two.

In **Step two** the changes in the accounting equation (equilibrium) are identified. For example, a credit purchase of merchandise leads to an increase of an asset (the company's inventory) and an increase in the company's liabilities (account payables).

**Step three** applies the double-entry technique of the account's functioning, in order to identify the impact of a transaction on relevant accounts. Here, transactions and events are recorded in chronological order through entries to the **General Journal**. To journalize a transaction is equivalent to recording it into the General Journal, through a **journal entry** ("înregistrare contabilă" in Romanian). A journal entry records information about each transaction, such as:

- the transaction's date;
- the source document and its number;
- a description of the transaction;
- accounts' names and codes;
- the amounts of each debit and credit.

For example, a raw material purchase on credit is recorded as in Table 4.5.

Journal entries may be simple, where one account is debited and another one is credited, as in the example above, or complex, where more than two accounts are debited or credited at the same time. Both simple and compounded journal entries must be balanced. A journal entry is balanced when the sum of debit equals to the sum of credit.

**Table 4.5** The Romanian format of the General Journal

| GENERAL JOURNAL | | | | | | |
|---|---|---|---|---|---|---|
| Date | Source document no. | Description | Journal entry | | Amounts (lei) | |
| | | | Debiting accounts | Crediting accounts | Debiting | Crediting |
| February 1st 20X1 | Invoice 203 | Purchase of raw materials | 301 raw materials | 401 accounts payable | 12,000 | 12,000 |

*Source* The authors

Therefore, the totals of the debit and credit columns of the journal must be equal.

**Step four**: The journal entries' amounts should then be **posted** into the "Ledger", meaning that in each specific "T" accounts impacted by the transaction, the debit or credit amounts are to be recorded. The Ledger is a journal that gathers all the "T" accounts of the company and the amounts are recorded either in the debit or credit side, as applicable.

**Example 2**: We shall now apply the steps of transaction analysis to obtain journal entries.

**Transaction 1**: On January 1st, 20X4 John and Peter founded Happiness S.R.L., each contributing with 2500 lei in cash. The newly established company will buy and resell IT accessories.

| Steps | Review questions | Answers |
|---|---|---|
| 1. | What is the nature of transaction or event? | The establishment of a company |
| 2. | What is the effect of the transaction on the fundamental accounting equation (A = E + L)? | $A + x = (E + x) + L$ <br> Increases an asset (Cash at Bank) <br> Increases equity (Capital) |
| 3. | Which side of the "Cash" account represents the increase in materials? | Debit side |
|    | Which side of the "Capital" account represents the increase in equity? | Credit side |
|    | What is the journal entry? | Lei 5000 "Cash" = "Capital" 5000 lei |
| 4. | Post the amounts into the Ledger | D Cash C / Lei 5000      D Capital C / 5000 lei |

**Transaction 2**: On January 2nd 20X4, Happiness S.R.L. purchased goods on credit for 14,000 lei. The supplier, Music Warehouse S.R.L., requires the payment in X days.

| Steps | Self-questions | Answers |
|---|---|---|
| 1. | What is the nature of this transaction or event? | A credit purchase |
| 2. | What is the effect of the transaction on the fundamental accounting equation (A = E + L)? | $A + x = E + (L + x)$ <br> It increases an asset (Goods) <br> It increases a liability (Account payables) |

## 4 ACCOUNTING PROCESS AND TRANSACTION ANALYSIS 75

| Steps | Self-questions | Answers |
|---|---|---|
| 3. | Which side of "Goods" account represents the increase in materials? | Debit side |
|  | Which side of "Account payables" account represents the increase in liabilities? | Credit side<br>Lei 14,000 "Goods" = "Acc payables" 14,000 lei |
|  | What is the journal entry? |  |
| 4. | Posting the amounts into the Ledger | D  Goods  C    D Account payables  C<br>Lei 14,000                                    14,000 lei |

**Transaction 3a**: On January 4th, 20X4, Happiness S.R.L. sold goods on credit for 10,000 lei.

| Steps | Self-questions | Answers |
|---|---|---|
| 1. | What is the nature of transaction or event? | A sale on credit |
| 2. | What is the effect of the transaction on the fundamental accounting equation (A=E+L)? | A+x=(E+x)+L<br>It increases an asset (Account receivables)<br>It increases a revenue (Revenues from Sales) |
| 3. | Which side of "Account receivables" account represents the increase in cash? | Debit side |
|  | Which side of "Revenue from Sales" account represents the increase in revenues? | Credit side<br>Lei 10,000 "Acc. Receivables" = "Rev. from sale" 10,000 lei |
|  | What is the journal entry? |  |
| 4. | Posting the amounts in the accounts (Ledger) | D  Acc receivables  C    D  Rev. from sale  C<br>Lei 10,000                                    10,000 lei |

**Transaction 3b**: The cost of the goods sold in transaction 3a was 8000 lei.

| Steps | Review questions | Answers |
|---|---|---|
| 1. | What is the nature of transaction or event? | Disposal of goods sold from inventory |
| 2. | What is the effect of the transaction on the fundamental accounting equation (A=E+L)? | A−x=(E−x)+L<br>It increases an expense (Expenses for goods)<br>It decreases an asset (Goods) |
| 3. | Which side of the "Expenses for Goods" account represents the increase in expenses? | Debit side |
|  | Which side of the "Goods" account represents the decrease in goods for resale? | Credit side |
|  | What is the journal entry? | Lei 8000 "Expenses for goods" = "Goods" 8000 lei |
| 4. | Post the amounts in the accounts (Ledger) | D Expenses for goods C    D Goods C<br>Lei 8000                      8000 lei |

**Transaction 4**: On January 6th, 20X4, Happiness S.R.L. receives half of the amount due by its debtor in its bank account.

| Steps | Review questions | Answers |
|---|---|---|
| 1. | What is the nature of transaction or event? | Receipt of the consideration owned to the client |
| 2. | What is the effect of the transaction on the fundamental accounting equation (A=E+L)? | A+x−x=E+L<br>It increases an asset (Cash or Bank Account)<br>It decreases an asset (Account receivables) |
| 3. | Which side of the "Cash" account represents the increase in cash? | Debit side |
|  | Which side of the "Account receivables" account represents the decrease in receivables? | Credit side |
|  | What is the journal entry? | Lei 5000 "Cash" = "Account receivables" 5000 lei |
| 4. | Post the amounts in the accounts (Ledger) | D Cash C    D Account receivables C<br>Lei 5000                    5000 lei |

**Transaction 5**: On January 7th, 20X4, Happiness S.R.L. only has 10,000 lei in its bank account to pay its supplier, Warehouse S.R.L. The payment is made through Happiness's bank account.

| Steps | Self-questions | Answers |
|---|---|---|
| 1. | What is the nature of transaction or event? | Payment of a liability |
| 2. | What is the effect of the transaction on the fundamental accounting equation $(A = E + L)$? | $A - x = E + (L - x)$<br>It decreases a liability (Account payables)<br>It decreases an asset (Cash at Bank) |
| 3. | Which side of the "Account payables" account represents the decrease in liabilities? | Debit side |
|  | Which side of the "Cash" account represents the decrease in cash? | Credit side |
|  | What is the journal entry? | Lei 10,000 "Acc payables" = "Cash" 10,000 lei |
| 4. | Post the amounts in the accounts (Ledger) | D Acc payables C    D Cash C<br>Lei 10,000                       10,000 lei |

**Transaction 6**: In exchange of the outstanding liability, Warehouse S.R.L. becomes a shareholder of Happiness S.R.L.

| Steps | Review questions | Answers |
|---|---|---|
| 1. | What is the nature of transaction or event? | Conversion of a liability into equity |
| 2. | What is the effect of the transaction on the fundamental accounting equation $(A = E + L)$? | $A = (E + x) + (L - x)$<br>It decreases a liability (Acc payables)<br>It increases equity (Capital) |
| 3. | Which side of the "Account payables" account represents the decrease in liabilities? | Debit side |
|  | Which side of the "Capital" account represents the decrease in cash? | Credit side |
|  | What is the journal entry? | Lei 4000 "Acc payables" = "Capital" 4000 lei |
| 4. | Post the amounts in the accounts (Ledger) | D Acc payables C    D Capital C<br>Lei 4000                        4000 lei |

## 4.5 The Ledger and the Trial Balance

Journal entries are posted (copied) to the Ledger in the following manner: debit amounts are posted to the left side of the debit account and credit amounts are posted to the right side of the credit account.

We shall now show the transactions journalized to the Ledger in Sect. 4.4, disclosing the correspondent account for each transaction and the dates of transactions:

**Cash**

| DEBIT | | CREDIT | |
|---|---|---|---|
| 01.01. Capital | 5000 | 07.01. Acc. payables | 10,000 |
| 06.01. Acc receivables | 5000 | | |

**Capital**

| DEBIT | | CREDIT | |
|---|---|---|---|
| | | 01.01. Cash at Bank | 5000 |
| | | 07.01. Acc payables | 4000 |

**Goods**

| DEBIT | | CREDIT | |
|---|---|---|---|
| 02.01. Acc payables | 14,000 | 04.01. Expenses with goods | 8000 |

**Account payables**

| DEBIT | | CREDIT | |
|---|---|---|---|
| 07.01. Cash at Bank | 10,000 | 02.01. Goods | 14,000 |
| 07.01. Capital | 4000 | | |

Account receivables

| DEBIT | | CREDIT | |
|---|---|---|---|
| 04.01. Revenue from Sale | 10,000 | 06.01. Cash at Bank | 5000 |
| | | | |

Revenue from Sales

| DEBIT | | CREDIT | |
|---|---|---|---|
| | | 04.01. Acc receivables | 10,000 |
| | | | |

Expenses with goods

| DEBIT | | CREDIT | |
|---|---|---|---|
| 04.01. Goods | 8000 | | |
| | | | |

As a consequence of the fundamental accounting equation, the sum of opening debit balances (asset accounts) equals the sum of opening credit balances (equity and liability accounts). Since each journal entry is balanced, the sum of the debit movement of all accounts equals the sum of the credit movement of all accounts. Therefore, the sum of closing debit balances equals the sum of closing credit balances.

All of these results are reviewed using the **trial balance**. The trial balance is a list of accounts, providing their debit and credit amounts and the balances at a point in time. The trial balance has a certain number of columns, that, in pairs of two, should have similar totals. The trial balance also condenses the information from the Ledger, facilitating the preparation of the financial statements. This is the reason why companies extract a trial balance usually before transferring the balances of revenues and expenses accounts to the Profit and Loss Account (Income Statement). When the totals of the columns do not match, one or several errors must have occurred while entering the journal entries to the ledger, transferring amounts from the ledger to the trial balance or while calculating account balances or trial balance totals. Today's software programs for data processing (ERP or other integrated computer software) have mitigated possible errors but, nevertheless, IT system errors still occur and sometimes are even be more difficult to be detected.

The main functions of the trial balance are:

a) to verify the accuracy of records made in the accounts;
b) to group and centralise the data recorded in the accounts.

Trial balances may be simple or more complex. A simple trial balance is a list of opening or closing balances of the T-accounts that have been used during the period, as in Table 4.6.

A more complex trial balance may contain several sets of columns. A rather common trial balance that has three sets of columns is illustrated in Table 4.7.

In some jurisdictions, companies may be required to disclose a more complex trial balance, together with their annual financial statements. Most of today's software systems provide this facility. This particular trial balance provides pairs of columns for opening debit and credit balances, current debit and credit amounts, total debit and credit amounts and closing debit and credit balances (Table 4.8).

**Table 4.6** Trial Balances format—one set of columns

| *The trial balance with one set of columns* | | | | | | |
|---|---|---|---|---|---|---|
| Name of account | Opening debit balance | Opening credit balance | or | Name of account | Closing debit balance | Closing credit balance |
| Account 1 | | | | Account 1 | | |
| Account 2 | | | | Account 2 | | |
| Account 3 | | | | Account 3 | | |
| ... | | | | ... | | |
| Total | ΣODB | ΣOCB | | Total | ΣCDB | ΣCCB |

ΣODB = ΣOCB
or
ΣCDB = ΣCCB
*Source* The authors

**Table 4.7** Trial Balances format—three sets of columns

*The trial balance with three sets of columns*

| Name of account | Opening debit balance | Opening credit balance | Total debit amount | Total credit amount | Closing debit balance | Closing credit balance |
|---|---|---|---|---|---|---|
| Account 1 | | | | | | |
| Account 2 | | | | | | |
| Account 3 | | | | | | |
| ... | | | | | | |
| Total | ΣODB | ΣOCB | ΣTDA | ΣTCA | ΣCDB | ΣCCB |

ΣODB = ΣOCB
ΣTDA = ΣTCA
ΣCDB = ΣCCB
*Source* The authors

## 4.6 THE BALANCE SHEET AND THE PROFIT AND LOSS ACCOUNT

Before the Balance Sheet and the Profit and Loss Account are drawn up, the following steps are necessary:

- balance the accounts, that is, work out closing (debit or credit) balances;
- extract the intermediate trial balance;
- book the adjusting entries (prepayments, accruals, provisions for risk and charges, missing items, declines in value etc.); more detail on the adjusting entries are provided by the Chapter 10;
- extract the final trial balance;
- transfer revenue and expense balances to the Profit and Loss account;
- record asset, equity and liability balances in the Balance Sheet.

We shall balance the accounts and extract the trial balance of Happiness S.R.L. This entity has no opening balances, therefore for each account we shall calculate only the current movement and closing balances. For the same reason, we shall only use a trial balance with two pairs of columns: one pair for the current movement and another for closing balances. The reader should note that expenses and revenues

**Table 4.8** Trial Balances format—four sets of columns

*The trial balance with four sets of columns (also called the trial balance with four sets of equalities)*

| Name of account | Opening debit balance | Opening credit balance | Current debit amount | Current credit amount | Total debit amount | Total credit amount | Closing debit balance | Closing credit balance |
|---|---|---|---|---|---|---|---|---|
| Account 1 | | | | | | | | |
| Account 2 | | | | | | | | |
| Account 3 | | | | | | | | |
| … | | | | | | | | |
| Total | ΣODB | ΣOCB | ΣCDA | ΣCCA | ΣTDA | ΣTCA | ΣCDB | ΣCCB |

ΣODB = ΣOCB
ΣCDA = ΣCCA
ΣTDA = ΣTCA
ΣCDB = ΣCCB

*Source* The authors

accounts have only temporary balances, since these will be transferred to the Profit and Loss Account.

### Cash

| DEBIT | | CREDIT | |
|---|---|---|---|
| 01.01. Capital | 5000 | 07.01. Acc payables | 10,000 |
| 06.01. Acc receivables | 5000 | | |
| Current debit amount | <u>10,000</u> | Current credit amount | <u>10,000</u> |
| | | | |

### Capital

| DEBIT | | CREDIT | |
|---|---|---|---|
| | | 01.01 Cash | 5000 |
| | | 07.01. Acc payables | 4000 |
| Closing balance | 9000 | Current credit amount | <u>9000</u> |
| | <u>9000</u> | | <u>9000</u> |
| | | | |
| | | Opening balance | 9000 |

### Goods

| DEBIT | | CREDIT | |
|---|---|---|---|
| 02.01. Acc payables | 14,000 | 04.01. Expenses for goods | 8000 |
| Current debit amount | 14,000 | Current credit amount | 8000 |
| | — | Closing balance | 6000 |
| | <u>14,000</u> | | <u>14,000</u> |
| | | | |
| Opening balance | 6000 | | |

### Accounts payables

| DEBIT | | CREDIT | |
|---|---|---|---|
| 07.01. Cash | 10,000 | 02.01. Goods | 14,000 |
| 07.01. Capital | 4000 | | |
| Current debit amount | <u>14,000</u> | Current credit amount | <u>14,000</u> |
| | | | |

## Account receivables

| DEBIT | | CREDIT | |
|---|---|---|---|
| 04.01.Revenue from Sale | 10,000 | 1.06. | Cash 5000 |
| **Current debit amount** | **10,000** | **Current credit amount** | **5000** |
| | | **Closing balance** | **5000** |
| | **10,000** | | **10,000** |
| Opening balance | 5000 | | |

## Revenue from Sales

| DEBIT | | CREDIT | |
|---|---|---|---|
| | | 04.01. Acc receivables | 10,000 |
| | | **Current credit amount** | **10,000** |

## Expenses for goods

| DEBIT | | CREDIT | |
|---|---|---|---|
| 04.01. Goods | 8000 | | |
| **Current debit amount** | **8000** | | |

To fill in the trial balance, we shall start with equity, asset and liability balances in a decreasing liquidity order (cash is the last) and continue with revenue and expense balances.

### Trial balance extracted from the books of Happiness S.R.L. as of 7 January 20X4 (lei)

| Name of account | Current debit amount | Current credit amount | Closing debit balance | Closing credit balance |
|---|---|---|---|---|
| Capital | | 9000 | | 9000 |
| Goods | 14,000 | 8000 | 6000 | |
| Account receivables | 10,000 | 5000 | 5000 | |

# 4 ACCOUNTING PROCESS AND TRANSACTION ANALYSIS

| Name of account | Current debit amount | Current credit amount | Closing debit balance | Closing credit balance |
|---|---|---|---|---|
| Account payables | 14,000 | 14,000 | | |
| Cash at bank | 10,000 | 10,000 | | |
| Revenue from sale | | 10,000 | | 10,000 |
| Expenses for goods | 8000 | | 8000 | |
| Total | 56,000 | 56,000 | 19,000 | 19,000 |

Happiness has no adjusting entries and therefore no final trial balance is needed. Revenue and expense balances will be transferred to the Profit and Loss Account (Income Statement) using the following two journal entries:

| 10,000 lei | Revenue from Sale | = | Profit and Loss Account | 10,000 lei |
|---|---|---|---|---|

| 10,000 lei | Profit and Loss Account | = | Expenses for Goods | 10,000 lei |
|---|---|---|---|---|

The revenue and expense accounts are now balanced:

### Revenue from Sales

| DEBIT | | CREDIT | |
|---|---|---|---|
| 07.01. P & L Account | 10,000 | 04.01. Acc receivables | 10,000 |
| **Current debit amount** | **10,000** | **Current credit amount** | **10,000** |
| | | | |

### Expense for Goods

| DEBIT | | CREDIT | |
|---|---|---|---|
| 04.01. Goods | 8000 | 07.01. P & L Account | 8000 |
| **Current debit amount** | **8000** | **Current credit amount** | **8000** |
| | | | |

The Profit and Loss Account and the Balance Sheet of Happiness S.R.L. are shown below:

**Profit and Loss account for the period ending January 7th, 20X4 (lei)**

| EXPENSES | | REVENUE | |
|---|---|---|---|
| 07.01. Expense for Goods | 8000 | 07.01. Revenue from Sale | 10,000 |
| **Closing balance profit** | 2000 | | |
| | **10,000** | | **10,000** |
| | | Opening balance profit | 2000 |

**Balance Sheet as of January 7th, 20X4 (lei)**

| ASSETS | | EQUITY AND LIABILITIES | |
|---|---|---|---|
| Goods | 6000 | Capital | 9000 |
| Acc payables | 5000 | Profit | 2000 |
| **Total assets** | **11,000** | **Total equity & liabilities** | **11,000** |

Only the accounts with a closing balance shall be disclosed in the Balance Sheet. In this example there is no liability at the Balance Sheet date, only assets and equity accounts. The formats of the Profit and Loss Account and the Balance Sheet used in the previous example are not the ones officially used by the economic entities, but their pedagogical merit is undoubtedly important.

It is important to remember that **assets, liabilities and owner's equity are Balance Sheet** items, whereas **revenue and expenses are Income Statement** items.

## 4.7 Conclusions

The following summary questions are intended to conclude this chapter. Please consider also our brief responses.

## Chapter summary questions:

| | |
|---|---|
| 1. What is the role of the accounting equation in the financial statements? | The accounting equation (equilibrium) shows the fundamental concept upon which accounting information is built: Assets = Equity + Liabilities. Every material transaction or event should be translated into the accounting system, based on this equation. |
| 2. What is the double-entry system in accounting? | The double-entry system means that every transaction or event should be represented by at least one debit account, in connection with at least one corresponding crediting account. |
| 3. What are the rules of using accounts? | Active accounts (assets and expenses) are debited by increasing events and credited by decreasing events. Passive accounts (equity, liabilities and revenues) work in the opposite way, meaning that they are credited by increasing events and debited by decreasing events. There are also bifunctional accounts (for example the Profit and Loss Account) that can have either a debit closing balance (a loss) or a credit closing balance (a profit). |
| 4. What are the steps of transaction analysis? | The steps of transaction analysis are as follows:<br>• Step one: determine the nature of the transaction<br>• Step two: determine how the accounting equation is impacted<br>• Step three: determine the appropriate accounts to be used<br>• Step four: determine which account should be debited and which one is to be credited and provide the journal entry<br>• Step five: post the journal entries into the Ledger.<br>At the end of the month/term/year, the closing balances of all accounts are computed and the temporary accounts are closed down. A trial balance is provided in preparation of the financial statements. |
| 5. What is the trial balance and how is it linked with the financial statements? | The trial balance is an important accounting tool, providing a list with all accounts that have been used during the period with the following figures related to each of them: initial balances, current debit amount, current credit amount, total debit amount, total credit amount and closing balances. The trial balance is also a revision instrument, used to assess the proper functioning of the accounts. All accounts with closing balances shall be disclosed in the Balance Sheet and temporary accounts, such as revenue and expense accounts, are disclosed in the Profit and Loss Account. |

**Quizzes (only one correct answer):**

1. A company started the year with total assets of 80 lei and total liabilities of 40 lei. During the period, the business earned revenues of 120 lei and incurred expenses of 70 lei. What is the amount of the owner's equity at the end of the period?
   a. 40 lei
   b. 50 lei
   c. 30 lei
   d. 90 lei
2. A company started the year with total assets of 80 lei and total liabilities of 40 lei. During the year, the business earned revenues of 120 lei and incurred expenses of 70 lei. The net change in owner's equity for the year is a:
   a. 10 lei decrease
   b. 40 lei increase
   c. 30 lei decrease
   d. 50 lei increase
3. Mr. M establishes a car service. During a period, the following transactions took place:
   a. Mr. M deposits 3500 lei into a new account for the company.
   b. The firm pays 2000 lei cash for equipment to be used for repairs.
   c. The firm borrows 7500 lei from a commercial bank and deposits the money in the account.
   d. The firm pays 300 lei rent for the first month.
   e. The firm pays 200 lei cash for supplies to be used.
   After all these transactions, which is the amount of cash is:
   a. 12,850 lei
   b. 8500 lei
   c. 12,100 lei
   d. 10,100 lei
4. The Balance Sheet, or Statement of Financial Position, is a snapshot of the entity. Which of the following items are included in this statement?
   a. Revenues
   b. Cash receipt
   c. Assets
   d. Withdrawals made

5. The account debited to record the purchase of a motor vehicle is:
   a. Cash
   b. Sundry Creditor
   c. Motor Vehicle
   d. Purchases
6. The purchase of an item of office equipment for cash is recorded as:
   a. Debit "Cash" and credit "Office Equipment"
   b. Debit "Cash" and debit "Office Equipment"
   c. Debit "Office Equipment" and credit "Cash"
   d. Credit "Cash" and credit "Office Equipment"
7. The account debited for payment of cash owed to suppliers is:
   a. Accounts Payable
   b. Accounts Receivable
   c. Cash
   d. Purchases
8. Cash received from debtors is recorded as:
   a. Debiting "Cash" and debiting to "Accounts Receivable"
   b. Debiting "Accounts Receivable" and crediting "Cash"
   c. Crediting "Cash" and crediting "Accounts Receivable"
   d. Debiting "Cash" and crediting "Accounts Receivable"
9. The account credited to record the purchase of a computer for cash is:
   a. Office Equipment
   b. Cash
   c. Other Payables
   d. Purchases
10. The trial balance is a list of all of the company's:
    a. "T" accounts used
    b. Assets
    c. Liabilities
    d. Equity

## Exercises

**Exercise 1**: Identify the following as assets, liabilities or owner's equity:
(a) Amounts owed to trade creditors; (b) Capital; (c) Motor vehicles; (d) Buildings; (e) Amounts due from trade debtors; (f) Mortgage;

(g) Cash at bank; (h) Equipment owned; (i) Bank overdraft; (j) Inventory; (k) Office supplies.

**Exercise 2**: In each of the following examples, you are required to calculate the owner's equity.

a. Land: lei 20,000; Building: lei 30,000; Cash at bank: lei 25,000; Mortgage loan: lei 16,000;
b. Inventory: lei 5000; Cash at bank: lei 4000; Motor vehicle: lei 3500; Equipment: lei 2000; Mortgage: lei 10,000;
c. Motor vehicle: lei 4000; Land: lei 20,000; Cash at bank: lei 5000;
d. Inventory: lei 600; Office equipment: lei 900; Trade debtors: lei 1200; Account Payables: lei 1000;
e. Cash at bank: lei 800; Furniture: lei 750; Inventory: lei 250; Bank loan: lei 300; Account Receivables: lei 200; Account Payables: lei 150.

**Exercise 3**: Provide the missing information below:

| Assets lei | Liabilities lei | Owner's equity lei |
|---|---|---|
| 7000 | 3000 | ? |
| 6000 | ? | 3600 |
| 9500 | 4700 | ? |
| ? | 3000 | 5000 |
| 10,500 | ? | 6000 |

**Case Studies**

**Case 1**: The initial financial position of a delivery company is: Capital: 20,000 lei, Warehouse: 10,000 lei, Cash: 1500 lei, Accounts payable: 1500 lei, Truck: 2500 lei, Office equipment: 1000 lei, Bank Account: 10,000 lei, Notes payable: 4000 lei, Accounts receivable: 500 lei.

Journalize and record the following transactions into the "T" accounts, regarding the delivery company, during a period, and prepare the trial balance, balance sheet and the income statement.

1. Purchased a delivery truck for 2300 lei cash.
2. Received a check of trucking charges as shown by the bill for 900 lei.
3. Paid to a radio station 300 lei cash for advertising services.
4. Sent a check for 230 lei in payment of an outstanding obligation.
5. Recorded and paid salaries amounted to 370 lei.

6. Sent a bill for 340 lei for goods transported.
7. Paid 120 lei for gasoline and oil used in trucks.
8. Received 1000 lei from a customer, for goods transported.

**Case 2**: Use the following elements and transactions to draw a correct Balance Sheet structure:

| | |
|---|---|
| Raw materials | 1000 |
| Long term credits | 20,000 |
| Salaries payable | 5000 |
| Patents | 2000 |
| Shareholders' capital | 10,000 |
| Cash | 16,000 |
| Accrued expenses | 300 |
| Notes receivable | 4000 |
| Dividends payable | 1500 |
| Legal reserves | 3800 |
| Land | 9000 |
| Merchandise | 3000 |
| Bank account | 60,000 |
| Notes payable | 11,000 |
| Accrued revenues | 500 |
| VAT payable | 2000 |
| Retained earnings (loss) | (18,000) |
| Accounts receivable | 5000 |
| Buildings | 14,000 |
| Share premium | 8000 |
| Accounts payable | 9000 |
| Shares | 12,000 |
| Salary tax payable | 1500 |

During the current month, the subsequent transactions occurred:

1. 30% account receivables are cashed into the bank account;
2. purchase of merchandise for 1000 lei, the payment being due later;
3. acquisition of raw materials for 3000 lei; half of them is paid immediately from cash, the other half after 2 weeks;
4. the supplier of merchandise is paid with a note payable;
5. a land is purchased and paid via a long-term credit of 10,000 lei;
6. a rent is cashed in advance for 500 lei;
7. all notes receivables are cashed in;

8. the salaries are paid from cash;
9. 10% from long term credits is converted into shares in shareholders' capital;
10. the VAT payable is paid from the bank account;
11. a long-term credit is cashed into the bank account for 7000 lei;
12. an invoice for special services is paid in advance for 5000 lei;
13. the rest of accounts receivable change the claim into notes receivable;
14. dividends are paid from bank account;
15. the company buys shares of company "Y" for 12,000 lei.

**Case 3**: The list below contains the transactions for Royal Advertising Co. during a month. Show how transactions are recorded in the accounts and analyse the transactions. Prepare the balance sheet and the income statement for the period.

1. Ms. M, the owner, invested 10,000 lei in her own advertising agency.
2. Rented an office, paying two months' rent in advance, 800 lei.
3. Hired a secretary and agreed to pay 600 lei every two weeks. The secretary agreed to work extra hours to make up the time for the first days of the month.
4. Purchased art equipment for 4200 lei in cash.
5. Purchased office equipment from Idea Equipment for 3000 lei paying 1500 lei in cash and agreeing to pay the rest next month.
6. Purchased from Dipro Supply Company on credit art supplies for 1800 lei and office supplies for 800 lei.
7. Paid 480 lei for one-year insurance policy.
8. Paid Dipro Supply Company 1000 lei of the amount owed.
9. Performed a service by placing advertisements for a coffee bar in the newspaper and collected a fee of 1400 lei.
10. Paid the secretary two weeks' salary, 600 lei.
11. Accepted an advance fee for art work to be done for another agency, 1000 lei.
12. Performed a service by placing several major advertisements for KAL Stores. The earned fees of 2800 lei will be collected next month.
13. Received and paid the utility bill of 100 lei.
14. Received (but did not pay) a telephone bill, lei 70.

CHAPTER 5

# Inventories

*Elena Nechita and Adriana Duțescu*

*Learning objectives:*

- *Understanding the accounting perspective of inventories*
- *Using and analysing various inventory cost methods*
- *Estimating the effects of different measurement techniques related to inventories that affect financial statements*
- *Assessing links with other management tools*

## 5.1 Definition

Inventories are assets that will be sold in the ordinary course of the business, including those in various stages of completion, and assets meant for consumption in production or rendering services.[1] Inventories are presented in the Balance Sheets of manufacturing companies as raw materials, work-in-progress (WIP) and finished goods, while goods for resale are common in wholesalers' and retailers' financial statements, called merchandise.

---

[1] According to the Romanian Accounting Regulations, inventories are defined similarly to the definition set forth in IAS 2 *Inventories*. IAS 2 mentions inventories include assets held for sale in the ordinary course of business (finished goods), assets in the production process for sale in the ordinary course of business (work in process), and materials and supplies that are consumed in production (raw materials).

Romanian Accounting Regulations provide the following classification of inventories:

- raw materials;
- consumables (i.e. fuel, packing materials, spare parts, seeds);
- work-in-progress (WIP);
- finished goods;
- merchandise/goods for resale;
- other inventories (animals, poultry, etc.).

## 5.2 Valuation and Measurement

### 5.2.1 Initial Valuation (Measurement) of Inventories

On initial recognition, **IAS 2 Inventories** and Romanian Accounting Regulations agree that inventories should be measured at their acquisition or production cost. The acquisition cost of purchased inventories comprises all costs incurred in bringing the inventories to their present location and state, such as: invoice net purchase price (without VAT), customs duties for imported goods, insurance, transportation and handling costs and other non-recoverable costs (i.e. inspection of inventories). Suppliers often give incentives to their customers to purchase certain products or large quantities; all these trade discounts are deducted from the cost of the inventories acquired.

**Exercise 1**: *Initial recognition of inventories—acquisition cost.* Stylish Shoes S.R.L. is a local shoes retailer. In October 20X8, the company purchases 5000 pairs of shoes from its Italian supplier LeScarpe at a purchase price of 25 euro/pair. Also, the supplier offers a 2% trade discount. The NBR exchange rate at the acquisition date is 4.6 lei/euro. For the delivery of the goods, Stylish Shoes S.R.L. uses a local supplier, Curier Rapid S.R.L., which issues an invoice in amount of 5000 lei, VAT 19%. Determine the acquisition cost of the shoes and present the corresponding accounting treatment.

**Solution**: Stylish Shoes S.R.L. will initially recognise the shoes as goods for resale (merchandise) valuated at their acquisition cost. Therefore, the acquisition cost of the shoes is to be determined as follows, in accordance to **IAS 2 Inventories** as well as with the Romanian accounting regulations:

Acquisition cost = Purchase price − Trade discounts + Delivery expenses
+all other direct costs needed to use the inventory
= (5000 pairs × 25 EUR/pair − 2% × 125,000 EUR) × 4.6 lei/euro + 5000 lei
= 122,500 euro × 4.6 lei/euro + 5000 lei = 568,500 lei

The total acquisition cost of inventories in amount of **568,500 lei** is split into:

- the equivalent of 563,500 lei due to the supplier LeScarpe and
- 5000 lei (plus the 950 lei VAT) due to the currier Curier Rapid S.R.L.

The company will then journalise the acquisition as follows:

- The invoice received from LeScarpe (the VAT implications related to this transaction will not be taken into consideration, as they are the subject to different fiscal regulations; further explanations shall be provided):

| 563,500 lei | Merchandise | = | Accounts payable/LeScarpe | 563,500 lei |
|---|---|---|---|---|

- The invoice received from Curier Rapid S.R.L.:

| 5950 lei | % | = | Accounts payable/Curier Rapid S.R.L. | 5950 lei |
|---|---|---|---|---|
| 5000 lei | Merchandise | | | 5000 lei |
| 950 lei | VAT deductible | | | 950 lei |

*Note 1.* The VAT amount from the delivery invoice is not included in the acquisition cost of merchandise, as this is an indirect tax which is deducted by Stylish Shoes S.R.L. and will be later recovered by the company from the local fiscal authorities

*Note 2.* The amount of the goods for resale recognised by the company, is of 563,500 Lei + 5000 Lei = 568,500 Lei, which represents the acquisition cost previously determined

The **production cost** of manufactured inventories (finished goods) includes costs with direct materials and conversion costs needed to bring these inventories in their present location and state. **Conversion costs** consist of costs directly related to the production, such as direct labour and production overheads allocated on a rational basis. Production overhead costs normally include indirect labour, indirect materials, depreciation, maintenance of factory buildings etc. These costs may be fixed, which means that they remain almost unchanged when production volume changes. This is the case of depreciation of equipment or factory maintenance costs. Fixed overheads should be allocated to units of production (ending products) on the basis of normal production capacity, for example, the average volume of production that may be obtained under normal, but not ideal, circumstances over a period of time. Variable overheads increase or decrease proportionally to the production volume. These overheads are allocated to each unit of production on the basis of actual production (the overheads allocation techniques are beyond the scope of this book).

**Example 2**: During the last years, Artisan S.A. has had technical problems that have led to only 80% of their production capacity being used. The company incurred the following costs for December 20X7 (5000 units raffia fruit baskets):

| Costs | Amounts (lei) |
|---|---|
| Costs for identifying a suitable supplier | 150 |
| Invoice price of raw materials | 10,000 |
| Customs duties for raw materials | 700 |
| VAT related to the purchase of raw materials | 2033 |
| Transportation costs for raw materials | 400 |
| Direct labour costs | 9000 |
| Indirect material and services costs, including 50 lei wasted materials | 1050 |
| Wages and contributions for auxiliary workers | 900 |
| Wages and contributions for factory staff | 300 |
| Depreciation of factory equipment and building | 800 |
| Share of general overheads | 200 |
| Storage costs | 150 |
| Transportation costs to distribution centre | 500 |

Production cost at 31 December 20X7 comprises (in lei):
Direct materials:

| | |
|---|---|
| • purchase price | 10,000 |
| • customs duties | 700 |
| • transportation | 400 |
| | 11,100 |
| Direct labour costs | 9000 |
| Variable production overheads (1050 − 50 + 900) | 1900 |
| Fixed production overheads (80% × 1100) | 880 |
| | **22,880** |

**Table 5.1** Production of inventories—comparison Romanian vs. IFRS approach

| Romanian (by nature P&L) (Consumptions are expensed in the moment of occurrence and when different stages of completion are incurred the finished goods account shall be debited and the Revenue account should be credited) | IFRS/international approach (by function P&L) (A new asset should embed all the costs related to this asset, therefore an account e.g. "Work-in-progress" or "Work-in-process (WIP)" shall capitalise all these costs) |
|---|---|
| 1. Use of raw materials in production (cost of raw materials):<br>11,100 lei Raw Materials Expense = Raw Materials 11,100 lei<br>2. Direct labour costs<br>9000 lei Salaries Expense = Salaries Payable 9000 lei<br>3. Production overheads (indirect materials, indirect labour, depreciation of equipment):<br>1000 lei Materials Expense = Materials 1000 lei<br>900 lei Salaries Expense = Salaries Payable 900 lei<br>4. General overheads (salaries of management, depreciation of headquarters etc.)<br>240 lei Salaries Expense = Salaries Payable 240 lei<br>640 lei Depreciation Expense of Buildings = Accumulated Depreciation 640 lei<br>5. Reception of finished goods at the warehouse (production cost = direct costs + share of production overheads)<br>22,800 lei Finished Goods = Revenues related to the 22,800 lei production cost of finished goods<br>6. Sale of finished goods at sale price (ignore VAT) and removal of finished goods from inventory at cost (let's suppose that all finished goods are sold at a 30,000 lei price):<br>30,000 lei Accounts receivable = Revenue from Sale 30,000 lei<br>22,800 lei Revenues related to the production cost of finished goods = Finished Goods 22,800 lei | 1. Use of raw materials in production (cost of raw materials):<br>11,100 lei WIP = Raw Materials 11,100 lei<br>2. Direct labour costs<br>9000 lei WIP = Salaries Payable 9000 lei<br>3. Production overheads (indirect materials, indirect labour, depreciation of equipment):<br>1900 lei WIP =    % <br>             Materials 1000 lei <br>             Salaries Payable 900 lei<br>4. General overheads (salaries of management, depreciation of headquarters etc.)<br>240 lei WIP/Administrative Costs = Salaries Payable 240 lei<br>640 lei WIP/Administrative Costs = Accumulated Depreciation 640 lei of Buildings<br>5. Reception of finished goods at the warehouse (production cost = direct costs + share of production overheads)<br>22,800 lei Finished Goods = WIP 22,800 lei<br>6. Sale of finished goods at sale price (ignore VAT) and removal of finished goods from inventory at cost:<br>30,000 lei Accounts receivable = Revenue from Sale 30,000 lei<br>22,800 lei Cost of Goods Sold = Finished Goods 22,800 lei |

*Source* The authors

Production cost per unit of finished goods = 22,880/5000 = 4576 lei

*Note 1*: the wasted materials cost is not included in the computation of the production cost of finished goods.
*Note 2*: the production overheads 1100 lei (wages and contributions for factory staff of 300 lei and depreciation of factory equipment and building of 800 lei), are allocated on an 80% basis to the current finished goods emerging from production, the other 20% being WIP (not yet finished products).
*Note 3*: General overheads, storage costs and transportation to the distribution centre are not included in the production cost because they are incurred after the production is completed. These costs are part of the full cost of products and they have a different impact in accounting statements.

The related accounting entries are presented in Table 5.1, emphasising a comparison between the Romanian approach and the IFRS/international approach.

*Note*: As it can be observed in this example, the effects on the production recordings and the sale recordings are different and this particularity is more obvious when the completion of finished goods occurs in a different period than the production process or when the completion of the production is in a different period than its sale.

Costs incurred in order to find a suitable supplier, general overhead costs, wasted materials costs, storage costs and transportation costs to the distribution centre are not included in the production cost of finished goods. The first two costs would have been incurred anyway; inefficiencies (wasted materials costs) could have been avoided, whereas the other costs go well beyond the process of production of finished goods. Such costs are also known as period costs, as opposed to product costs. A product generates product costs, but period costs are linked to other operations within the company.

The example above demonstrates the calculation of a production cost by adding up relevant costs that have actually occurred. Another possibility is to use standard costs based on normal levels of material, labour and overhead costs.[2] If variances are significant, standards need to be revised (this issue is beyond the scope of this book, therefore is not going to be exemplified).

---

[2] Although less common, standard costs can be used for purchased goods as well.

## 5.2.2 Assigning Costs to Inventories

Assigning costs is an issue whenever inventories are sold or otherwise consumed, as the underlying assumption of accruals requires the matching of expenses with associated revenues. Costs are easily assigned when dealing with unique and expensive items, such as jewellery, paintings and cars. Each such item has a tag attached to it that allows the exact matching of its cost with the sale price.

When inventories initially measured at standard cost are sold, the Simplified Accounting Regulations require that a proportional amount of variances be included in the inventory expense.[3]

**Example 3**: Let us assume that, on December 1st, 20X4, Artisan S.A. has 1000 units in inventories at 4544 lei standard cost per unit while variances between actual and standard cost amount to 22,720 lei. The company produced 5000 units during the month; the differences between the actual production cost and standard cost add up to 160,000 lei. The variance is considered to be favourable. The company sold 5600 units in December. What is the cost of sales and the cost of inventories unsold?

**Solution**: One possibility is to assign variances proportionally to goods sold and those left in inventory using a coefficient that gives the variance per unit of item in inventory:

$K = (OB_{VAR} + I_{VAR})/(OB_Q + I_Q)$, where $OB_{VAR}$ is the amount of variances corresponding to the opening inventory, $I_{VAR}$ is the increase of variances owed to production during the period, $OB_Q$ is the quantity of items in the opening inventory and $I_Q$ is the increase in quantity (quantity produced) during the period.

$K = (22,720 + 160,000)/(1000 + 5000) = 30.45$ lei
Variances allocated to cost of sales (COS):
30.45 lei * 5600 units = 170,520 lei
Variances assigned to closing inventory:
(22,720 + 160,000) − 170,520 = 12,200 lei

Therefore, the cost of goods sold is:

5600 units * 4544 lei/unit + 170,520 lei = 25,616,920 lei
and the cost of the goods left in inventory:
400 units * 4544 lei/unit + 12,200 lei = 1,829,800 lei

---

[3] This has been a traditional practice in Romanian accounting and although the specific Accounting Regulations are silent about it, we believe that it is widely used.

Anglo-Saxon enterprises tend to transfer variances to cost of sales, if small in amount (unfavourable variances are expected to balance with favourable variances[4]). If the variances are significant, they are apportioned between cost of sales and inventory accounts (raw materials, WIP, finished goods).

For interchangeable goods measured at actual purchase/production costs, the accountant should find a method to assign costs to inventories that are sold or consumed. These accounting conventions, also called "inventory's cost methods", do not need to directly correspond to the physical flows of inventories. There are three such methods: a) weighted average cost method, b) first-in-first-out, and c) last-in-first-out. Companies are free to choose one of these methods for their inventories with the condition of using it consistently. The chosen method has an effect on the inventory's expense (cost of sales) and the profit figure in the profit and loss account, but also on the number of inventories shown in the Balance Sheet.

Romanian Accounting Regulations allow Weighted Average Cost, FIFO and LIFO[5] methods, which should be used **consistently** from one accounting period to another. The change of method is permitted in exceptional circumstances (either because it is required by a new Standard or because it increases the quality of the financial information) and requires justification by the company's management, which must also indicate the effects of the change on financial statements. A company may use different inventory's cost methods at the same time for items that have different natures and uses. Inventories methods used for accounting purposes are also accepted for the calculation of taxable income.

a) *Weighted Average Cost Method (W.A.C.)*

Under this method, both inventory expense and closing inventory are measured at the weighted average cost (W.A.C.) commonly calculated after each purchase. The closing balance of one accounting period becomes the opening inventory of the next period.

---

[4] Romanian manufacturers tend to have higher variances mainly due to two factors: the volatility of prices and the infrequent revision of standards.

[5] According to the Romanian Accounting Regulations, the use of LIFO is allowed, while in accordance with IFRS this cost assigning method is not accepted any more.

**Example 4**: Assume Scented S.A. is a dealer in cosmetics. Its opening inventory on December 1st, 20X3, comprises 100 boxes of soap at an average cost of 50 lei per unit. On December 15th, 20X3, it purchases 200 boxes at 60 lei each and on 21 December 21st, 20X3, 100 boxes at 61 lei per box. On December 28th, 20X3, it sells 310 boxes. Calculate the cost of the boxes sold and the amount of closing inventory.

| Explanation | Amounts | Obs. |
|---|---|---|
| December 1st opening inventory | 100 boxes * 50 lei/box = 5000 lei | |
| December 15th purchase | 200 boxes * 60 lei/box = 12,000 lei | WAC = (5000 + 12,000)/(100 + 200) = 17,000/300 = 56.67 lei |
| December 21st purchase | 100 boxes * 61 lei/box = 6100 lei | WAC = (17,000 + 6100)/(300 + 100) = 23,100/400 = 57.75 lei |
| December 28th sale | 310 boxes * 57.75 lei/box = 17,902.5 lei | Shown as inventory expense in the Profit and Loss Account |
| December 31st closing inventory | 90 boxes * 57.75 lei/box = 5197.5 lei | Disclosed as inventories in the Balance Sheet |

b) *First-In-First-Out (FIFO)*

The FIFO method assumes that the earliest purchased inventories are sold first, in other words, the closing inventory will comprise the most recently acquired items. We shall come back to the example above.

| | | |
|---|---|---|
| December 1st opening inventory | 100 boxes * 50 lei/box = 5000 lei | |
| December 15th purchase | 200 boxes * 60 lei/box = 12,000 lei | |
| December 21st purchase | 100 boxes * 61 lei/box = 6100 lei | |
| December 28th sale | 310 boxes | 100 boxes * 50 lei/box + 200 boxes * 60 lei/box + 10 boxes * 61 lei/box = 17,610 lei |
| December 31st closing inventory | 90 boxes | 90 boxes * 61 lei/box = 5490 lei |

c) *Last-In-First-Out (LIFO)*

LIFO assumes that the most recently purchased goods are sold first; if inventory levels have been maintained, the closing inventory may consist of items that do not exist anymore from a physical point of view.

| | | | |
|---|---|---|---|
| December 1st opening inventory | 100 boxes * 50 lei/box = 5000 lei | | |
| December 15th purchase | 200 boxes * 60 lei/box = 12,000 lei | | |
| December 21st purchase | 100 boxes * 61 lei/box = 6100 lei | | |
| December 28th sale | 310 boxes | 100 boxes * 61 lei/box + 200 boxes * 60 lei/box + 10 boxes * 50 lei/box = 18,600 lei | |
| December 31st closing inventory | 90 boxes | 90 boxes * 50 lei/box = 4500 lei | |

**Evaluation of cost methods**

In the case of Scented S.A., a comparison of alternative inventory's cost methods gives the table below:

Cost assigning methods—comparison

| W.A.C. | | FIFO | | LIFO | |
|---|---|---|---|---|---|
| Inventory expense | Closing inventory | Inventory expense | Closing inventory | Inventory expense | Closing inventory |
| 17,902.5 lei | 5197.5 lei | 17,610 lei | 5490 lei | 18,600 lei | 4500 lei |

It now becomes obvious that in a period of price increases (as in our example), FIFO shows a lower inventory expense/cost and thus a bigger profit than LIFO and average cost. This is an interesting observation for managers who get bonuses based upon the company's profit. However, as the most recently acquired items are deemed to be in inventory at the end of the year, the closing inventory figure is closer to current prices, giving a more realistic picture of the balance sheet. Under LIFO, inventories in the balance sheet are considered the earliest (oldest) purchased; due to inflation, their Balance Sheet value may become not material.

To make up for this disadvantage, **IAS 2 Inventories** requires a company to present either the lower of FIFO or WAC and net realisable value or the lower of current cost and net realisable value. Be aware that the LIFO method is forbidden under IFRS but allowed under US GAAP and other local reporting frameworks (including the Romanian one).

The strongest argument for using LIFO[6] in a period of rising prices is that, where tax authorities allow it, the inventory expense is higher, leading to a lower profit and profit tax.

**Exercise 5**: *Cost methods—determining the cost of goods sold.* Top Printer S.R.L. is a local wholesaler of printers. On December 1st, 20X8, the opening inventory of model X300 printers consists of 100,000 lei (100 printers × 1000 lei/piece). In December 20X8, the company carried out the following transactions involving the X300 printers:

- On December 3rd, the company purchased 100 pieces at the unit price of 1100 lei/piece, an acquisition which involved delivery costs in amount of 10,000 lei;
- On December 15th, 120 printers were sold at a selling price of 1500 lei/piece;
- On December 18th, the company purchased 20 printers at the unit cost of 1600 lei/piece;
- On December 23rd, 90 printers were sold at a selling price of 1800 lei/piece.

A 19% VAT is applicable to all of the above transactions.

Determine the X300 printers closing inventory as of December 31st, the cost of the printers sold, as well as the profit of Top Printer S.R.L. under each of the cost formulas that can be used and interpret the obtained results.

**Solution**: The following cost formulas can be used in order to determine the cost of the goods sold by the company:

a) FIFO;
b) WAC after each purchase;
c) WAC at the end of the accounting period;
d) LIFO—this method is allowed only according to the national accounting regulations (OMPF 1802/2014).

---

[6] These considerations are overturned in a period of declining prices.

a) The impact of applying FIFO as cost formula for model X300 printers is reflected in following table

*Merchandise inventory—X300 printers—December 20X8*

| Date | Acquisitions[a] | | | Disposals | | | Closing inventory | | |
|---|---|---|---|---|---|---|---|---|---|
| | Q (units) | UC (lei/unit) | TC (lei) | Q (units) | UC (lei/unit) | TC (lei) | Q (units) | UC (lei/unit) | TC (lei) |
| 1.12.20X8 | | | | | | | 100 | 1000 | 100,000 |
| 3.12.20X8 | 100 | 1200[b] | 120,000 | | | | 100 | 1000 | 100,000 |
| | | | | | | | 100 | 1200 | 120,000 |
| | | | | | | | 200 | | 220,000 |
| 15.12.20X8 | | | | 100 | 1000[c] | 100,000 | 80 | 1200 | 96,000 |
| | | | | 20 | 1200 | 24,000 | | | |
| | | | | 120 | | 124,000 | | | |
| 18.12.20X8 | 20 | 1600 | 32,000 | | | | 80 | 1200 | 96,000 |
| | | | | | | | 20 | 1600 | 32,000 |
| | | | | | | | 100 | | 128,000 |
| 23.12.20X8 | | | | 80 | 1200 | 96,000 | 10 | 1600 | 16,000 |
| | | | | 10 | 1600 | 16,000 | | | |
| | | | | 90 | | 112,000 | | | |
| 31.12.20X8 | | | | | | | 10 | 1600 | 16,000 |

[a]where: Q—quantity, UC—unit cost, TC—total cost;
[b]For each acquisition, the initial recognition of the inventory implies determining the acquisition cost as follows:
Acquisition cost = Purchase price − Trade discounts + Expenses directly related to the acquisition which are not to be recovered
Therefore, acquisition cost 03.12.2018 (TC) = 100 × 1100 + 10,000 = 120,000 lei => UC = TC/Q = 120,000/100 = 1200 lei/unit;
[c]On the disposals column the cost of the goods sold is disclosed, determined by using one of the cost formulas. The selling price of the sales transaction is not to be disclosed in the disposals column

After applying the FIFO cost formula, the final closing inventory of X300 printers as of December 31st, 20X8, consists of 10 pieces of 1600 lei/piece, having a total cost of 16,000 lei.

b) The impact of applying WAC (weighted average cost) after each purchase as a cost formula for the model X300 printers is reflected in the following table:

*Merchandise inventory excerpt—X300 printers—December 20X8*[a]

| Date | Acquisitions | | | Disposals | | | Closing inventory | | |
|---|---|---|---|---|---|---|---|---|---|
| | Q (units) | UC (lei/unit) | TC (lei) | Q (units) | UC (lei/unit) | TC (lei) | Q (units) | UC (lei/unit) | TC (lei) |
| 1.12.20X8 | | | | | | | 100 | 1000 | 100,000 |
| 3.12.20X8 | 100 | 1200 | 120,000 | | | | 100 | 1000 | 100,000 |
| | | | | | | | 100 | 1200 | 120,000 |
| | | | | | | | 200 | | 220,000 |
| | | | | | | | $WAC_1 = TC/Q$ | | |
| | | | | | | | = 220,000/200 = 1100 lei/pc | | |
| 15.12.20X8 | | | | 120 | 1100 | 132,000 | 80 | 1100 | 88,000 |
| 18.12.20X8 | 20 | 1600 | 32,000 | | | | 80 | 1100 | 88,000 |
| | | | | | | | 20 | 1600 | 32,000 |
| | | | | | | | 100 | | 120,000 |
| | | | | | | | $WAC_2 = TC/Q$ | | |
| | | | | | | | = 120,000/100 = 1200 lei/pc | | |
| 23.12.20X8 | | | | 90 | 1200 | 108,000 | 10 | 1200 | 12,000 |
| 31.12.20X8 | | | | | | | 10 | 1200 | 12,000 |

[a]Comments from previous table apply here as well

After applying the WAC after each purchase, the closing inventory of X300 printers as of December 31st, 20X8, consists of 10 pieces valued at 1200 lei/piece, resulting in a final account balance of 12,000 lei.

c. The impact of applying WAC (weighted average cost) at the end of the accounting period as cost formula for model X300 printers is reflected as follows:

*Merchandise inventory excerpt—X300 printers—December 20X8*[a]

| Date | Acquisitions | | | Disposals | | | Closing inventory | | |
|---|---|---|---|---|---|---|---|---|---|
| | Q (units) | UC (lei/unit) | TC (lei) | Q (units) | UC (lei/unit) | TC (lei) | Q (units) | UC (lei/unit) | TC (lei) |
| 1.12.20X8 | | | | | | | 100 | 1000 | 100,000 |
| 3.12.20X8 | 100 | 1200 | 120,000 | | | | 100 | 1000 | 100,000 |
| | | | | | | | 100 | 1200 | 120,000 |
| | | | | | | | 200 | | 220,000 |
| 15.12.20X8 | | | | 120 | 1145 | 137,400 | | | |
| 18.12.20X8 | 20 | 1600 | 32,000 | | | | 100 | 1000 | 100,000 |
| | | | | | | | 100 | 1200 | 120,000 |
| | | | | | | | 20 | 1600 | 32,000 |
| | | | | | | | 200 | | 252,000 |
| 23.12.20X8 | | | | 90 | 1145 | 103,050 | | | |

| Date | Acquisitions | | | Disposals | | | Closing inventory | | |
|---|---|---|---|---|---|---|---|---|---|
| | Q (units) | UC (lei/unit) | TC (lei) | Q (units) | UC (lei/unit) | TC (lei) | Q (units) | UC (lei/unit) | TC (lei) |
| 31.12.20X8 | | | | | | | 100 | 1000 | 100,000 |
| | | | | | | | 100 | 1200 | 120,000 |
| | | | | | | | 20 | 1600 | 32,000 |
| | | | | | | | 220 | | 252,000 |
| | | | | | | | WAC=TC/Q = = 252,000/220=1145 lei/pc | | |
| | | | | | | | 10 | 1145 | 11,450 |

[a]Comments from previous table apply there as well

After applying the WAC at the end of the accounting period, the closing inventory of X300 printers as of December 31st, 20X8, consists of 10 pieces valued at 1145 lei/piece, resulting in a final account balance of 11,450 lei.

    d. The impact of applying LIFO as a cost formula for the model X300 printers is reflected as follows:

*Merchandise inventory excerpt—X300 printers—December 20X8*[a]

| Date | Acquisitions | | | Disposals | | | Closing inventory | | |
|---|---|---|---|---|---|---|---|---|---|
| | Q (units) | UC (lei/unit) | TC (lei) | Q (units) | UC (lei/unit) | TC (lei) | Q (units) | UC (lei/unit) | TC (lei) |
| 1.12.20X8 | | | | | | | 100 | 1000 | 100,000 |
| 3.12.20X8 | 100 | **1200** | 120,000 | | | | 100 | 1000 | 100,000 |
| | | | | | | | 100 | 1200 | 120,000 |
| | | | | | | | 200 | | 220,000 |
| 15.12.20X8 | | | | 100 | 1200 | 120,000 | 80 | 1000 | 80,000 |
| | | | | 20 | 1000 | 20,000 | | | |
| | | | | 120 | | 140,000 | | | |
| 18.12.20X8 | 20 | 1600 | 32,000 | | | | 80 | 1000 | 80,000 |
| | | | | | | | 20 | 1600 | 32,000 |
| | | | | | | | 100 | | 112,000 |
| 23.12.20X8 | | | | 20 | 1600 | 32,000 | 10 | 1000 | 10,000 |
| | | | | 70 | 1000 | 70,000 | | | |
| | | | | 90 | | 102,000 | | | |
| 31.12.20X8 | | | | | | | 10 | 1000 | 10,000 |

[a]Comments from previous table apply there as well

After applying the LIFO cost formula, the closing inventory of X300 printers as of December 31st, 20X8, consists of 10 pieces valued at 1000 lei/piece, resulting in a final account balance of 10,000 lei.

The impact of each cost formula in the entity's financial statements is reflected in the following table:

*The impact of the inventory cost formula in the financial statements of Top Printers S.R.L*

| Cost formula | Closing inventory[a] | Cost of goods sold[b] | Revenues from the sale of merchandise[c] | Profit from the sale of X300 printers (revenues − cost of goods sold) |
|---|---|---|---|---|
| FIFO | 16,000 lei | 124,000 + 112,000 = 236,000 lei | 120 × 1500 + 90 × 1800 = 342,000 lei | 106,000 lei |
| WAC after each purchase | 12,000 lei | 132,000 + 108,000 = 240,000 lei | 342,000 lei | 102,000 lei |
| WAC at the end of the period | 11,450 lei | 137,400 + 103,050 = 240,450 lei | 342,000 lei | 101,950 lei |
| LIFO | 10,000 lei | 140,000 + 102,000 = 242,000 lei | 342,000 lei | 100,000 lei |

[a]Representing the value of goods for resale as part of current assets in the balance sheet (statement of financial position)
[b]Representing the value of expenses with merchandise in the income statement (Profit & Loss Account)
[c]Revenues from the sale of merchandise are determined as unit selling price multiplied by quantity sold for each selling transaction

The numbers confirm the previously highlighted impact in a context of an inflationist economy. Hence, applying the FIFO method results in the lowest expense amount and, therefore, the highest profit level. Analysing the amounts in comparison to the other three methods going down towards LIFO, the expenses of merchandise exponentially increase, reaching the highest value using LIFO and the profit decreases to its lowest value using LIFO. Furthermore, using LIFO, the company would have to disclose the lowest value of goods for resale, which is not consistent with the market price evolution at the end of the financial year, thus altering the true and fair view.

### 5.2.3 Valuation of Inventories in the Balance Sheet

Balance Sheet disclosure inventories are valued at the lower of cost and net realisable value. As previously established, a standard cost or an actual cost may be used. The net realisable value of goods bought for resale and the net realisable value of finished goods is their estimated selling price minus estimated selling costs; for goods that are in production, expected completion costs are also deducted from the estimated selling price. Several factors may lead to a lower net realisable value than the cost:

- An increase of costs (raising costs of inputs) or a reduction of their selling price (a negative change in the demand for a specific inventory);
- Poor inventory management that has resulted in excessive inventory levels;
- Physical damage of inventories (i.e. when paint containers are damaged without affecting the quality of the product; also showroom items sale);
- Obsolescence (i.e. fashion textiles);
- A strategic decision to sell under cost in order to penetrate new markets.

The net realisable value should be calculated for each item of inventory, although grouping with related items is possible (such as spare parts for a custom-made piece of equipment) and is useful when it is not practical to estimate it on an item by item basis.

**Example 6**: Assume that on December 1st 20X3, Artisan SA has a beginning inventory of 2000 units at 4400 lei each. During December, the company manufactured 5000 units with a production cost of 4576 lei per unit and sold 6000 units. The company uses the periodic inventory and FIFO method for assigning costs. At the end of the financial year, the expected selling price of these products is 4800 lei. In order to sell its products, the company estimates packaging and distribution costs of 300 lei. What is the balance sheet value of these inventories?

**Solution**: The net realisable value of one unit of the closing inventory is:
4800 lei − 300 lei = 4500 lei

The balance sheet value of one unit of the closing inventory is thus:
Min (Cost; Net Realisable Value) = Min (4576 lei; 4500 lei) = 4500 lei

The Balance Sheet value of the closing inventory:

1000 units * 4500 lei/unit = 4,500,000 lei

**Exercise 7**: *Balance sheet valuation of inventories.*

Considering the case of Top Printer S.R.L., the wholesaler in Exercise 5 (Sect. 5.2.2), and assuming that the company's managers decide that FIFO is the cost assigning model which best fits to valuating X300 printers, determine the value of these printers to be disclosed in the statement of financial position as of December 31st, 20X8, knowing that the X300 printer reaches a net realisable value of 1450 lei/unit at the financial year end of 20X8 (based on the assumption that there are no other transactions related to merchandise). Journalise the corresponding accounting entry.

**Solution**: As shown in Exercise 5, there is a disclosure of a closing inventory for X300 printers after applying FIFO of 10 units at the unit cost of 1600 lei/unit, leading to a total amount of 16,000 lei.

For the Balance Sheet valuation of its inventories, the company will compare the cost of the X300 printers remaining in inventory to their net realisable value, as follows:

Cost = 10 units × 1600 lei/unit = 16,000 lei
Net realisable value = 10 units × 1450 lei/unit = 14,500 lei

Therefore, the value which will be disclosed in the Statement of Financial Position of Top Printer S.R.L. is the lowest value between cost and net realisable value (NRV):
Min (Cost; Net Realisable Value) = min (16,000 lei; 14,500 lei) = 14,500 lei

Hence, the entity has to record an impairment adjustment (write-down) in the amount of: 16,000 lei − 14,500 lei = 1500 lei.

A write-down in a company's inventory is recorded by reducing the amount reported by the asset account (IFRS approach) or by recognising an increase of a contra inventory account (the approach of Romanian accounting regulations). The debit in the entry to record an impairment adjustment of an inventory is an expense account which affects the company's income statement.

Therefore, the accounting entry to be recorded is the following:

- under Romanian accounting regulations:

| 1500 lei | Expenses with the impairment of current assets | = | Accumulated impairment of merchandise | 1500 lei |
|---|---|---|---|---|

- according to IFRS:

| 1500 lei | Expenses with the Write-down of Inventories | = | Merchandise | 1500 lei |

When the financial statements are prepared, merchandise will be disclosed at its net value in the Balance Sheet, an amount determined as the difference between its cost and the recorded impairment adjustment, as follows:

Net value of merchandise December 31st, 20X8 = Debit Ending Balance of Merchandise − Credit Ending Balance of Accumulated Impairment of Merchandise = 16,000 lei − 1500 lei = 14,500 lei (NRV).

## 5.3 Acquisition, Production and Sale of Inventories

Before moving on to accounting for transactions involving inventories, we shall clarify the role of value added tax (VAT), which accompanies almost every purchase and sale of inventories. VAT[7] is a consumption tax, that is, a tax included in the prices of consumer goods and services and thus paid by consumers. VAT is levied on the value added (VA) by each participant in the chain of production and distribution of a good or service. The value added by an enterprise may be calculated using the formula below:

$$VA = \text{Sale Price} - \text{Intermediate Consummations}$$

where intermediate consummations are purchases of materials and services needed for the production of a good or for the provision of a service.

Next, the value-added tax is obtained by applying a percentage[8] to the value added by an enterprise. Currently, this percentage is 19%:

$$VAT = 19\% \times (\text{Sale Price} - \text{Intermediate Consummations})$$

Some transactions involving inventories are acquisitions of materials for production and goods for resale. Since these inventories will be used in production, sold or otherwise consumed for business purposes, the VAT paid on acquisition is recoverable: from an accounting point of view it is treated as a receivable. Other transactions are sales of goods:

---

[7] In Chapter 7 we provide more explanations and examples related to VAT

[8] Established by a government as a matter of tax policy.

where the VAT collected from customers is a liability towards the state budget. Companies act as mere agents for the taxation authority: having deducted VAT paid on purchases from VAT collected on sales, the balance is settled with the taxation authority.

### 5.3.1 Transactions Involving Purchased Inventories

Once the valuation issues have been sorted out, accounting for purchased inventories is straightforward.

**Example 8**: Computer Warehouse S.A., a wholesaler, purchased 100 scanners from a manufacturer. The catalogue price is 3000 lei per piece, but the company received a trade discount of 10%. Computer Warehouse S.A. is subject to 19% VAT. A quantity of 40 scanners is delivered to a retailer: the normal sale price is 4000 lei per scanner, but the company offers a 5% trade discount for purchases of more than 30 units. Provide the journal entries of all transactions.

**Solution**: The purchase of goods for resale[9] at 2700 lei each (catalogue price less trade discount):

| 321,300 lei | % | = | Accounts payable[a] | 321,300 lei |
|---|---|---|---|---|
| 270,000 lei | Merchandises | | | |
| 51,300 lei | VAT deductible | | | |

[a]Other terms used for Accounts Payable are Trade Payables and Suppliers

The resale of 40 scanners at sale price 3800 lei (sale price less trade discount):

| 180,880 lei | Accounts receivable[a] | = | % | 180,880 lei |
|---|---|---|---|---|
| | | | Revenue from the sale of merchandises | 152,000 lei |
| | | | VAT collected | 28,880 lei |

[a]Other terms used for Accounts Receivable are Trade Receivables, Clients and Customers

---

[9] Another term commonly used to name goods for resale is merchandise.

Disposal of items sold from inventory: 40 units * 2700 lei/unit = 108,000 lei

| 108,000 lei | Cost of goods sold/Expenses with merchandises | = | Merchandises | 108,000 lei |

**Exercise 9**: Taking into account the information provided in Exercise 5 related to transactions performed by Top Printers S.R.L., journalise all the transactions for December 20X8 if the company's management decides to apply FIFO.

**Solution**: Considering the case Top Printers S.R.L. is applying FIFO for determining the cost of goods sold, the following transactions are recorded by the entity:

1. December 3rd, 20X8, a purchase of 100 pieces at the unit price of 1100 lei/piece, involving delivery costs in the amount of 10,000 lei and resulting an acquisition cost of 1200 lei/piece previously computed; 19% VAT is applied;

| 142,800 lei | % | = | Accounts payable | 142,800 lei |
| 120,000 lei | Merchandise | | | |
| 22,800 lei | VAT deductible | | | |

2. December 15th, 20X8, a sale of 120 printers at the selling price of 1500 lei/piece, VAT 19%;

The selling transaction implies the following two steps:

a) Recognising the revenue (the actual sale): the selling price is in the total amount of 120 units × 1500 lei/unit = 180,000 lei:

| 214,200 lei | Accounts receivable | = | % | 214,200 lei |
| | | | Revenues from the sale of merchandise | 180,000 lei |
| | | | VAT collected | 34,200 lei |

b) Recognising the expense (the disposal of the goods sold)—if FIFO is applied, the cost of goods sold is in the amount of 124,000 lei, as determined in Exercise 5 (Sect. 5.2.2):

| 124,000 lei | Cost of goods sold/Expenses with merchandise | = | Merchandise | 124,000 lei |

3. December 18th, 20X8, an acquisition of 20 printers at a unit cost of 1600 lei/piece, VAT 19%;

| 38,080 lei | % | = | Accounts payable | 38,080 lei |
| 32,000 lei | Merchandise | | | |
| 6080 lei | VAT deductible | | | |

4. December 23rd, 20X8, a sale of 90 printers at the selling price of 1800 lei/piece, VAT 19%:

The same two steps of the selling transaction are applied:

a) Recognising the revenue (the actual sale) – the selling price is in the total amount of 90 units × 1800 lei/unit = 162,000 lei:

| 192,780 lei | Accounts receivable | = | % | 192,780 lei |
| | | | Revenues from the sale of merchandise | 162,000 lei |
| | | | VAT collected | 30,780 lei |

b) Recognising the expense (the disposal of the goods sold) – if FIFO is applied, the cost of goods sold is in the amount of 112,000 lei, as determined in Exercise 5 (Sect. 5.2.2):

| 112,000 lei | Cost of goods sold/Expenses with merchandise | = | Merchandise | 112,000 lei |

### 5.3.2 Transactions Involving Manufactured Goods

Accounting for production varies according to the method of presenting operating expenses in the Profit and Loss Account. One way is to present operating expenses by their nature, as expenses with materials, salaries, utilities, depreciation etc. Another way is to allocate these expenses to the functions of the enterprise (production, distribution, and administration). The Profit and Loss Account will then show a different classification of operating expenses: cost of goods sold, administration cost, distribution expenses and other operating expenses. The second analysis is a typical international (IFRS) approach to Profit and

Loss Accounts and it's more in line with the management perspective. Romanian Accounting Regulations require a "by-nature" analysis of operating expenses on the face of the Profit and Loss Account, together with a "by-function" presentation of the same expenses in the notes.[10] We shall now turn to accounting for production in a by-nature Profit and Loss Account, followed by a comparative presentation of accounting for production under both analyses of operating expenses. The underlying assumption of accruals requires the matching of expenses with associated revenues. It should be noted that under both analyses of operating expenses, expenses are matched with revenues at the time of sale.

**Example 10**: Jouet S.R.L., a toy manufacturer, produces and sells 1000 baby dolls each month. The direct costs incurred in December 20X7, comprised raw materials of 50,000 lei, direct wages of 36,000 lei and social charges associated with direct wages of 16,000 lei. The management accountant in charge with finished goods allocated production overheads of 48,000 lei consisting of:

| | |
|---|---|
| Salaries of supervisors | 10,000 lei |
| Social charges in respect of above salaries | 4000 lei |
| Depreciation of equipment | 18,000 lei |
| Electricity | 16,000 lei |

These costs (overheads) are not individualised to products or services. Except for the cost of raw materials, they were included in the company's total expenses with salaries, social charges, depreciation and electricity. The respective entries were those below:

| 50,000 lei | Raw material expense | = | Raw materials | 50,000 lei |
|---|---|---|---|---|

| 60,000 lei | Salaries expense | = | Salaries payable | 60,000 lei |
|---|---|---|---|---|

(out of which 46,000 lei included in the production cost of toys)

---

[10] One reason for this requirement that goes well beyond those set out in **IAS 1 Preparation of Financial Statements**, could be the desire to attract foreign investors that are more familiar with the by-function presentation. Another purpose could have been that of enforcing the use of management accounting in Romanian companies.

| 25,000 lei | Social expense | = | Social costs payable | 25,000 lei |

(out of which 20,000 lei incorporated in the production cost of finished goods)

| 24,000 lei | Depreciation expense | = | Accumulated depreciation of equipment | 24,000 lei |

(including 18,000 lei allocated to the production cost of toys)

| 22,610 lei | % | = | Accounts payable | 22,610 lei |
| 19,000 lei | Electricity expense | | | 19,000 lei |
| 3610 lei | VAT deductible | | | 3610 lei |

(including 16,000 lei electricity consumed allocated to the production cost of toys)

The production cost of the toys obtained during the month amounted to:
50,000 lei + 46,000 lei + 20,000 lei + 18,000 lei + 16,000 lei = 150,000 lei.

The production cost per unit was: 150,000 lei/1000 units = 150 lei.
The production obtained generates the accounting entry below:

| 150,000 lei | Finished goods | = | Revenues related to the production cost of finished goods | 150,000 lei |

Now, let us assume that Jouet S.R.L. sold all 1000 toys on credit to a wholesaler for 200 lei per unit, VAT 19%. Accounting for such a transaction consists of two steps: the credit sale (the recognition of revenue) and the removal of items sold from inventory (the recognition of the related expense). The customer, who will in turn invoice it to his customers, pays VAT.

The credit sale at sale price:

| 238,000 lei | Accounts receivable | = | % | 238,000 lei |
| | | | Revenue from sale of finished goods | 200,000 lei |
| | | | VAT collected | 38,000 lei |

Removal of items sold from inventory at cost:

| 150,000 lei | Revenues related to the production cost of finished goods | = | Finished goods | 150,000 lei |
|---|---|---|---|---|

The profit and loss account of Jouet S.R.L. is shown below:

| Profit and loss A/c | | | |
|---|---|---|---|
| Expenses (lei) | | Revenues (lei) | |
| Raw materials | 50,000 | Revenue from sale | 200,000 |
| Salaries | 60,000 | | |
| Social charges | 25,000 | | |
| Depreciation | 24,000 | | |
| Electricity | 19,000 | | |
| Total expenses | 178,000 | | |
| Profit | 22,000 | | |

We will now convert this by-nature Profit and Loss Account into a by-function Profit and Loss Account, considering that the cost of production sold was 150,000 lei and the remaining 28,000 lei were administrative expenses. The flow of journal entries is adapted as follows:

a) Raw materials consumption:

| 50,000 lei | WIP | = | Raw materials | 50,000 lei |
|---|---|---|---|---|

b) Salaries related to production:

| 46,000 lei | WIP | = | Salaries payable | 46,000 lei |
|---|---|---|---|---|

c) Additional salary contribution related to production:

| 20,000 lei | WIP | = | Social costs payable | 20,000 lei |
|---|---|---|---|---|

d) Depreciation of non-current assets related to production:

| 18,000 lei | WIP | = | Accumulated depreciation of equipment | 18,000 lei |
|---|---|---|---|---|

e) The electricity consumed (allocated to) in the production:

| 16,000 lei | WIP | = | Accounts payable | 16,000 lei |
|---|---|---|---|---|

f) Completion of Finished Goods:

| 150,000 lei | Finished goods | = | WIP | 150,000 lei |
|---|---|---|---|---|

g) Sale of Finished Goods:

| 238,000 lei | Accounts receivable | = | % | 238,000 lei |
|---|---|---|---|---|
| | | | Revenue from sale of finished goods | 200,000 lei |
| | | | VAT collected | 38,000 lei |

| 150,000 lei | Cost of goods sold | = | Finished goods | 150,000 lei |
|---|---|---|---|---|

| 28,000 lei | Administrative expenses | = | Other payables | 28,000 lei |
|---|---|---|---|---|

*Profit and loss A/c*

| Expenses (lei) | | Revenues (lei) | |
|---|---|---|---|
| Cost of sales | 150,000 | Revenue from sale | 200,000 |
| Administrative expenses | 28,000 | | |
| Total expenses | 178,000 | | |
| Profit | 22,000 | | |

As we move on to the comparative illustration, it should be noted that in the by-nature presentation, expenses are recognised during production, when they occur. However, this is a false pretence, since expenses are then cancelled by crediting the technical account "Revenues related to the production cost of finished goods" (formerly known as Variation of Inventories, term used by national accounting regulations previous to OMPF 1802/2014), each time finished goods are obtained. Expenses are recognised when manufactured goods are sold, as the account Revenues related to the production cost of finished goods is debited, thus allowing the offsetting of revenue against the expenses that make up the production cost. In the by-function analysis, the "WIP" account collects all production costs and these are expensed, through the "Cost of goods Sold", at the time of the sale.

### 5.3.3 *Perpetual and Periodic Inventory*

In the previous two paragraphs, we have assumed that acquisitions, production and sales had an immediate effect on the inventory accounts:

they were debited or credited each time inventories were involved. The perpetual inventory system updates the inventory balance each time an item of inventory is sold. At any time, the accounting department knows the inventory inflows, outflows and the inventory balance based on invoices and other supporting documents. Warehouses also keep inventory information, generally in quantitative terms. **Perpetual inventory** is easier to use within a computerized integrated system, such as CRM, or ERP. Romanian Accounting Regulations require a physical inventory review to be undertaken at least annually. This is not the only way in which one can account for transactions with inventories. We will discuss another scheme of accounting for transactions involving inventory accounts next.

A **periodic inventory** system relies on the inventory count to determine on what was actually sold during the period. This system might be relevant for restaurants, small shops, low value - big volumes businesses. For purchased inventories, the accountant books only the purchases. The closing figure arises from the physical inventory assessment, while the inventory expense (cost of sales) is a residual amount from the equation below:

**Inventory expense (COS) = Opening balance + Purchases − Closing balance**

Periodic inventory is suitable for small entities, as the costs for running it are much lower than those implied by the perpetual inventory. In most of the cases though, companies prefer the perpetual inventory since it proves to be advantageous in a digital environment.

**Example 11**: To illustrate perpetual and periodic inventory for purchased inventories, assume that on December 1st, 20X9, Mir S.R.L., a wholesaler, has an opening inventory of 100 boxes of chocolate at 50 lei each. On December 15th, 20X9, the company purchases 500 boxes at 55 lei per box. On December 20th, 20X9, 540 boxes are sold for 60 lei each. At the end of the year, the physical inventory review shows that 50 boxes are unsold. Mir S.R.L. uses FIFO for assigning inventory costs. For simplicity reasons, VAT is ignored.

| Perpetual inventory | Periodic inventory |
|---|---|
| 1. Opening inventory:<br>100 boxes * 50 lei/box = 5000 lei | 1. Opening inventory:<br>100 boxes * 50 lei/box = 5000 lei |
| 2. Purchase of goods for resale:<br>500 boxes * 55 lei/box = 27,500 lei<br>27,500 lei Merchandises = Accounts Payable 27,500 lei | 2. Purchase of goods for resale:<br>500 boxes * 55 lei/box = 27,500 lei<br>27,500 lei Merchandises = Accounts Payable 27,500 lei |
| 3. Sale of goods for resale<br><br>3a. Shipment of inventories:<br>540 boxes * 60 lei/box = 32,400 lei<br>32,400 lei Accounts Receivable = Revenue from Sale 32,400 lei<br><br>3b. Disposal of inventories sold:<br>100 boxes * 50 lei/box + 440 boxes *55lei /box = 29,200 lei<br><br>29,200 lei Cost of goods sold/ = Merchandises 29,200 lei<br>Expense with goods | 3. Sale of goods for resale<br>Only the revenue recognition from the actual sale is recorded:<br>3a. Shipment of inventories:<br>540 boxes * 60 lei/box = 32,400 lei<br>32,400 lei Accounts Receivable = Revenue from Sale 32,400 lei<br><br>3b. Removal of inventories sold:<br>No accounting entry regarding the disposal of goods, but data regarding this transaction is physically recorded at the warehouse. |
| 4. On December 31st, 20X9, before the physical inventory review, the closing balance of the inventory account shows a closing balance of:<br><br>60 boxes * 55 lei /box = 3300 leia | 4. On December 31st, 20X9, before the physical inventory taking, the inventory account shows only opening balance and purchases:<br><br>100 boxes * 50 lei/box + 500 boxes *55 lei/box = 32,500 lei |
| 5. The physical inventory review highlights the need to adjust accounting data to the (lower) inventory levels in the warehouse:<br>(60 – 50) boxes * 55 lei/box = 550 lei<br><br>550 lei Expense with Merchandise = Merchandise 550 lei | 5. The physical inventory review gives the closing balance figure; the inventory account will be credited with the amount necessary to obtain the closing inventory (also the inventory expense for the period):<br><br>Closing inventory:<br>50 boxes * 55 lei/box = 2750 lei<br><br>Change in inventory (inventory expense):<br>29,750 lei Expense with Merchandises = Merchandises 29,750 lei |
| 6. Transfer of Goods for Resale Expense to P&L A/c<br>29,750 lei Profit and Loss = Expense with Merchandise 29,750 lei | 6. Transfer of Goods for Resale Expense to P&L A/c<br>29,750 lei Profit and Loss = Expense with Merchandise 29,750 lei |

These accounting entries are summarized in the accounts below:

| Merchandises A/c | | | | Merchandises A/c | | | |
|---|---|---|---|---|---|---|---|
| Debit | | Credit | | Debit | | Credit | |
| December 1st Balance b/d | 5000 | December 20th Revenue from sale | 29,200 | December 1st Balance b/d | 5000 | December 31st Inventory expense | 29,750 |
| December 15th | 27,500 | December 31st Inventory expense | 550 | December 15th Purchase | 27,500 | | |
| TDA | 32,500 | TCA Dec. 31st Balance c/d | 29,750 2750 | TDA | 32,500 | TCA December 31st Balance c/d | 29,750 2750 |
| December 31st Balance b/d | 2750 | | | December 31st Balance b/d | 2750 | | |

| Merchandises expense A/c | | | | Merchandises expense A/c | | | |
|---|---|---|---|---|---|---|---|
| Debit | | Credit | | Debit | | Credit | |
| December 20th Goods for resale | 29,200 | December 31st P&L A/c | 29,750 | December 31st Goods for resale | 29,750 | December 31st P&L A/c | 29,750 |
| December 31st Goods for resale | 550 | | | | | | |
| TDA | 29,750 | TCA | 29,750 | TDA | 29,750 | TCA | 29,750 |

**Exercise 12**: *Physical inventory review.* Present the accounting treatment that Top Printers S.R.L. (the company from Exercise 5, Sect. 5.2.2) will apply for the X300 printers if the physical inventory determines only 9 pieces of printers in inventory on December 31st, 20X8.

**Solution**: As previously mentioned in Exercise 5, at the end of October 20X8, the ending balance of X300 printers consists of 10 pieces. However, the physical inventory performed on December 31st, 20X8, shows that only 9 pieces are found at the company's warehouse. We take into account the former assumptions that Top Printers S.R.L. applied FIFO and no transactions occurred during October 31st, 20X8, and December 31st, 20X8.

Therefore, a specific journal entry must be recorded for the missing piece, as the closing inventory of merchandise must disclose the exact number of units existing in the warehouse (1 piece × 1600 lei/piece = 1600 lei):

| 1600 lei | Expenses with merchandise | = | Merchandise | 1600 lei |
|---|---|---|---|---|

## 5.4 Conclusions

The following summary questions are intended to conclude the main topics of this chapter:

**Chapter summary questions:**

| | |
|---|---|
| 1. What are inventories? | Inventories are assets:<br>(a) held for sale in the ordinary course of business;<br>(b) in the process of production for such sale; or<br>(c) in the form of materials or supplies to be consumed in the production process or in the rendering of services. |
| 2. Provide examples of inventories. | Examples of inventory:<br>• raw materials;<br>• consumables (i.e. fuel, packing materials, spare parts, seeds);<br>• work-in-progress (WIP);<br>• finished goods;<br>• merchandise/goods for resale. |
| 3. How are inventories initially recognised? | Inventories are initially recognised at their cost, either acquisition cost or production cost. The cost of inventories is comprised of all costs of purchase, costs of conversion and other costs incurred in bringing the inventories to their present location and condition (according to **IAS 2 Inventories**). The costs of purchase of inventories is comprised of the purchase price, import duties and other taxes (other than those subsequently recoverable by the entity from the taxing authorities), transportation, handling and other costs directly attributable to the acquisition of finished goods, materials and services. Trade discounts, rebates and other similar items are withdrawn in determining the costs of purchase. |
| 4. How are inventories valuated in the Balance Sheet? | Inventories shall be measured at the lower of cost and net realisable value.<br>Estimates of net realisable value are based on the most reliable evidence available at the time the estimates are made, of the amount the inventories are expected to realise (according to IAS 2 Inventories). The practice of writing inventories down below cost to net realisable value is consistent with the view that assets should not be carried in excess of amounts expected to be realised from their sale or use. |

| | |
|---|---|
| 5. Which cost assessing models can be used to determine the cost of the inventories sold? | The cost of inventories shall be assigned by using the first-in, first-out (**FIFO**), weighted average cost (**WAC**) or last-in, first-out (**LIFO**) formula. An entity shall use the same cost formula for all inventories which have a similar nature and use to the company. For inventories with a different nature or use, different cost formulas may be justified.<br>The Romanian accounting regulations allow the application of LIFO, but according to IAS 2 Inventories the use of the last-in, first-out (LIFO) formula to measure the cost of inventories is prohibited. |
| 6. What advantages and disadvantages are incurred when choosing FIFO or LIFO or WAC? | For companies looking for higher profits in an increasing price environment FIFO would be the best option because it is proving the lower cost of goods sold and, consequently, the higher profit. As a down-size one can be the fact that the related expense is an "old" one. The advantages of FIFO become the disadvantages of LIFO and vice versa. The best advantage of WAC, other than its simplicity, is that it "smooths" the expenses related to inventories, providing a less volatile P & L Account. |
| 7. What is the difference between perpetual and periodic inventory? | Perpetual inventory is an on-going method to track all inventory movements as they incur, whereas periodic inventory provides the cost of goods sold at intervals, after the physical inventory review, as a net amount equal to opening balance + purchase of inventories – ending balance. |
| 8. What happens when inventories are missing at the annual physical checking procedure? | When inventories are missing at the annual physical checking procedure an expense (a loss) should be disclosed. |
| 9. What are the effects of inventory' sale in the annual financial statements? | The effects of inventory' sale in the annual financial statements are: revenues from sale and cost of goods sold in the Profit and Loss Account, a decrease of Inventories and the disclosure of either Accounts receivables or Bank Accounts in the Balance Sheet. In the Cash-Flow Statement only the cash -flow from customers should be disclosed, when received. |
| 10. What is the meaning of WIP and when is it used? | WIP refers to the production that is not 100% completed and is an important intermediary item to journalise the production of goods. |

**Quizzes (only one of the options is correct)**

1. Which of the following inventory cost methods provides the highest profit when prices have an increasing trend?
   a. FIFO;
   b. LIFO;
   c. WAC after each purchase;
   d. WAC at the end of the accounting period.
2. Inventories are valuated in the balance sheet at:
   a. Max (Cost; Fair value);
   b. Min (Price; Net realisable value);
   c. Max (Price; Fair value);
   d. Min (Cost; Net realisable value).
3. An inventory of 200 Smart TVs is purchased at the unit price of 1500 lei/unit with a trade discount of 5% and a delivery fee of 2000 lei. Also, handling expenses in the amount of 500 lei are incurred. The VAT applicable is 19%. Considering all of the above, the acquisition cost of the smart TVs for a VAT-paying company is in the amount of:
   a. 287,500 lei;
   b. 287,000 lei;
   c. 342,125 lei;
   d. 341,625 lei.
4. On October 1st, 20X8, there is an opening balance of perfumed candles of 5000 units valuated at a cost of 5 lei/unit. On October 5th, 20X8, 15,000 units are purchased at the cost of 4 lei/unit and then a sale of 12,000 perfumed candles takes place on October 15th, 20X8. On October 25th, 20X8, 200 units are purchased at the acquisition cost of 6 lei/unit. Which of the following assessments is true?
   a. If WAC after each purchase is applied, the closing balance of perfumed candles is in the amount of 53,750 lei;
   b. If FIFO is applied, the expenses with merchandise are in the amount of 53,000 lei;
   c. If WAC after each purchase is applied, the expenses with merchandise are in the amount of 50,250 lei;
   d. If FIFO is applied, the closing balance of perfumed candles is in the amount of 44,000 lei.

5. Which of the following is the correct accounting entry for recording a negative difference of 5000 lei obtained after performing the physical inventory of raw materials:
   a. Finished goods = Raw materials 5000 lei;
   b. Expenses with raw materials = Raw materials 5000 lei;
   c. Raw materials = Expenses with raw materials 5000 lei;
   d. Expenses with raw materials = Finished goods 5000 lei.
6. Which of the following is the correct accounting entry for recording the disposal of finished goods sold at a cost of 15,000 lei, according to the Romanian Accounting Standards:
   a. Finished goods = Revenues from the sale of finished goods 15,000 lei;
   b. Expenses with finished goods = Finished goods 15,000 lei;
   c. Revenues related to the production cost of finished goods = Finished goods 15,000 lei;
   d. Accounts receivable = Finished goods 15,000 lei.
7. On December 31st, 20X7, the net realisable value of a merchandise inventory was in the amount of 10,000 lei, while its cost raised to the amount of 12,000 lei. At the end of financial year 20X8, the net realisable value of the same inventory is of 11,500 lei. For evaluating the merchandise inventory in the balance sheet of financial year 20X8, the following transaction has to be recorded:
   a. An impairment adjustment in the amount of 1500 lei;
   b. A reversal of the impairment adjustment in the amount of 500 lei;
   c. A reversal of the impairment adjustment in the amount of 1500 lei;
   d. An impairment adjustment in the amount of 500 lei.
8. Which is the correct journal entry for recording the impairment of merchandise in the amount of 1500 lei:
   a. Expenses with the impairment of current assets = Impairment of merchandise 1500 lei;
   b. Expenses with merchandise = Merchandise 1500 lei;
   c. Expenses with merchandise = Accumulated impairment of receivables 1500 lei;
   d. Accumulated impairment of merchandise = Expenses with impairment of current assets 1500 lei.

9. At the end of the manufacturing process, 500 units of finished goods are obtained, after incurring the following costs: direct materials of 5000 lei, direct labour of 7500 lei, variable overheads of 2500 lei and fixed overheads in amount of 3500 lei. Only 75% of the normal production capacity was used for manufacturing the finished goods. Which is the production cost?
   a. 18,500 lei;
   b. 17,625 lei;
   c. 15,225 lei;
   d. 17,000 lei.
10. On November 1st, 20X8, there is an opening balance of finished goods in the amount of 100 units valuated at a cost of 50 lei/unit. On November 10th, 20X8, 250 units are obtained at the production cost of 60 lei/unit. On November 15th, 20X8, 325 units are sold at a selling price of 75 lei/unit. On November 30th, 20X8, 20 units are found in the warehouse when performing the physical inventory. If LIFO is applied for assessing the cost of goods sold and, assuming there were no other expenses recorded except for the ones included in the production process, the profit obtained in November 20X8 is in the amount of:
   a. 20,375 lei;
   b. 6625 lei;
   c. 5375 lei;
   d. 9375 lei.

## Exercises

**Exercise 1**: On December 1st, 20X8, Art Furniture S.R.L., a local furniture wholesaler, purchased an inventory of 2000 oak chairs at a total acquisition price of 1,560,000 lei. The supplier offered a 2% trade discount and the delivery costs involved were in the amount of 20,000 lei. Also, the acquisition involved handling expenses in the amount of 40,000 lei. 19% VAT is applied to all received invoices. The company's depreciation expenses are in the amount of 250,000 lei. What is the value at which the oak chairs will be recognised by Art Furniture S.R.L.? Present the accounting treatment correspondent to the oak chairs inventory.

**Exercise 2**: Fine Furniture S.R.L., a furniture manufacturer, reflects the following information related to three different types of finished goods at the end of the financial years 20X7 and 20X8:

| Finished good | Cost (lei) | Net realisable value 2017 (lei) | Net realisable value 2018 (lei) |
|---|---|---|---|
| Oak chairs | 100,000 | 110,000 | 120,000 |
| Oak dining tables | 350,000 | 320,000 | 340,000 |
| Oak coffee tables | 230,000 | 210,000 | 200,000 |
| **Total** | **680,000** | **640,000** | **660,000** |

What are the amounts at which the finished goods will be disclosed at in the company's balance sheet of 20X7 and 20X8? Present the corresponding accounting entries for both years.

**Exercise 3**: For the production of 500 units of 5th generation laptops A301, Delta Technology S.R.L. incured the following expenses in November 20X8:

- total direct expenses (raw materials and labour) of 1,080,000 lei;
- total overheads of 920,000 lei, out of which 400,000 lei variable expenses.

Knowing that in November 20X8, the entity has used only 60% of its normal production capacity, determine the production cost of A301 laptops.

**Exercise 4**: On December 1st, 20X8, the opening balance of merchandise in the warehouse of Coffee House S.R.L. consists of 2000 packs of coffee capsules, which the company previously purchased at the total acquisition price of 22,500 lei, with a trade discount of 2% and a delivery cost of 750 lei. Also, the advertising expenses the company recorded in the first week of December 20X8 are in amount of 550 lei. During December 20X8, Coffee House S.R.L. conducts the following transactions:

a. on December 5th, 20X8, a purchase of 2500 packs of coffee capsules at the acquisition prices of 15 lei/pack, 19% VAT;
b. on December 15th, 20X8, a sale of 3000 packs at the selling price of 20 lei/pack, 19% VAT;
c. on December 20th, 20X8, an acquisition of 1500 units at the purchase price of 14 lei/pack, delivery fee of 750 lei, 19% VAT;
d. on December 25th, 20X8, a sale of 2000 units at the selling price of 23 lei/unit, 19% VAT.

On December 31st, 20X8, the company performs the physical inventory review and determines a closing balance of 980 remaining packs at the warehouse. Furthermore, on December 31st, 20X8, the net realisable value of the inventory is estimated at 12 lei/pack, as in December 20X8 a new type of coffee capsules was launched by the entity's supplier.
Requirements:

1. Determine the acquisition cost of the opening inventory on December 1st, 20X8;
2. Prepare the merchandise expenses for the coffee capsules packs in December 20X8, knowing that the company is using the weighted average cost for assessing the cost of goods sold;
3. Journalise all the transactions involving the packs of coffee capsules for December 20X8;
4. Determine the value of the coffee capsules which will be disclosed in the entity's statement of financial position at the end of financial year 20X8. Present the necessary accounting entries.

**Case study.** *The accounting treatment of inventories.*

On December 1st, 20X8, Pana Box S.R.L., a jewellery manufacturer, has an opening inventory of silver bracelets of 2000 units, valuated at the production cost of 90 lei/unit. For the production of bracelets, the company uses 925 silver as raw material, which has an opening inventory of 20 kg at the acquisition price of 1800 lei/kg. Also, the company sells custom-made jewellery boxes which are purchased from a supplier. The opening inventory of those boxes is of 250 units valuated at the acquisition cost of 50 lei/unit. The trial balance of the entity shows the following opening account balances on December 1st, 20X8:

- Accounts receivable 150,000 lei;
- Finished goods 180,000 lei;
- Merchandise 12,500 lei;
- Accounts payable 235,000 lei;
- Salaries payable 145,000 lei;
- Raw materials 36,000 lei;
- Cash at bank 250,000 lei;
- Equipment 55,000 lei;
- Accumulated depreciation of equipment 15,000 lei;
- Buildings 900,000 lei;

- Accumulated depreciation of buildings 775,000 lei
- VAT payable 13,500 lei;
- Sundry creditors 90,000 lei;
- Profit of the current financial year 310,000 lei.

During December 20X8, Pana's Box S.R.L. conducts the following transactions (19% VAT is applied to all purchases and sales):

a. on December 2nd, 20X8, the company purchases 25 kg of 925 silver from its supplier at the acquisition price of 1900 lei/kg, with 2% trade discount and delivery costs of 2000 lei;
b. on December 5th, 20X8, the entity records salaries expenses for December 20X8 in the amount of 93,750 lei, out of which 75,000 lei salaries of employees directly involved in the manufacturing process of finished goods;
c. on December 6th, 20X8, the company consumes 36 kg of silver;
d. on December 8th, 20X8, a purchase of 50 jewellery boxes is made at the acquisition price of 45 lei/piece;
e. on December 10th, 20X8, the silver supplier is partially paid through bank transfer in the amount of 50,000 lei which was due at this date;
f. on December 15th, 20X8, the company sells 1500 bracelets at the selling price of 190 lei/bracelet;
g. on December 18th, 20X8, a client paies through bank transfer in the amount of 150,000 lei;
h. on December 20th, 20X8, 80 jewellery boxes are sold at the selling price of 75 lei/piece;
i. on December 25th, 20X8, the invoice of electricity consumption is received in the amount of 60,000 lei, 19% VAT. Management estimates that 22,500 lei of the energy expenses are directly attributable to equipment used in the manufacturing process and the rest can be attributed to the lighting in the company's headquarters;
j. on December 31st, 20X8, the entity records the monthly depreciation as follows: depreciation of buildings in the amount of 56,250 lei and depreciation of equipment in the amount of 12,000 lei;
k. on December 31st, 20X8, the company obtains 3000 bracelets from the production process;

l. on December 31st, 20X8, a sale of 2500 bracelets takes place, at the selling price of 190 lei/unit;
m. on December 31st, 20X8, the company performs the physical inventory and determines a closing inventory of 995 bracelets at the warehouse. No differences are found for the other types of inventories. Also on December 31st, 20X8, the net realisable value of the finished goods is estimated at 75 lei/bracelet.

In December 20X8, the company used 80% of its production capacity and the equipment is used for production purposes only. Also, FIFO is used for assigning the cost of disposals for all types of inventories.

*Requirements*:

1. Determine the production cost of the bracelets obtained on December 31st, 20X8;
2. Journalise all the above transactions of Pana's Box S.R.L. in December 20X8;
3. Determine the closing account balances on December 31st, 20X8 of all the accounts involved and then prepare both balance sheet and income statement at the end of financial year 20X8.

CHAPTER 6

# Non-current Assets

*Elena Nechita and Adriana Duțescu*

*Learning objectives:*

- *Understanding the accounting perspective of non-current assets*
- *Using and analysing various categories of non-current assets and their impact*
- *Estimating the effects of different depreciation and amortisation techniques*
- *Analysing different valuation policies applicable to non-current assets and their influence in financial statements*
- *Links with other management tools*

## 6.1 Introduction

According to some accounting frameworks (Romanian Accounting Regulations included), non-current assets (also known as "fixed assets" or "long-term assets"), assets to be used in the company for more than one year, may be divided into three categories: intangible non-current assets, tangible non-current assets and financial assets (relating to financial assets being held in the company for more than one year). Financial assets are discussed in detail in Chapter 9. To simplify, we shall use "tangible assets", "intangible assets" and "financial assets" to refer to various categories of non-current assets in this chapter.

Most tangible and intangible assets have a limited useful life. The economic usefulness embodied into these assets are systematically allocated, via depreciation or amortisation, to the accounting periods which overlap the useful life of the asset. Also, factors internal and external to the enterprise may indicate that a tangible or an intangible asset is impaired. We shall explain a procedure later in this chapter, which will determine the recognition of impairment losses.

As previously explained, all material transactions included in the accounting information system are based on supporting documents.

## 6.2 Tangible Non-current Assets

**Tangible assets**, also called Property, Plant and Equipment, are non-current assets[1] with a tangible shape, that are held by an enterprise for use in production activities, for rental to others or for administrative purposes. **IAS 16 Property, Plant and Equipment** gives example of types of tangible non-current assets, namely assets of similar nature and function:

- land;
- land and buildings;
- machinery;
- ships;
- aircraft;
- motor vehicles;
- furniture and fixture;
- office equipment.

Romanian accounting regulations classify this category into the following groups: land, buildings, technical equipment, vehicles, furniture, office equipment, protection equipment, investment properties, tangible assets for exploring and assessing mineral resources, productive biological assets and other fixed assets.

The recognition of property, plant and equipment is based on the following criteria: the probability of future economic benefits and the reliability of measurement.

---

[1] An asset is a resource controlled by an enterprise as a result of a past event and from which economic benefits are expected to flow to the enterprise (IASB Framework, par. 4.4.a); normally the expectation is that this asset to be used in the company for more than 1 year.

## 6.3 Intangible Non-current Assets

### 6.3.1 Definitions

Companies enjoy the benefits provided by items without a tangible substance, such as patents, copyrights, trademarks, licenses, computer software, motion picture films, market shares, skilled workforce and so on. At the moment, most multinational companies have intangible assets as an important assets category (e.g. Procter & Gamble or Bayer). Simultaneously, companies with high R&D (Research and Development) costs are considered innovative and on the edge of progress. Before discussing the recognition of these items for accounting purposes, some clarifications related to subcategories of intangible assets are necessary.

**A patent** is a government grant which gives the owner the exclusive right to make, use or sell an invention, as described and claimed by the patent. Patents are granted for inventions "in all fields of technology, provided that they are new, involve an inventive step and are susceptible of industrial application".[2] A form of government granted monopoly for a fixed number of years,[3] patents are meant to encourage inventors to disclose their inventions to the public. Following the expiration of the grant, anyone can make, use or sell the invention as described in the expired patent. A patent may not be renewed.

Allergan, the company that produces Botox, also produces a prescription eye drop for chronic dry eyes called Restasis, which reduces inflammation. There are six patents on Restasis, all of which expire in 2024. Generic drug companies have tried to sue Allergan, claiming its patents are invalid. If the patents don't hold up, then cheaper, generic versions could be on the market well before 2024. In a unique legal manoeuvre, Allergan sold the patents to the Saint Regis Mohawk Tribe, a Native American tribe in upstate New York, in September. The tribal government received $13.75 million from Allergan to take on the patents, according to

---

[2] European Patent Convention of 5 October 1973, as revised by the Act revising Article 63 EPC of 17 December 1991 and the Act revising the EPC of 29 November 2000, art. 52.

[3] The standard term of a European patent is twenty years as from the date of filing. Provided that the annual renewal fees are duly paid, patents remain in force for the maximum term (European Patent Convention, art. 63). In Romania, 20 years as from the date of filing of the application, according to Patent Law no. 64/1991, republished in the Romanian Official Journal, Part I, no. 471 of 26 June 2014 (art. 30).

Allergan. The tribe's extraordinary place in federal law could shut the patent lawsuits down (the Mohawk tribe has claimed that sovereign immunity shields the patents from challenges under that process). If all would have gone according to Allergan's plan, the company would have received $15 million per year until the patents expired. However, a federal judge in Texas invalidated four key patents for the dry-eye treatment Restasis, dealing a blow to its manufacturer, Allergan. The ruling does not mean that generic versions of the drug will be available soon, however. Allergan said that it would appeal the decision, and the Food and Drug Administration has not yet approved copycat versions of the drug. Still, the decision was a setback for the company, whose stock dipped more than 5% upon the news. Restasis is Allergan's second best-selling product, behind the wrinkle treatment Botox, bringing in nearly $1.5 billion in 2016 (*New York Times*, 16.10.2017; newsweek.com, 09.10.2017).

**A copyright** is a form of legal protection to the authors of literary, dramatic, musical, artistic, and certain other intellectual works, such as computer programs. Such works are commonly protected for the duration of the author's life plus an additional number of years after the author's death. The copyright owner may transfer one, a group or all of his exclusive rights.

**Example 1**: FixSoft SRL, a software company, has developed a computer program for on-line global income tax filing. The company has registered its product with the National Office for Patents and Trademarks. What are its options to realise this copyrighted work?

- The company may decide to sell copies of this copyrighted computer program or it may lease, rent or lend them to the Ministry of Finance. A software product license grants the legal right to run or access the software program.[4] A license agreement governs the use of the licensed software program.
- The company may choose to transfer one, some or all of the copyright rights to the Ministry of Finance, such as:
  - The right to make copies of the computer program and offer them to the public by sale, rental, lease or lending;
  - The right to modify the copyrighted computer program;
  - The right to organise public performances of the computer program etc.

---

[4] Selling software is actually selling a limited license to use and copy the software.

A **trademark** is a word, symbol or phrase "capable of graphic representation serving to distinguish the goods or services"[5] of a particular manufacturer or seller. For example, the trademark "L'Orèal," identifies the beauty products made by the French group L'Orèal and distinguishes them from those made by other manufacturers (e.g. Nivea or Clarins). By utilising trademarks, companies aim to enhance their public recognition through advertisement and quality control. In Romania, the exclusive use of a trademark is guaranteed for 10 years from the national filing date and may be renewed at the end of each ten year period upon the payment of a fee.[6] However, the rights to a trademark can be lost due to a lack of supervision or quality control by the trademark owner. Sometimes, trademarks may lose their original distinctiveness: the word ceases to identify a specific source or manufacturer but denotes a broad category or type of product. Terms such as "thermos", "aspirin" and "cellophane" have become generic and are no longer entitled to trademark protection.

From an accounting standpoint, intangible fixed assets are *identifiable*, non-monetary assets that *lack physical substance* and are used by enterprises in production, rents to others or for administrative purposes (**IAS 38 Intangible Assets**). Therefore, the asset should be *identifiable*, it must be *controlled* by the company, it should generate future economic benefits and its cost should be able to be measured reliably (IAS 38, par. 8).

Some identifiable items are not intangible assets because they do not fulfil the basic criteria set forth in the definition of that particular asset. A company may have won a stable market share, but consumer tastes and loyalty cannot be controlled. Although in common language it is right to say that a skilled management team is an "asset of a business", from an accounting point of view it is not. A company cannot control the behaviour of individuals or the length of time it will benefit from their services.

**Example 2**: The 2017 Annual Report of Microsoft Corporation reveals that on December 8th, 2016 the company completed the acquisition of LinkedIn Corporation for a total purchase price of $27.0 billion. LinkedIn has been included in the consolidated results of operations since the date of acquisition. LinkedIn contributed with revenues of $2.3 billion. The allocation of the purchase price to goodwill was completed

---

[5] Article 29 from Law no. 84/1998 on Marks and Geographical Indications.
[6] Article 3(a) from Law no. 84/1998 on Marks and Geographical Indications.

as of June 30th, 2017. The major classes of assets and liabilities to which the purchase price was allocated were as follows[7]:

| (In millions) | $ |
| --- | --- |
| Cash and cash equivalents | 1328 |
| Short-term investments | 2110 |
| Other current assets | 697,000 |
| Property and equipment | 1529 |
| Intangible assets | 7887 |
| Goodwill[a] | 16,803 |
| Short-term debt | −1323 |
| Other current liabilities | −1117 |
| Deferred income taxes | −774,000 |
| Other | −131,000 |
| Total purchase price | 27,009 |

[a]Goodwill was assigned to the Productivity and Business Processes segment. The goodwill was primarily attributed to increased synergies that are expected to be achieved from the integration of LinkedIn. None of the goodwill is expected to be deductible for income tax purposes

### 6.3.2 Recognition

As with a tangible asset, an intangible asset is included in the financial statements if it meets the definition above and the general recognition criteria.

It now becomes apparent that expenditure such as start-up costs, training, advertising and promotional activities does not lead to the creation of an intangible asset and therefore is not recognised as such. In addition, those economic benefits, generated by the synergy between the various parts of the business, also known as internally generated goodwill, cannot be reliably measured and thus do not qualify as an intangible asset.

Assets which result from the general development of the business, such as internally generated brands, publishing titles or customer lists, are not recognised as intangible assets. It is improbable that the costs attributable to maintaining and developing a brand such as L'Oréal can be separated and reliably measured.

As a general rule, an identifiable item internally generated by a business may find itself in one of the following phases:

---

[7] Microsoft Corporation 2017 Annual Report, Note 9—Business Combinations, available at https://www.microsoft.com/investor/reports/ar17/index.html.

- the research phase; or
- the development phase.

IAS 38 takes the view that the eventual benefits generated by a project currently in the research phase are too uncertain and no asset should be recognised. Research activities are those conducted with the aim at obtaining new knowledge and/or applying results, the search for alternatives for materials, systems, processes and activities like the design, evaluation and final selection of such alternatives. The development phase starts after the final selection has been made and the testing, pre-production activities or pilot production have begun.

As for the development phase, the standard lays a set of cumulative conditions in order to ascertain that both asset recognition criteria are met. For that reason, the enterprise should demonstrate:

1. that the realisation of the asset is technically feasible;
2. its intention to realise the asset;
3. its ability to use or sell the asset;
4. the particular pattern in which the future economic benefits will arise (the existence of a market or a specific internal use);
5. the availability of resources to complete the asset; and
6. the reliable measurement of the costs involved.

The first five conditions are linked to the first recognition criterion, i.e. the probability of economic benefits arising in the future, whereas the last condition is coupled to the second criterion, the reliability of measurement.

**Example 3**: Software Development Ltd. is developing a software application for which the following expenses are involved:

| Period | Description | Amount (lei) |
| --- | --- | --- |
| 01.03.–31.03.2018 | The purchase of several apps for analysing similar software | 2000 |
| 01.04.–30.04.2018 | Previous results are inconclusive, therefore additional research is conducted on the internet for similar software | 3000 |
| 01.05.–15.05.2018 | Conclusion of the analysis is presented in a report and the conceptual layout of the future application is prepared | 4300 |

| Period | Description | Amount (lei) |
|---|---|---|
| 16.05.–31.10.2018 | A first version of the software is designed, but the IT experts do not guarantee the technical feasibility of the project. Also, there are uncertainties regarding the resources needed to finalise the software | 4000 |
| 01.11.–30.11.2018 | Programming and software analysis are conducted | 9000 |
| 01.12.–31.12.2018 | Final software testing | 12,000 |

The first step is to classify the conducted activities between research and development stages, as follows:

| Activity | Research phase (lei) | | Development phase (lei) |
|---|---|---|---|
| The purchase of several apps for analysing similar software | The scope is obtaining new information | 2000 | |
| Previous results are inconclusive, therefore additional research is conducted on the internet for similar software | The scope is obtaining new information | 3000 | |
| Conclusion of the analysis is presented in a report and the conceptual layout of the future application is prepared | Assessing the final selection of alternatives | 4300 | |
| A first version of the software is designed, but the IT experts do not guarantee the technical feasibility of the project. Also, there are uncertainties regarding the resources needed to finalise the software | Normally this step is included in the development stage, but the IT experts do not guarantee the technical feasibility of the project and there are uncertainties regarding the resources needed to finalise the software. Therefore, the asset recognition criteria are not met | 4000 | |

| Activity | Research phase (lei) | Development phase (lei) | |
|---|---|---|---|
| Programming and software analysis are conducted | | Testing, pre-production activities or pilot production have begun | 9000 |
| Final software testing | | Testing, pre-production activities are conducted. | 12,000 |
| Total expenses | Research 13,300 | Development | 21,000 |

After classifying the activities, the following transactions are recorded:

a) The research phase—all related expenses are recognised as costs in the income statement:

| 13,300 lei | Expenses with studies and research | = | Accounts payable/ Cash at banks | 13,300 lei |
|---|---|---|---|---|

b) Development phase—an intangible non-current asset is recognised (the Romanian version):

| 21,000 lei | Development cost/ Other intangible assets | = | Revenues from the production of intangible non-current assets | 21,000 lei |
|---|---|---|---|---|

Or the IFRS version

| 21,000 lei | Development cost/Other intangible assets | = | WIP* | 21,000 lei |
|---|---|---|---|---|

WIP* are detailed in Chapter 5

Romanian accounting regulations are somewhat ambivalent. The Romanian Accounting Regulations include start-up costs among intangible assets and a company may choose to capitalise them. Development costs are capitalised if the conditions set forth in IAS 38 are met. The Simplified Accounting Regulations also allow the capitalization of start-up costs and other organization costs, but only assets resulting from the development phase of a project may be recognised as intangibles. Examples of development activities are included (identical to those in IAS 38), but without any conditions for their recognition.

## 6.4 The Recognition and Valuation of Tangible and Intangible Non-current Assets

### 6.4.1 *Initial Recognition and Valuation*

Regardless of their specific allocated category or subcategory, non-current assets are valuated in the following moments:

- initial recognition
- subsequent expenditure
- Balance Sheet moment/date
- disposal/exchange/sale moment

**The initial recognition** of non-current assets, according to IAS 16, should be based upon their **cost**. If acquired, the appropriate value is the ***purchase cost***; if self-produced, the ***production cost*** will be relevant. In some cases, non-current assets might be brought into the business as shareholders' capital contribution and, therefore, the initial recognition should be based on the specific ***utility value*** or ***market value***.

The **acquisition cost** of a non-current asset includes:

- purchase cost;
- import duties (custom taxes);
- transportation and insurance costs to get the asset to its site;
- costs of site preparation;
- installation;
- testing costs;
- the estimated cost of dismantling and removing the asset and restoring the site if the enterprise has the obligation to perform such operations; and
- other similar costs.

**Example 4**: Developer SA purchases a plot of land for 100 million lei with the intention to build a fast-food restaurant. The previous owner had erected a hangar on it to host a fruit market. Developer has no use for this construction, which is also in bad condition and will dismantle it at a cost of 4 million lei. For accounting purposes, the cost of the land is 104 million lei, as the costs to remove an old building or otherwise prepare the land for use are capitalised to the cost of the land (as it is necessary for the construction of the future building on the land).

How does one arrive from the acquisition price to the acquisition cost of an asset? The following example will clarify this issue.

**Example 5**: Company ABC purchases equipment from the supplier of 119,000 lei (VAT 19% included). A transportation invoice of 10,000 lei plus 19% VAT is paid to TRANS SRL to deliver the equipment to the ABC location; an amount of 10,000 lei is due for installation procedures and 5000 lei is calculated to be future possible losses in use. a) What is the acquisition cost of the equipment for the initial recognition? b) What are the effects of these transactions in the financial statements?

**Solution**:

a) What is the acquisition cost of the equipment?

While answering this question, it is imperative to be aware of the stipulations IAS 16 imposes when measuring costs: the asset's cost should include all *costs directly attributable to the asset, in order to be at the necessary location and in its condition of use*. There is a number of costs that should never be capitalised, for e.g. administration and general overheads, repairs, idle time, costs incurred after the asset is ready for use, initial operating losses or future losses in use, advertising and promotional costs, training costs, relocations costs etc. (IAS 16, par. 16–17).

Computation of the acquisition cost of the equipment:

- Net acquisition invoice amount....................................100,000 lei (without VAT[8]).
- Net transportation cost from invoice ...........................10,000 lei (without VAT)

---

[8] VAT should not be included in the initial cost of any asset, because this is an indirect tax which can be recovered from the fiscal authorities. Additional information is provided in Chapters 5 and 7

- Checking procedures............................................10,000 lei
- **Total initial cost (depreciable cost)....................120,000 lei.**[9]

b) What are the effects of these transactions in the financial statements?

b.1. Acquisition invoice
Step 1: How is the accounting equilibrium affected by this transaction?

$$\begin{array}{ll} \text{ASSETS} = \text{EQUITY} + \text{LIABILITIES} \\ +100,000 \text{ lei} = 0 \quad\quad + 119,000 \text{ lei} \\ +19,000 \text{ lei} \end{array}$$

Step 2: Journal entry

| 119,000 lei | % | = | Accounts payable for non-current assets | 119,000 lei |
|---|---|---|---|---|
| 100,000 lei | Equipment | | | |
| 19,000 lei | VAT deductible | | | |

Step 3: Impact in the financial statements

The impact on the Balance Sheet of the company is the following: assets increase by 100,000 lei, VAT deductible increase by 19,000 lei and liabilities increase by 119,000 lei.

b.2. Transportation invoice

*The accounting analysis is based on the same procedure, however, for simplification, only the journal entry is provided*

Step 2. Journal entry

| 19,000 lei | % | = | Other payable for non-current assets | 19,000 lei |
|---|---|---|---|---|
| 10,000 lei | Equipment | | | |
| 9000 lei | VAT deductible | | | |

---

[9] The possible future loss of 5000 lei should not be capitalised, being one specific cost exemption by IAS 16.

b.3. Installation procedures

| 10,000 lei | Equipment = | Other payable for non-current assets | 10,000 lei |

Apart from the *cost model* at the initial recognition, IAS 16 also offers the choice of the *revaluation model*. An example of non-current assets' revaluation and its benefits shall be provided further on.

**Self-constructed assets** are initially valued at production cost. The production cost consists of the direct costs and a fraction of indirect costs. Direct costs are those costs which can be traced to the asset under construction, such as direct material costs (e.g. raw materials) and direct labour costs (e.g. workers on the assembly line). Indirect costs are production overhead costs (such as factory maintenance costs, depreciation and factory administration costs). These costs should be systematically allocated to the self-constructed asset on a rational basis. For example, if a factory is working below its normal production capacity, this aspect should be taken into account when allocating overheads. To avoid overcharging the production cost, overheads are then allocated, taking into account the actual production capacity used. General overhead costs (depreciation and maintenance of administrative buildings and general administration) are not included in the production cost. These costs would have occurred anyway even without a fixed asset under construction.

The Romanian Accounting Regulations include some particular cases of initial valuation that are listed below.

1. Assets representing contribution to the share capital are valued according to the valuation made pursuant by the Romanian Company Law, subject to market price, usefulness, condition and location of the goods;
2. Assets obtained gratuitously are valued at their utility value[10] subject to market price, condition and location of the goods;
3. Assets acquired through exchange with other assets are recorded at the fair value of the assets received in exchange;

---

[10] Fair value, in the Simplified Accounting Regulations.

4. Borrowing costs which are directly attributable to the acquisition, construction or production of certain assets.[11] This may be capitalised as part of that asset's cost if the policy is consistently applied to all similar assets.

### 6.4.2 Subsequent Expenditure

An enterprise continues to disburse amounts of money for its items of property, plant and equipment after they have been brought to working condition. The question is how to treat this subsequent expenditure: *capitalise* it, i.e. add it to the cost of the asset involved, or *expense* it, i.e. add it as an expense in the profit and loss account? This question should rather be rephrased to: "Will the enterprise obtain additional economic benefits a result of the expenditure?" If benefits in excess of the original performance are probable, the expenditure should be added to the cost of the existing asset. This is the case with improvements, which may prolong the useful life or increase the quantity or quality of the output of a plant item. Sometimes the expenditure relates to the adoption of a production process that leads to the material reduction of operating costs.

**Example 6**: The management of a weaving mill decides to fit all the machines with energy saving devices that will cut down electricity costs by 15%. The cost of the device will be added (capitalised) to the gross carrying amount of the weaving machines because there is a material reduction in operating costs.

**Example 7**: A sewing machine part is replaced with one that creates better and a greater variety of seams. Its cost will be added to the cost of the original asset because it enhances the quality of the products.

All other subsequent expenditures should be recognised as expenses in the period when incurred and deducted from revenues in the current period's Profit and Loss Account. This is the case with ordinary repairs (cleaning, repainting, and lubricants) because they only maintain the original appearance or performance of the assets.This specific accounting treatment, rooted in IAS 16, is also required by Romanian Accounting Regulations.

---

[11] Assets that inevitably take a long time to be ready for their intended use, e.g. a power plant (IAS 23 *Borrowing Costs*).

**Example 8**: A building, with a cost of 22 mil. lei, is depreciated over 20 years via the straight-line method (a residual value of 2 mil. lei is estimated). The following events occur: (a) during the 3rd year of use its internal walls are repainted, the overall cost is 80,000 lei (no VAT added) (b) on December 31st, 20X9, a general repair and full renovation project ended, the overall cost of it being 1.19 million lei (VAT of 19% included). Requirements: Which subsequent costs should be capitalised and what effect would this have on the annual financial statements?

**Solution**: The painting process by the end of the third year of use does not qualify for cost capitalisation, it is just a maintenance cost and is to be expensed. However, the renovation cost does qualify for capitalisation because it provided additional benefits, for e.g., prolonging the useful life of the building. Therefore, the amount of 1 mil. lei (VAT excluded) increases the value of the non-current asset and its depreciable amount (depreciation shall be reassessed, based on the new value).

- Journal entries for wall painting:

| 80,000 lei | Other operating expenses | = | Accounts payable | 80,000 lei |
|---|---|---|---|---|

- Journal entry for consolidation cost:

| 1,190,000 lei | % | | = | Accounts payable for non-current assets | 1,190,000 lei |
|---|---|---|---|---|---|
| 1,000,000 lei | Buildings | | | | |
| 190,000 lei | VAT deductible | | | | |

### 6.4.3 Measurement at the Balance Sheet Date

At the **Balance Sheet date**, the value of the non-current assets is reassessed in order to provide their "true and fair amount". If companies use the cost model for their non-current assets, the Balance Sheet value (also called the ***net carrying amount***) is the difference between the initial cost and the accumulated depreciation[12] of the asset. For example, a piece of equipment with an initial cost of 100,000 lei and an accumulated

---

[12] Depreciation concept and examples will be provided further on this chapter.

depreciation of 20,000 lei will have a Balance Sheet value of 80,000 lei (100,000 lei − 20,000 lei). If the asset is considered to be impaired,[13] then the impairment value should be subtracted from the net carrying amount, for Balance Sheet purposes. If the business uses the **revaluation model**, the Balance Sheet value of the asset is its new revaluation amount. For instance, a building which costs 1 million lei in 2009 and is revalued at 1.5 million lei the end of 2013 (market value), is recognised in the Balance Sheet at the end of 2013 in the amount of 1.5 million lei.[14]

**Example 9**: A piece of equipment was purchased for 20,000 lei and its accumulated depreciation is 8000 lei. There are no indications that the asset is impaired. The asset will be included in the financial statements at its carrying amount of 12,000 lei.

**Example 10**: An assembly line costing 100,000 lei, with accumulated depreciation of 20,000 lei, is negatively affected by a change in market conditions. Impairment losses of 10,000 lei are calculated. The carrying amount of the asset is 70,000 lei.

Under alternative accounting regulations, the cost of the non-current asset is substituted by its fair value.[15] The fair value is the amount for which an asset could be exchanged between knowledgeable, willing parties in an arm's length transaction (**IFRS 13 Fair Value Measurement**). The fair value is generally understood as the asset's market value, as determined by qualified evaluators.

When a company chooses the fair value as the valuation basis for a class of tangible or intangible assets, it has to perform valuations regularly, with a frequency that reflects the volatility of the market prices of those assets. It is obvious that the fair value of the company's car fleet is more sensitive to price changes than the fair value of its lathes. In a stable economy, property items like land and buildings could be revalued every three to five years, whereas revaluations of items with fluctuating prices should be done more often.

For assets which do not have a fluctuating competitive market price, the replacement cost is considered its fair value. The calculation of the

---

[13] Impairment concept and examples are discussed further on in the chapter.

[14] Specific examples will be provided further on in this chapter.

[15] "Fair value" in the Simplified Accounting Regulations and a value that takes into account "inflation, the utility of the asset, its condition and the market price" in the Harmonised Accounting Regulations.

depreciated replacement cost starts with establishing the replacement cost of a new asset and then deducting the respective accumulated depreciation.

**Example 11**: A company owns a custom-made power generator costing 40 million lei and depreciated 40%. There is no market for such an asset; a new one could be built for 4.5 million lei. Thus, the replacement cost is:

$$4,500,000 * 60\% = 2,700,000 \text{ lei}$$

There is also a valuation principle that prevents companies to present assets with a value greater than their recoverable amount at the Balance Sheet date. Examples are provided at the end of this chapter in Sect. 6.8, Impairment of current assets.

### 6.4.4 Measurement at Disposal, Exchange or Sale

A non-current asset is **disposed** at its **net carrying amount** (cost minus accumulated depreciation), when its use ended, or the business decided to replace it or sell it. If the asset is sold at a price higher than its net carrying amount, the company will incur a profit; if the selling price is below the net carrying amount, the company will incur a loss.

For example, a car with an acquisition cost of 50,000 lei and an accumulated depreciation of 45,000 lei, sold for 4000 lei, will incur a loss of 1000 lei (4000 lei − 5000 lei) in the Profit and Loss Account of the company.

## 6.5 Acquired and Produced Non-current Assets

### 6.5.1 Purchase of Non-current Assets

The journal entries are based on the invoice and on the reception documents (handover receipt, certificate of acceptance, certificate of temporary acceptance etc.).

**Example 12**: Ninva SA, a juice and jam producer, wishes to purchase an air conditioning system in the amount of 75,000 lei (net of VAT, 19%) for the administrative building. The supplier requires an advance payment of 10% of the price net of VAT. The supplier will deliver and install the system without additional costs.

Based on the bank statement, the journal entry of the advance payment is:

| 7500 lei | Advance payment for non-current assets | = | Cash/Bank account | 7500 lei |
|---|---|---|---|---|

Based on the invoice, the reception documents and the installation of the air conditioning system, the following journal entry is made:

| 89,250 lei | % | = | Non-current assets suppliers | 89,250 lei |
|---|---|---|---|---|
| 75,000 lei | Property, plant and equipment | | | |
| 14,250 lei | VAT deductible | | | |

The sum of the transaction should generate:

| 89,250 lei | Non-current assets suppliers | = | % | 89,250 lei |
|---|---|---|---|---|
| | | | Advance paid for non-current assets in progress | 7500 lei |
| | | | Cash | 81,750 lei |

### 6.5.2 Production of Non-current Assets

The production of non-current assets is accounted for similar to the production of goods, with the difference that the production of a non-current asset takes longer to complete, often longer than one financial year. The principle reinforced by IFRS is that, at the end of the year, the costs incurred for the production of a non-current asset should not influence the Profit and Loss account.

In the Romanian accounting system, the account "Revenue from the Production of Non-Current Assets" was introduced. This national journalising method differs from the IFRS's requirements, but it is still compatible in terms of the effects in the financial statements. The title of this account is somewhat misleading as, in spite of its name, this is not a "real" revenue account. It serves only to neutralise the costs already recognised as expenses for the production of a non-current asset, at the end of the year. This peculiar situation occurs even though there are accounts called "Work-in-progress for tangible and intangible assets". However, these accounts do not incorporate the appropriate expenditure of production when incurred. Therefore, the Work-in-progress accounts are debited in connection with the "Revenue from Non-Current-Assets Production" accounts. Also, only the production cost is credited to this account and not the sale price.

**Example 13**: AGNA SA, a car manufacturer, builds a new warehouse for its spare parts. The construction started on November 1st, 20X6. On December 31st of the same year, the building was 60% finished. The management accountant in charge of this project collected and attributed the following costs to the construction of the warehouse:

| | |
|---|---|
| Materials | 500,000 lei |
| Wages of the builders | 80,000 lei |
| Social charges in respect of direct labour | 33,600 lei |
| Salaries of the supervisors | 15,000 lei |
| Social charges in respect of indirect labour | 6400 lei |
| Depreciation of equipment used | 20,000 lei |
| Fuel and electricity | 10,000 lei |

From a financial accounting point of view, these costs are not individualised. They are included in the company's total costs with materials, salaries, social charges, depreciation, fuel and electricity. The Romanian method thus is different from the International method (pursuant to IFRS) which is emphasised by the following solution. The respective entries could be journalised as the following:

| Romanian (by nature P&L) (consumption is expensed in the moment of occurrence and, when incurred at different stages of implementation, the Work-in-progress account shall be debited and the Revenue account shall be credited) | IFRS/international approach (by function P&L) (A new asset should include all the costs related to this asset, therefore an account e.g. "Work-in-progress" or "Work-in-process" shall capitalise all these costs) |
|---|---|
| 1. Use of raw materials for the production of a non-current asset (cost of raw materials) of 500,000 lei<br>500,000 lei Raw Materials Expense = Raw Materials 500,000 lei | 1. Use of raw materials for the production of a non-current asset (cost of raw materials) of 500,000 lei:<br>500,000 lei WIP for tangible assets = Raw Materials 500,000 lei |

| Romanian (by nature P&L) (consumption is expensed in the moment of occurrence and, when incurred at different stages of implementation, the Work-in-progress account shall be debited and the Revenue account shall be credited) | IFRS/international approach (by function P&L) (A new asset should include all the costs related to this asset, therefore an account e.g. "Work-in-progress" or "Work-in-process" shall capitalise all these costs) |
|---|---|
| 2. Direct labour costs of 133,600 lei (80,000+33,600) 133,600 lei Salaries Expense = Salaries Payable 133,600 lei 3. Indirect labour cost of 21,400 lei (15,000+6400) 15,000 lei Salaries Expense = Salaries Payable 15,000 lei 6400 lei Other expenses with salaries = Other salary payables 6400 lei 4. Depreciation of the equipment used 20,000 lei Depreciation Expense = Accumulated depreciation of equip. 20,000 lei 5. Fuel and electricity 10,000 lei Fuel Expense = Account payable 10,000 lei 6. On December 31st N, if the asset is still in progress (production cost to date): Work in Progress for Assets = Revenue from the Production of Tangible 7. The end of the production process and the recognition of the non-current asset, in N+1 (production cost) 665,000 lei Non-current Asset = Revenue from the Production of Tangible Assets 665,000 lei | 2. Direct labour costs of 133,600 lei (80,000+33,600) 133,600 lei WIP for tangible assets = Salaries Payable 133,600 lei 3. Indirect labour cost of 21,400 lei (15,000+6400) 15,000 lei WIP for tangible assets = Salaries Payable 15,0000 lei 6,400 lei WIP for tangible assets = Other Salaries Payable 6400 lei 4. Depreciation of the equipment used 20,000 lei WIP for tang. assets = Accumulated depreciation of equip. 20,000 lei 5. Fuel and electricity 20,000 lei WIP for tang. assets = Account payable 20,000 lei 6. On December 31st N, if the asset is still in progress: No entry 7. The end of the production process and the recognition of the non-current asset, in N+1 (production cost) 665,000 lei Non-current Asset = WIP 665,000 lei for Tangible Assets |

## 6.6 Depreciation, Amortisation and Depletion of Tangible and Intangible Non-current Assets

All assets with an estimated useful life eventually exhaust their lifespan. Different types of assets, such as intangible and mineral assets, are systematically reduced in value throughout their useful life. A distinction is made between depreciation, depletion and amortisation, depending on the type of asset in question:

| Method of reduction | Type of asset | Examples |
|---|---|---|
| Depreciation | Tangible assets (property, plant and equipment) | Buildings, equipment, machinery etc. |
| Amortisation | Intangible assets | Patents, copyrights, development costs etc. |
| Depletion | Mineral assets | Mines, oil fields etc. |

### 6.6.1 Depreciation of Tangible Assets

The principle behind depreciation is to offset the cost of an asset with the benefits from its use. Not all non-current assets are depreciated. Land has an indefinite useful life and is not depreciated. There are several fallacies regarding the concept of depreciation. Firstly, an appropriate valuation of non-current assets through depreciation is neither possible, nor intended (although most non-current assets will decrease in value as they are used). A machine's market value may increase due to a shortage, but it would still be depreciated over its useful life.

Secondly, funds are not set aside for the replacement of a depreciating non-current asset. Also, a company may decide not to replace a certain non-current asset and replacement costs may be very different from its previous price. Depreciation charges are rather made to insure a correct calculation of the net profit.

Professional judgement is heavily involved in establishing the depreciation of an asset. Therefore, accounting depreciation is not always equal to tax depreciation. The latter is linked to economic policy aims, such as providing incentives for capital investment or balancing the national budget.

When calculating depreciation for accounting purposes, estimates are made with respect to useful life, depreciation method and residual value. An asset is normally amortised over its useful life, namely the number of years that the entity expects to get useful service from the asset or the number of units that the asset is expected to produce. Though based on the physical life of the asset, its useful life is often limited by its rate of obsolescence (e.g., a computer system), operational factors (e.g. number or shifts or maintenance programs) or legal factors, such as the duration of a financial lease. The useful life is subject to periodical reviews which include changes to the depreciation amount for the current and future periods.

**Example 14**: On January 1st, 20X3, Ramas SA purchased a printing press for 150,000 lei and had an estimated useful life of 15 years. After 3 years, on January 1st, 20X6, the company reviewed the useful life and, following the investigation of the market value of printing equipment, decreased it to 9 years.

According to IAS 16, this change of the estimation only affects current and future financial statements. The revised useful life on January 1st, 20X6 is 9 years (revised useful life of 12 years minus the expired useful life of 3 years). It is applied to the net carrying amount of the equipment on January 1st, 20X7, in the amount of 120,000 lei (150,000 − 150,000 * 3 * 1/15).

The considerations above apply to companies operating under the Romanian Accounting Regulations. When estimating the useful life of a non-current asset, the other companies refer to the guidelines included in a Catalogue regularly updated by the Ministry of Finance.

The *residual value* (the estimated price to be obtained by selling the asset at the end of its useful life) is expected to be low or non-existent in Romania, as opposed to the Anglo-Saxon economic view. At the end of their useful life, some assets may generate cash if sold. Companies often sell their computers that have reached the expected useful life to private users.

The depreciable amount of an asset is, in general, its original cost minus its residual value. Because of immateriality, the residual value is not discounted when calculating the depreciable amount.

The depreciation method should mirror the pattern in which the asset's economic benefits are consumed by or flow to the enterprise. It should be consistently applied unless there is a significant change of the scheme according to which economic benefits expire. The selected method should be rational and systematic. It should be reviewed periodically and when the method is changed and has effects on the current and future periods.

There are several different methods of depreciation:

- straight-line;
- reducing balance;
- sum of the years' digits;

- units of production/activity; and
- other methods.

The accounting standards **IAS 16 Property, Plant and Equipment** (and also the Romanian Accounting Regulations) does not express a preference about which method should be used. The method chosen should be the one which is the most appropriate in regard to the type of asset and its use in the business and should be consistently applied on an annual basis, across both the Profit and Loss Account and the Balance Sheet.

The Simplified Accounting Regulations in Romania offer a choice between the following methods to small companies, namely:

- straight-line;
- diminishing balance methods;
- accelerated;
- number of units of production.

The depreciation methods are also influenced by tax considerations: for example, the accelerated method allows a 50% write off in the first year of service, followed by the straight-line method, for the outstanding balance.

The depreciation method should be reviewed periodically and changed if the pattern in which the economic benefits are consumed changes. Similar to the revaluation of the depreciation period, only the current and the ensuing accounting periods are affected.

The following table discloses the explanatory note related to property, plant and equipment from the Telekom 2017 Consolidated Annual Report.[16]

---

[16] Deutsche Telekom Consolidated Annual Report for Financial Year 2017, Explanatory Note 6—Property, Plant and Equipment, available at https://www.annualreport.telekom.com/site0218/notes/notes-to-the-consolidated-statement-of-financial-position/property-plant-and-equipment.html.

*Deutsche Telekom Financial Year 2017*

Property, plant and equipment

| millions of € | Land and equivalent rights, and buildings including buildings on land owned by third parties | Technical equipment and machinery | Other equipment, operating and office equipment | Advance payments and construction in progress | Total |
|---|---|---|---|---|---|
| **Cost** | | | | | |
| At December 31, 2015 | 18,516 | 116,013 | 8597 | 3468 | 146,594 |
| Currency translation | 80 | 928 | 47 | 38 | 1093 |
| Changes in the composition of the Group | 0 | 15 | (2) | 2 | 15 |
| Additions | 133 | 5357 | 482 | 5384 | 11,356 |
| Disposals | 157 | 4786 | 1240 | 82 | 6265 |
| Change from non-current assets and disposal groups held for sale | (200) | (9) | (106) | (8) | (323) |
| Reclassifications | 168 | 4196 | 636 | (5037) | (37) |
| **At December 31, 2016** | **18,540** | **121,714** | **8414** | **3765** | **152,433** |
| Currency translation | (294) | (3342) | (209) | (165) | (4010) |
| Changes in the composition of the Group | 23 | 7 | 2 | 9 | 41 |
| Additions | 104 | 4954 | 469 | 5994 | 11,521 |
| Disposals | 206 | 5053 | 596 | 57 | 5912 |
| Change from non-current assets and disposal groups held for sale | (526) | (32) | 0 | (1) | (559) |

|   |   |   |   |   |   |
|---|---|---|---|---|---|
| Reclassifications | 246 | 4874 | 761 | (5927) | (46) |
| At December 31, 2017 | 17,887 | 123,122 | 8841 | 3618 | 153,468 |

**Accumulated depreciation and impairment losses**

|   |   |   |   |   |   |
|---|---|---|---|---|---|
| At December 31, 2015 | 11,082 | 84,785 | 6063 | 27 | 101,957 |
| Currency translation | 51 | 503 | 23 | (2) | 575 |
| Changes in the composition of the Group | 0 | 5 | (3) | 0 | 2 |
| Additions (depreciation) | 684 | 7148 | 724 | 1 | 8557 |
| Additions (impairment) | 63 | 138 | 11 | 8 | 220 |
| Disposals | 163 | 4165 | 1046 | 24 | 5398 |
| Change from non-current assets and disposal groups held for sale | (139) | (8) | (73) | (8) | (228) |
| Reclassifications | (41) | (68) | 110 | (1) | 0 |
| Reversal of impairment losses | (8) | (2) | 0 | 0 | (10) |
| At December 31, 2016 | 11,529 | 88,336 | 5809 | 1 | 105,675 |
| Currency translation | (200) | (1809) | (115) | (1) | (2125) |
| Changes in the composition of the Group | 9 | 0 | 1 | 0 | 10 |
| Additions (depreciation) | 635 | 6905 | 772 | 0 | 8312 |
| Additions (impairment) | 35 | 42 | 3 | 0 | 80 |
| Disposals | 173 | 4234 | 532 | 0 | 4939 |
| Change from non-current assets and disposal groups held for sale | (369) | (31) | 0 | 0 | (400) |
| Reclassifications | (84) | (11) | 83 | 0 | (12) |

| | | | | | |
|---|---|---|---|---|---|
| Reversal of impairment losses | (11) | 0 | 0 | 0 | (11) |
| At December 31, 2017 | 11,371 | 89,198 | 6021 | 0 | 106,590 |
| Net carrying amounts | | | | | |
| At December 31, 2016 | 7011 | 33,378 | 2605 | 3764 | 46,758 |
| At December 31, 2017 | 6516 | 33,924 | 2820 | 3618 | 46,878 |

a) **Straight-line method**

Straight-line depreciation (also available for the amortisation of intangible assets) is calculated by dividing the depreciable amount (cost less estimated residual value) to the asset's estimated number of years of useful life. The figure derived from this calculation then becomes a fixed charge, written off each year from the initial cost of the asset.

As an equal amount is charged each year, a graph plotting the upward accumulation of depreciation year by year would appear as a straight line.

Depreciation is recorded as a debit to Depreciation Expense and a credit to Accumulated Depreciation. Depreciation Expense is shown in the Profit and Loss Account, while Accumulated Depreciation adjust the original cost or revalued amount of an asset, thus giving the carrying amount in the Balance Sheet.

**Example 15**: MarCom SA purchased a new commercial vehicle with an estimated useful life of five years. The cost of the asset was 22,500 lei (net of VAT) and its residual value after five years was estimated to be 2500 lei. Show the effects of the annual depreciation.

**Solution:** Using the straight-line method, the annual depreciation expense would be:
$(22,500 - 2500)/5 = 20,000/5 = 4000$ lei

Thus, profits would bear an annual expense of 4000 lei, while the cost of the vehicle would be reduced by the same amount each year in the Balance Sheet.

The journal entry to deal with the purchase of the asset would be:

| 26,775 lei | % | = | Non-current asset suppliers | 26,775 lei |
| 22,500 lei | Vehicles | | | |
| 4275 lei | VAT deductible | | | |

At the end of the year, the Depreciation Expense account is debited with 4000 lei and the Accumulated Depreciation account is credited with the same amount. On the basis of this prerequisite, the financial statements will include the non-current assets with the carrying amount of 18,500 lei in the Balance Sheet (disclosed as vehicles at cost 22,500 lei – less accumulated depreciation to date 4000 lei).

Journal entries would include:

| 4000 lei | Depreciation expense | = | Accumulated depreciation | 4000 lei |

The depreciation expense for the year is closed into the P&L Account by the end of the year:

| 4000 lei | Profit and Loss Account | = | Depreciation expense | 4000 lei |

### Extract from Ledger Accounts

*Depreciation Expense a/c*

December 31st  
Accumulated depreciation 4000 lei

December 31st  
Profit and Loss a/c 4000 lei

*Accumulated Depreciation a/c*

December 31st  
Balance c/d 4000 lei

December 31st  
Depreciation Exp. a/c 4000 lei  
January 1st  
Balance b/d 4000 lei

### Extract from the Profit and Loss Account

| Depreciation | 4000 lei |
| Heating and electricity | * |
| Motor vehicle running costs | * |

### Extract from the Balance Sheet

| Non-current assets | Cost | Depreciation | Carrying amount (NBV) |
|---|---|---|---|
| Motor vehicles | 22,500 lei | 4000 lei | 18,500 lei |

**Assets acquired during an accounting period**

A business may purchase a new non-current asset at any time during the course of an accounting period. To reflect the limited use the business has had from the asset in that period, it will charge depreciation on a pro rata basis.

**Example 16**: A business with an accounting period which runs from January 1st to December 31st, purchases a new intangible asset on April 1st, 20X8, in the amount of 24,000 lei. The expected useful life of the asset is 4 years and its residual value is nil. What should the amortisation charge for 20X8 be?

**Solution**: The amortisation expense per year of service will be 24,000/4 = 6000 lei

However, since the asset was acquired on April 1st, 20X8, the business has only benefited from the use of the asset for 9 months instead of the full 12 months. It would therefore seem fair to charge amortisation in 20X8 of only 9 months:

9 * 6000/12 = 4500 lei

**b) Diminishing balance methods**

Diminishing balance methods apply either a constant (fixed) depreciation percentage to a decreasing (variable) amount or a decreasing (variable) depreciation percentage to a constant (fixed) amount. The rationale of diminishing balance methods is that some non-current assets, mainly equipment items, tend to depreciate more in the earlier years than they do in the later years of their useful life. The reducing balance method and sum of the years' digits are the most used diminishing balance methods.

**b.1. Reducing balance method/double declining method**

This method applies a constant percentage to the carrying amount of the asset (cost minus accumulated depreciation) brought forward at the beginning of each year. Since the percentage is applied to a reducing balance, the depreciation amount will be less each successive year. Generally, the percentage used is double the straight-line percentage, that is, a double declining rate.

**Example 17**: On January 1st, 20X2, Industrial SA purchases metal processing equipment in the amount of 90,000 lei plus 10,000 lei installation and testing costs. The estimated useful life is 5 years, giving a straight-line percentage of 20%. A residual value of 5000 lei is estimated. Management believes that the economic benefits embodied in this asset are consumed at a decreasing rate. The diminishing balance method is used at a double declining rate. The rate is therefore 40%.

**Solution:**

Acquisition cost = Purchase price + expenses directly related to the acquisition − Commercial discounts

= 90,000 + 10,000 = 100,000 lei

Depreciable value (Carrying amount to be depreciated) = Acquisition cost − Residual value = 100,000 − 5000 = 95,000 lei

The following table discloses the way the annual depreciation (lei) based on the double declining method is computed during the asset's useful life:

| Year | Carrying amount to be depreciated | Diminishing balance depreciation | Remaining value (closing NBV) |
|---|---|---|---|
| 20X2 | 95,000 lei | 95,000 × 40% = 38,000 lei | 100,000 − 38,000 = 62,000 lei |
| 20X3 | 62,000 − 5000 = 57,000 lei | 57,000 × 40% = 22,800 lei | 62,000 − 22,800 = 39,200 lei |
| 20X4 | 39,200 − 5000 = 34,200 lei | 34,200 × 40% = 13,680 lei | 39,200 − 13,680 = 25,520 lei |
| 20X5 | 25,520 − 5000 = 20,520 lei | 20,520 × 40% = 8,208 lei | 25,520 − 8208 = 17,312 lei |
| 20X6 | 17,312 − 5000 = 12,312 lei | 12,312 lei | 17,312 − 12,312 = 5000 lei |

To observe the 5 year useful life, the depreciation amount in 20X6 is a balancing figure.

**b.2. Sum of years' digits method**

In order to charge a higher depreciation rate in the early years of the asset's life, a decreasing rate is applied to a constant depreciable amount. One possible option is called "sum of the digits" and consists in the calculation of the percentage applied based on the sum of years of use, as shown in the following example:

**Example 18**: We shall use the same data as in the example above.

| | |
|---|---|
| Cost | 100,000 lei |
| Estimated residual value | 5000 lei |
| Depreciable amount | 95,000 lei |

Sum of the years' digits of the useful life:
$5+4+3+2+1=15$

| Year | Rate | Depreciation charge | Accumulated depreciation | Closing NBV |
|---|---|---|---|---|
| 1 | 5/15 | 95,000×5/15=31,667 lei | 31,667 lei | 100,000–31,667=68,333 lei |
| 2 | 4/15 | 95,000×4/15=25,333 lei | 57,000 lei | 100,000–57,000=43,000 lei |
| 3 | 3/15 | 95,000×3/15=19,000 lei | 76,000 lei | 100,000–76,000=24,000 lei |
| 4 | 2/15 | 95,000×2/15=12,667 lei | 88,667 lei | 100,000–88,667=11,333 lei |
| 5 | 1/15 | 95,000×1/15=6333 lei | 95,000 lei | 100,000–95,000=5000 lei |
| Sum of years' digits=15 | | | | |

A formula can also be used for the sum of years' digits: $n(n+1)/2$, where n is the number of years of useful life. Thus, in our example: 5 * 6/2=15

Journal entries of the first year of use would include:

| | | | | |
|---|---|---|---|---|
| 31,667 lei | Depreciation expense | = | Accumulated depreciation | 31,667 lei |

The journal entries for the following years will have the same corresponding accounts but different amounts, based on the previous table.

### c. Units of production/activity method

Another depreciation method, extensively used for non-current assets used in operations (production, main activities of the business) is the **"units of activity" method**; this method provides annual depreciation directly correlated to the way the asset is used or based on the output generated (e.g. km or miles driven, volume of output provided etc., no. of hours worked etc.). This method is considered more relevant because it is based on the specific outputs of the non-current asset, e.g. number of copies on an annual basis for printer machine, number of miles/km accumulated by a car/airplane/train, tones of refined oil for refining equipment, number of bottles of beverages etc.

**Example 19**: Let's use the **units of activity method** now to calculate and disclose annual depreciation. A printer, costing 100,000 lei, was put in use on February 1st, 20X1. Its useful life is estimated at 5 years and 100,000 standard copies. In the first year, 24,000 copies were printed; in the second year, 20,000 were printed; in the third year, 21,000 copies were printed; in the fourth year, 22,000 copies were printed and in the fifth and final year, 13,000 copies were printed.

The annual depreciation is shown in the following table:

| Year | Rate (thousand copies) | Depreciation charge | Accumulated depreciation |
| --- | --- | --- | --- |
| 1 | 24/100 | 24,000 lei | 24,000 lei |
| 2 | 20/100 | 20,000 lei | 44,000 lei |
| 3 | 21/100 | 21,000 lei | 65,000 lei |
| 4 | 22/100 | 22,000 lei | 87,000 lei |
| 5 | 13/100 | 13,000 lei | 100,000 lei |

The journal entry of the first year of use is:

| 24,000 lei | Depreciation expense | = | Accumulated depreciation | 24,000 lei |
| --- | --- | --- | --- | --- |

The journal entries for the following years will have the same corresponding accounts but different amounts, based on the previous table.

There are other depreciation methods that emphasise the tax/fiscal approach and are considered to offer a tax allowance (tax relief) for companies. This may apply in the case of the accelerated methods and the diminishing balance methods with diminishing coefficients (determined based on the assets' useful life) used in Romanian business practices.

### 6.6.2  Amortisation of Intangible Assets and Depletion

A subcategory of non-current assets is "intangible assets", such as patents, copyrights, goodwill and software. These assets fulfil the characteristics of a non-current asset, therefore, they should be used for a longer period of time (more than one year) and are expected to bring future benefits to the company. These intangible assets are therefore amortised, in order to depict their way of being used, via expenses disclosed in the P&L Account.

The principle behind amortisation is to match the cost of an asset with the related benefits of its use. This is also the definition of depreciation!

Is there a difference between depreciation and amortisation? The concepts are the same but relate to different assets: "depreciation" relates to tangible non-current assets, "amortisation" relates to intangible non-current assets, both concepts have the same rationale: to show the way the specific asset is used and impacts the Profit and Loss Account.

A third concept, which is used in relation to natural resources, is "**depletion**". For example, an oil field shall deplete throughout the extraction process of crude oil every year from the field (it is similar to the units of activity depreciation method but based on the annual quantity extracted).

**Example 20**: A patent was purchased for 100,000 lei and is estimated to bring straight-line future economic benefits in the following 10 years. The annual amortisation is 100,000 lei * 1/10 years = 10,000 lei

Journal entries are:

| 10,000 lei | Amortisation expense | = | Accumulated amortisation | 10,000 lei |
|---|---|---|---|---|

Its effect in the P&L Account:

| 10,000 lei | Profit and Loss Account | = | Amortisation expense | 10,000 lei |
|---|---|---|---|---|

In the annual Balance Sheet, the patent is disclosed at its net carrying amount, i.e. cost minus the accumulated depreciation. By the end of the first year, the Balance Sheet value of the patent is 90,000 lei (100,000 lei − 10,000 lei).

## 6.7 Revaluation of Non-current Assets

IAS 16 provides two valuation models for non-current assets: the cost model and the revaluation model (IAS 16, par. 31). As the first model has already been explained and exemplified, we shall now focus on the revaluation model. IAS 16 provides the option that non-current assets can be carried on at their fair value minus any accumulated depreciation. The following criteria must be fulfilled: the revaluation should be provided with sufficient regularity: if one non-current asset is revaluated, then the entire class must be revaluated (IAS 16, par. 36); the increasing amount is disclosed as other comprehensive income; the decreasing amount should be recognised immediately in the P&L Account or as a diminution of a previous revaluation reserve (IAS 16, par. 39).

**Example 21**: A complex piece of equipment for a car plant was purchased, checked and put into operation. The following data are provided:

- Invoice amount owed to supplier 119,000 lei. (VAT of 19% included)
- Transportation cost to the plant location 11,900 lei. (VAT of 19% included)
- Checking procedures in the amount of 10,000 lei. (no VAT involved)
- Accounting policy settled: 10 years, double-decline method, immaterial residual value
- By the end of the year 4 the equipment is revaluated at 52,000 lei.

**Requirements**: provide the impact of the acquisition, annual depreciation and revaluation of the equipment advantages and disadvantages of NCA revaluation on the financial statements.

**Solution**:

Step 1. Computation of the initial cost of the equipment

- Net acquisition invoice amount............................... 100,000 lei (without VAT)
- Net transportation cost from invoice .........................10,000 lei (without VAT)
- Checking procedures............................................. 10,000 lei
- Total initial cost (depreciable cost)..........................**120,000 lei.**

Step 2. Depreciation, based on a 10 years useful life, double-decline method

| Useful life (0) | Carrying amount (1) | Depreciation expense (2= 1 * 20%) | Accumulated depreciation (3) | Carrying amount (4= 1 – 2) |
| --- | --- | --- | --- | --- |
| Year 1 | 120,000 lei | 24,000 lei | 24,000 lei | 96,000 lei |
| Year 2 | 96,000 lei | 19,200 lei | 43,200 lei | 76,800 lei |
| Year 3 | 76,800 lei | 15,360 lei | 58,560 lei | 61,440 lei |
| Year 4 | 61,440 lei | 12,288 lei | 70,848 lei | 49,152 lei |
| ........ | | | | |

## Step 3. Revaluation of the equipment by the end of the 4th year

- Carrying amount of equipment end year 4..................49,152 lei
- Market value of the equipment end year 4..................52,000 lei
- Revaluation reserve (revaluation difference).....................2848 lei

## Step 4. Effects on the financial statement

a) Acquisition of equipment:
  • Acquisition invoice:

| Method 1 |
|---|
| a) ASSETS = EQUITY + LIABILITIES |
| + 100,000 lei    =    0          + 119,000 lei |
| +   19,000 lei |
| ↓                                        ↓ |
| 119,000 lei        % =    Accounts payable for non-current assets 119,000 lei |
| 100,000 lei equipment |
| 19,000 lei VAT deductible |
| The impact is on the Balance Sheet of the company, assets increase by 100,000 lei, VAT increase by 19,000 lei, liabilities increase by 119,000 lei. |

  • Transportation invoice

| Journal entry |
|---|
| 11,900 lei %                = Account payables for non-current assets 11,900 lei |
| 10,000 lei equipment |
| 1900  lei VAT deductible |
| The impact is on the Balance Sheet of the company, assets increase by 10,000 lei, VAT increase by 1900 lei, liabilities increase by 11,900 lei. |

  • Checking procedures:

| Journal entry |
|---|
| ASSETS         =   EQUITY    +   LIABILITIES |
| + 10,000 lei          =   0              + 10,000 lei |
| ↓                                         ↓ |
| 10,000 lei Equipment     =   Account payables  10,000 lei |
| The impact is on the Balance Sheet of the company, assets increase by 10,000 lei, and liabilities increase by 10,000 lei |

## b) Annual depreciation[a]

| Journal entry |
|---|
| 24,000 lei   "Expenses with        =    "Accumulated         24,000 lei.<br>         equip. depreciation"                 depreciation of equip"<br>              ↓                                    ↓<br>**Effect in the Income Statement**    **Effect in the balance sheet**<br>         (Expense +)                        (Equipment value -)<br><br>There is a significant impact on the Income Statement, because the Depreciation expense of 24,000 lei decreases the Profit and, in the end, the Equity. The other impact is on the Balance Sheet of the company: the equipment value declines by 24,000 lei and amounts to 96,000 lei by the end of the first year of use; additionally the equity is diminished by the same amount, 24,000 lei. |

[a]The transaction related to the annual depreciation is repeated each year with a different amount, based on the annual depreciation computation (see depreciation table).

c) **Method 1. Revaluation of the equipment by the end of the 4th year**—using the **revaluation of the net book value method**

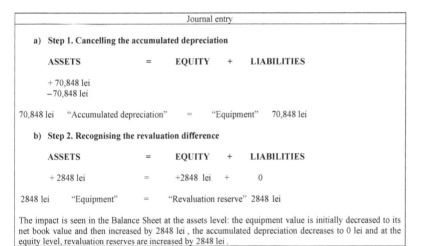

**Method 2. Revaluation of the equipment by the end of the 4th year**—using the **revaluation of the initial cost and the accumulated depreciation**

| Journal entry |
|---|

This revaluation method is based on determining a revaluation coefficient as follows:
Revaluation coefficient = Fair value/carrying amount = 52,000/49,152 = 1.058

The revaluation coefficient is then applied to both the initial cost of the equipment and the accumulated depreciation, as shown in the following table:

| Elements | Initial values | Revalued amounts | Differences | Impact |
|---|---|---|---|---|
| Equipment | 120,000 lei | 120,000 x 1.058 = 126,960 lei | 126,960 – 120,000 = 6960 lei | Increase of equipment with 6960 lei |
| Accumulated depreciation of equipment | 70,848 lei | 70,848 x 1.058 = 74,957 lei | 74,957 – 70,848 = 4109 lei | Increase of accumulated depreciation with 4109 lei |
| Revaluation reserve | 0 lei | 0 lei | 6960 – 4109 = 2851 lei | Increase of the revaluation reserve with 2851 lei |

```
    ASSETS           =      EQUITY     +   LIABILITIES
    + 6960
    - 4109 lei       =      + 2851 lei


6960 lei    "Equipment"    =         %                          6960 lei
                                "Accumulated depreciation of    4109 lei
                                      equipment"
                                "Revaluation reserve"           2851 lei
```

The impact is seen in the Balance Sheet at the assets level and consists of the equipment value, which is increased by 6960 lei, and the depreciation of equipment, which is increased by 4109 lei; and at the equity level, where revaluation reserves are increased by 2851 lei.

## Advantages and disadvantages of the revaluation procedure

a) Advantages:
- The asset's value in the Balance Sheet is its market price/fair value;
- The assets and equity levels of the company are increased (the company's balance sheet "looks" better);
- The true and fair principle is applied;

b) Disadvantages:
- The depreciation expense increases in the following years (the depreciable amount is now 52,000 lei), therefore the operation profit declines;
- The future market value of the asset might decline and this should be recorded; the revaluation process cant's the "stopped" when the company is not satisfied with its outcome

## 6.8 Impairment of Non-current Assets

The concept of "impairment" is described and exemplified in the **IAS 36 Impairment of assets**. This concept emerged from the Balance Sheet valuation rules, stating that a non-current asset should be disclosed at the minimum of its net carrying amount and recoverable amount. If the carrying amount of the asset is higher than its recoverable amount, the asset is considered to be impaired and the Balance Sheet value of the asset should be stated at its minimum, which is the recoverable amount. Based on companies' accounting policies, the impairment tests may differ for different subcategories; some tests are provided on a regular basis, even on an annual basis (e.g. the goodwill)

We have already seen that the net carrying amount is the cost of the assets minus the accumulated depreciation. What is the **recoverable amount**? Based on **IAS 36 Impairment of assets**, the **recoverable amount** is the maximum of the assets' **fair value** minus the cost of disposal and the **value in use** (IAS 36, par. 6). The fair value is the price to be received when selling an asset or paid to transfer a liability, in a normal transaction between market participants (IFRS 13 Fair Value Measurement) and the value in use is the present value of future cashflows expected to flow from the use of the asset or from the cash-generated unit group.[17]

When is an impairment test performed? IAS 36 gives the appropriate indications: an asset is considered impaired at the Balance Sheet moment when it is adversely affected by **external factors**, such as market value declines, negative changes in technology and increase in market rates; or **internal factors**, such as obsolescence and worse economic performances (IAS 36, par. 13)

**Example 22**: An assembly line of a car manufacturer, costing 1 million lei, depreciated straight-line for 10 years and tested for impairment by the end of year 5. At that moment, the fair value of the assembly line is 300,000 lei and the value in use is 390,000 lei. Is the asset impaired? What is the Balance Sheet disclosure amount at the end of year 5?

**Solution**: The net carrying amount by the end of year 5 is 500,000 lei = 1,000,000 cost − (1,000,000/10) * 5 years.

---

[17] Cash generated unit is the smallest identifiable group of assets that generate cash inflows, independent form other assets or group of assets (IAS 36, par. 6).

The recoverable amount is 390,000 lei and is the maximum of the fair value 300,000 lei and the value in use, 390,000 lei.

The net carrying amount is 500,000 lei, greater than the recoverable amount, 390,000 lei, therefore, the asset is considered impaired and its Balance Sheet amount should be 390,000 lei (500,000 lei − 390,000 lei). The asset's value should decrease by 110,000 lei.

The journal entry is:

| 110,000 lei | Expenses with the impairment of non-current assets | = | Assembly line (non-current asset) | 110,000 lei |
|---|---|---|---|---|

For the next year, the depreciation shall be based on the new value, 390,000 lei, and the annual depreciation will be 78,000 lei. If a new impairment test is performed and a new recoverable amount is provided, then the figures will be adjusted accordingly.

## 6.9 SALE/DISPOSAL AND EXCHANGE OF ASSETS

When non-current assets are disposed of, sold or exchanged, the net carrying amount is the benchmark valuation.

**Example 23**: A piece of equipment for the car plant, purchased for the price of 100,000 lei (net of VAT), with net custom taxes of 10,000 lei, chequing procedures of 10,000 lei (net of VAT), estimated to be used for 10 years, applying the double-decline method (no residual value) is sold by the end of the 4th year of use for 40,000 lei, plus 19% VAT. Show the effects of the sale in the annual financial statements.

**Solution:**

Step 1. Computation of the initial cost of the equipment

- Net acquisition invoice amount...................................100,000 lei (without VAT)
- Net transportation cost from invoice ........................... 10,000 lei (without VAT)
- Checking procedures............................................ ...10,000 lei.
- **Total initial cost (depreciable cost)...........................120,000 lei.**

## Step 2. Depreciation, based on a 10-year useful life, applying the double-decline method

| Useful life | Carrying amount (1) | Depreciation expense (2= 1 * 20%) | Accumulated depreciation 3 | Carrying amount (4= 1 – 2) |
|---|---|---|---|---|
| Year 1 | 120,000 lei | 24,000 lei | 24,000 lei | 96,000 lei |
| Year 2 | 96,000 lei | 19,200 lei | 43,200 lei | 76,800 lei |
| Year 3 | 76,800 lei | 15,360 lei | 58,560 lei | 61,440 lei |
| Year 4 | 61,440 lei | 1288 lei | 70,848 lei | 49,152 lei |
| ........ | | | | |

## Step 3. The sale effect
Net selling price....................................................40,000 lei
Net carrying amount.............................................49,152 lei
Loss..........................................................................9152 lei
Journal entry

- Sale

| 47,600 lei | Other receivables = | % | | 47,600 lei |
|---|---|---|---|---|
| | | Revenues from the sale of non-current assets | | 40,000 lei |
| | | VAT Collected | | 7600 lei |

- Disposal of the non-current asset

| 120,000 lei | % = | | Non-current asset | 120,000 lei |
|---|---|---|---|---|
| 70,848 lei | | Accumulated depreciation | | |
| 49,152 lei | | Expenses with the disposal of non-current assets | | |

- Effects on the financial statements:
  - A loss of 9152 lei in the P&L Account (40,000 lei revenues from sale – 49,152 lei expenses with non-current asset)
  - A zero balance sheet value for the non-current asset and a minus 9152 lei in the equity of the business

## 6.10 Other Special Cases Related to Non-current Assets: IAS 20, IAS 40, IAS 36

### 6.10.1 Assets Obtained on a Grant (IAS 20 Government Grants)

Through international, national or local agencies, governments often provide incentives for the development of certain industries or geographic areas. Sometimes, this government assistance may consist of financing the purchase or the construction of fixed assets that are to be used in specified locations and periods. Also, a non-monetary asset, such as land, may be granted for use to a business.

Grants are recognised only if there is reasonable assurance that: (1) the company will comply with the conditions imposed when awarded and (2) they will actually be received.

Accounting issues arise in relation to the presentation of the asset and of the respective grant in the financial statements. **IAS 20 Government grants** offers two alternatives:

- The asset is initially recognised at its cost, while the grant is set up as deferred income. The asset is depreciated as usual and the grant is recognised as income over the life of the asset. If the grant matches the cost of the asset, the impact on the Profit and Loss Account is nil. If the grant is lower, the Profit and Loss Account will bear only the uncovered fraction spread over the useful life of the asset.
- The grant is offset against the cost of the asset and only the net amount, if any, is shown in the balance sheet. The profit and loss account will thus bear a lower depreciation charge.

**Example 24**: As provided in the pre-accession strategy, one of the ways in which the European Union supports the development of Candidate States is by co-financing projects for small and medium sized enterprises. Assume that on December 5th, 20X3, Construct SRL is awarded a grant of 5000 euros through the EU programme for the purchase of a micro rolling mill for small steel structures. Construct SRL orders the equipment the same day. The grant is received in the company's bank account on December 20th, 20X3. Acquisition and installation costs of the rolling mill amount to 10,000 euros as shown in the manufacturer's invoice dated December 20th 20X3. The invoice is paid immediately.

The rolling mill is ready for use in January, 20X4. How should Construct SRL account for the grant and the related transactions?

**Solution**: a) The company intends to use the grant for the purpose it has been awarded and there is reasonable assurance that the grant will be received (all previously awarded grants have reached their recipients). Upon issue by the EU authority, the company recognises the investment grant at the exchange rate on December 5th, 20X3:

5000 euros * 3.6 lei/euro = 18,000 lei

| 18,000 lei | Investment grants receivable | = | Investment grants (Deferred revenue) | 18,000 lei |
|---|---|---|---|---|

b) On December 20th, the amount of the grant is transferred to the company's bank account. In the company's Cash in Foreign Currency account the amount is exchanged for lei (exchange rate 3.63 lei/euro):

| 18,150 lei | Bank account in foreign currency | = | % | 18,150 lei |
|---|---|---|---|---|
| | | | Investment grants receivable | 18,000 lei |
| | | | Exchange gain | 150 lei |

c) The company receives the micro rolling mill and the invoice from its manufacturer, ElectricWerk NV, on December 20th (exchange rate 3.63 lei/euro). The amount payable is translated in lei at the spot exchange rate:

10,000 euros * 3.63 lei/euro = 36,300 lei

| 36,300 lei | Equipment | = | Current asset suppliers | 36,300 lei |
|---|---|---|---|---|

d) The equipment is exempted from customs tax, but not from VAT, which must be paid on imported goods at the rate of 19% (36,300 lei * 19%).

| 6897 lei | VAT deductible | = | Cash | 6897 lei |
|---|---|---|---|---|

e) Construct SRL immediately pays 10,000 euros to the manufacturer of the equipment.
10,000 euros * 3.63 lei/euro = 36,300 lei

| 36,300 lei | Non-current asset suppliers | = | Cash in foreign currency | 36,300 lei |
|---|---|---|---|---|

**Extract from the Profit and Loss Account for the year 20X3**

Exchange gain    150 lei

**Extract from the Balance Sheet as of December 31st, 20X3**

| *Non-current assets* | Cost | Accumulated depreciation | Carrying amount |
|---|---|---|---|
| Equipment | 36,300 lei | – | 36,300 lei |

| *Deferred revenues* | | |
|---|---|---|
| Investment grants | 18,000 lei | |

f) and g) Construct SRL estimates a useful life of 10 years and a straight-line depreciation pattern. As the rolling mill is ready for use in January 20X4, parallel to accounting for the depreciation of the rolling mill, the company amortises the investment grant. The Profit and Loss Account of the year 20X4 will thus only show the company's contribution towards the cost of the equipment spread over the useful life, that is:
36,300/10 – 18,000/10 = 1830 lei

| 3630 lei | Depreciation expense | = | Accumulated depreciation of equipment | 3630 lei |
|---|---|---|---|---|

| 1800 lei | Investment grants (deferred revenue) | = | Revenue from investment grants | 1800 lei |
|---|---|---|---|---|

**Extract from the Profit and Loss Account for the year 20X4 (lei)**

Revenue from investment grants    1800 lei
Depreciation expense              (3630) lei

### Extract from the Balance Sheet as of December 31st, 20X4 (lei)

| Non-current assets | Cost | Accumulated depreciation | Carrying amount |
|---|---|---|---|
| Equipment | 36,300 lei | 3630 lei | 32,670 lei |

| Deferred revenues | | |
|---|---|---|
| Investment grants | 16,200 lei | |

Alternatively, under the second option provided by IAS 20, the company could have deducted the grant from the acquisition cost of the asset. Entries a) through e) remain unchanged.

f) A different carrying amount of the asset emerges:

| 18,000 lei | Investment grants | = | Equipment | 18,000 lei |
|---|---|---|---|---|

### Extract from the Profit and Loss Account for the year 20X3 (lei)

Exchange gain           150 lei

### Extract from the Balance Sheet as of December 31st, 20X3 (lei)

| Non-current assets | Cost | Investment grant | Carrying amount |
|---|---|---|---|
| Equipment | 36,300 lei | (18,000) lei | 18,300 lei |

g) As the equipment is ready to use in January 20X4, the carrying amount of 18,300 lei (36,300 − 18,000) will be depreciated from the estimated useful life, resulting in an annual depreciation charge of:
(36,300 − 18,000)/10 = 1830 lei

| 1830 lei | Depreciation expense | = | Accumulated depreciation of equipment | 1830 lei |
|---|---|---|---|---|

### Extract from the Profit and Loss Account for the year 20X4 (lei)

Depreciation expense           (1830) lei

### Extract from the Balance Sheet as of December 31st, 20X4 (lei)

| Non-current assets | Cost | Accumulated depreciation | Carrying amount |
|---|---|---|---|
| Equipment | 36,300 lei | 3630 lei | 32,670 lei |

### 6.10.2  Investment Property (IAS 40)

Investment property is property (land, a building, part of a building, or all) held (by the owner or by the lessee under a finance lease) to receive rents or for capital appreciation or both. (IAS 40, par. 5).

Examples of investment property include (IAS 40, par. 8):

- land held for long-term capital appreciation;
- land held for a currently undetermined future use;
- building leased out under an operating lease;
- vacant building held to be leased out under an operating lease;
- property that is being constructed or developed for future use as investment property.

a) **Initial measurement**

Investment property is initially measured at cost, including transaction costs. Such cost should not include start-up costs, abnormal waste, or initial operating losses incurred before the investment property achieves the planned level of occupancy (IAS 40, par. 20 and 23).

b) **Measurement subsequent to initial recognition**

IAS 40 permits entities to choose between a fair value model, and a cost model (IAS 40, par. 30).

a) Fair value model

Investment property is re-measured at fair value, which is the price that would be received by selling an asset or paid to transfer a liability in an orderly transaction between market participants at the measurement date (IAS 40, par. 5). Gains or losses arising from changes in the fair value of investment property must be included in net profit or loss for the period in which it arises (IAS 40, par. 35).

b) Cost model

After initial recognition, investment property is accounted for in accordance with the cost model as set out in IAS 16 Property, Plant and

Equipment: cost minus accumulated depreciation minus accumulated impairment losses (IAS 40, par. 56).

**Example 25**: Company ALFA purchased a piece of land in the amount of 280,000 lei, commission expenses amounted to 22,000 lei and notary fees amounted to 8000 lei. The land is meant to be rented to third parties. On March 1st, 20X1, immediately after the purchase, the fair value of the asset is 325,000 lei. On December 31st, 20X1, the fair value increases to 337,000 lei and on December 31st, 20X2, the fair value decreases to 330,000 lei.

How does ALFA treat the transactions regarding the land in terms of the accounting treatment, noting that the company uses the fair value model for its investment property in the financial years 20X1 and 20X2?

**Solution:**

1) March 1st, 20X1—Acquisition of investment property

The initial recognition of the land as investment property is made at its acquisition cost, determined as follows:
Acquisition cost = Acquisition price + Directly attributable expenses
= 280,000 + 22,000 + 8000 = 310,000 lei

| 310,000 lei | Investment property | = | Accounts payable for non-current assets | 310,000 lei |
|---|---|---|---|---|

2) On March 1st, 20X1—Evaluation of the investment property at fair value

Carrying amount ...................... 310,000 lei
Fair value ...............................325,000 lei
Increase of the asset's value by ......15,000 lei

| 15,000 lei | Investment property | = | Gains from the valuation of investment property at fair value | 15,000 lei |
|---|---|---|---|---|

3) On December 31st, 20X1—Evaluation of the investment property at fair value (337,000 lei)

Carrying amount ....................... 325,000 lei (previous fair value)
Fair value ...............................337,000 lei (new fair value)
Increase of the asset's value by .........12,000 lei

| 12,000 lei | Investment property | = | Gains from the valuation of investment property at fair value | 12,000 lei |
|---|---|---|---|---|

4) On December 31st, 20X2—Evaluation of the investment property at fair value (330,000 lei)

Carrying amount ....................... 337,000 lei (previous fair value)
Fair value ...............................330,000 lei (new fair value)
Decrease of the asset's value with ......7000 lei

| 7000 lei | Losses from the valuation of investment property at fair value | = | Investment property | 7000 lei |
|---|---|---|---|---|

c) **Classification of transfers to or from investment property**

Transfers to or from investment property should only be made when there is a change in the property's use. For a transfer from investment property carried at fair value to owner-occupied property or inventories, the fair value at the change of use is the 'cost' of the property under its new classification (IAS 40, par. 57 and 60).

**Example 26**: Company GAMMA owns a building (investment property) which was rented to third parties. On December 31st, 20X2, the managers decide to start using this building for the company's administrative purposes. The building's fair value at December 31st, 20X1, amounts to 22,000 lei and on December 31st, 20X2, 22,500 lei. The carrying amount of the investment property on December 31st, 20X1, is 20,000 lei. At the beginning of financial year 20X3, the useful life of the building is estimated to be 20 years. On December 31st, 20X3, the building's recoverable value amounts to 19,500 lei.

Disclose the accounting aspects of the building for financial years 20X1 to 20X3.

**Solution:**
Based on the information provided, the company will apply the accounting treatment for investment property measured at fair value from 20X1 to 20X2 pursuant to IAS 40. On December 31st, 20X2, the building will be reclassified from investment property to buildings used by the entity. From January 1st, 20X3, the building will be held for the company's own use and will be evaluated at cost minus accumulated depreciation minus impairment adjustments according to IAS 16 and IAS 36.

Therefore, Gamma will journalise the following transactions:

1) On December 31st, 20X1—Evaluation of the investment property at fair value (22,000 lei)

Carrying amount ............................. 20,000 lei
Fair value .........................................22,000 lei
Increase of the asset's value with ............ 2000 lei

| 2000 lei | Investment property | = | Gains from the valuation of investment property at fair value | 2000 lei |
|---|---|---|---|---|

2) On December 31st, 20X2—Reclassification of the investment property to buildings held for the company's own use

According to IAS 40, the fair value of the building at the change of use is the 'cost' of the property under its new classification. Therefore:

Assigned cost of the building ............... 22,500 lei (the new fair value)
Carrying amount before transfer ............22,000 lei (previous fair value)
Increase of the asset's value with ................500 lei

| 22,500 lei | Buildings | = | % Investment property Gains from the valuation of investment property at fair value | 22,500 lei 22,000 lei 500 lei |
|---|---|---|---|---|

3) On December 31st, 20X3, annual depreciation is recorded after 1 year of use

Annual depreciation = Carrying amount/Useful life = 22,500 lei/20 years = 1125 lei/year

| 1125 lei | Expenses with the depreciation of NCA | = | Accumulated depreciation of buildings | 1125 lei |
|---|---|---|---|---|

4) On December 31st, 20X3, an impairment test takes place and the recoverable value is 19,500 lei pursuant to IAS 36[18]

Carrying amount = Cost − Accumulated depreciation = 22,500 − 1125 = 21,375 lei
Recoverable value = 19,500 lei
=> Decrease of the asset's value with 1875 lei
The company will record an impairment adjustment as follows:

| 1875 lei | Expenses with impairment adjustments of NCA | = | Impairment adjustments of buildings | 1875 lei |
|---|---|---|---|---|

At the end of financial year 20X3, the value of the building which is to be disclosed in the Balance Sheet is:
Cost − Accumulated depreciation − Impairment adjustments = 22,500 − 1125 − 1875 = 19,500 lei.

## 6.11 Conclusions

The following summary questions are providing conclusions to this chapter.

---

[18] For the accounting treatment according to IAS 36 see Sect 6.6. Impairment of non-current assets.

## Chapter summary questions:

| | |
|---|---|
| 1. What are non-current assets? | Non-current assets are assets used for more than one year. |
| 2. How are non-current assets classified? | The non-current assets can be divided into intangible assets (without physical shape), tangible assets (with physical shape) and financial assets. |
| 3. Provide examples of non-current assets. | Examples of non-current assets: land, buildings, equipment, cars, computers furniture, patents, copyrights, goodwill, investments in associates. |
| 4. How are non-current assets initially measured? | The non-current assets are initially measured at cost (acquisition cost or production cost). The VAT should always be excluded. There are some assets that are initially measured at fair-value or utility value (e.g. capital contribution in non-current assets or non-current assets received for free). |
| 5. What is depreciation (or amortisation) and what are the effects in the annual financial statements? | The depreciation concept refers to tangible assets and amortisation concept refers to intangible assets. Both depreciation and amortisation show the way the asset is used in the business. Their effects in the financial statements are an expense in the P&L Account and a decrease of the asset's amount in the annual Balance Sheet. |
| 6. What is the best depreciation method? | There is no specific answer to this question: every method is relevant, according to the way the asset is used. I.g.: a building should be depreciated based on the straight-line method, whereas an airplane is depreciated based on the units-of-activity method (number of miles). |
| 7. How are non-current assets measured in the Balance Sheet? | For Balance Sheet purposes, the non-current assets are measured by comparing the net carrying amount to the recoverable amount. When the carrying amount is higher than the recoverable amount, that assets is impaired. |
| 8. What is the revaluation of an asset and what are the effects on the annual financial statements? | A company can decided to revaluate a non-current asset. In this respect, the asset should be measured at its fair value and the differences between the carrying amount at the fair value must be disclosed either as equity (revaluation reserve) if the fair value is higher, or as expenses, if the carrying amount is higher. |
| 9. What happens when a non-current asset is sold before the end of its useful life? | When a non-current asset is sold before the end of its useful life, either a loss (when revenues from sale is lower than the expense with the asset) or a gain (when revenues from sale is higher than the expense with the asset) on sale is disclosed. |

## Quizzes (only one correct answer)

1. According to IAS 36, the recoverable value is:
   a. Max (value in use; net book value);
   b. Min (value in use; fair value less costs to sell);

c. Max (value in use; fair value less costs to sell);
d. Min (value in use; net book value).
2. On January 1st, 20X1, the company GAMMA purchases a piece of production equipment for which the following information is given: the purchase price is 22,500 lei, expenses related to the instalment of the equipment amount to 2500 lei, the equipment has a useful life of 6 years, the straight line method is used for the depreciation and the residual value is 1000 lei. On December 31st, 20X2, the company applies the impairment test. The fair value is estimated at 15,500 lei and the costs related to the sale amount to 300 lei, the value in use is of 15,400 lei. On December 31st, 20X3, there are clues that the equipment regained its value and the recoverable value is estimated at 17,500 lei. What is the value of the production equipment which is to be disclosed in the financial statements of 20X2 and 20X3?
a. 15,400 in 20X2, 17,500 in 20X3;
b. 15,400 in 20X2 13,000 in 20X3;
c. 15,200 in 20X2, 17,500 in 20X3;
d. 15,200 in 20X2, 17,000 in 20X3.
3. The acquisition cost of a non-current asset is determined as:
a. Purchase price – directly related expenses – trade discounts;
b. Purchase price + directly related expenses – residual value;
c. Purchase price + directly related expenses – trade discounts;
d. Purchase price – accumulated depreciation.
4. The carrying amount of a non-current asset to be depreciated is determined as:
a. Cost – Accumulated depreciation – Impairment adjustments – Residual value;
b. Cost – Accumulated depreciation – Impairment adjustments;
c. Cost – Accumulated depreciation – Impairment adjustments – Recoverable value;
d. Cost – Accumulated depreciation.
5. On January 1st, 20X1, the company ALFA owns a building purchased at the cost of 200,000 lei, having accumulated depreciation in the amount of 20,000 lei and an estimated remaining useful life of 20 years. The depreciation method used is the straight-line method. On December 31st, 20X1, the company revaluates the building at the fair value of 175,000 lei. What is the

value of the annual depreciation of financial year 20X1 and the value of the revaluation reserve?
a. Annual depreciation 9000 lei; revaluation reserve 5000 lei;
b. Annual depreciation 8750 lei; revaluation reserve 5000 lei;
c. Annual depreciation 9000 lei; revaluation reserve 4000 lei;
d. Annual depreciation 8750 lei; revaluation reserve 4000 lei.

6. On December 31st, 20X1, a company holds a piece of land purchased at the cost of 100,000 lei. On December 31st, 20X2, the company revaluates the land at the fair value of 90,000 lei. Taking into account that this is the first revaluation of the land, which revaluation entry is correct?
a. Lands = Revenues from the revaluation 10,000 lei;
b. Revaluation reserves = Lands 10,000 lei;
c. Expenses from the revaluation = Lands 10,000 lei;
d. Lands = Revaluation reserves 10,000 lei.

7. What is the correct journal entry for cancelling the accumulated depreciation of equipment, if an entity applies the method of revaluating the net carrying amount?
a. Accumulated depreciation = Expenses with depreciation;
b. Accumulated depreciation = Equipment;
c. Expenses with depreciation = Equipment;
d. Equipment = Accumulated depreciation.

8. On December 31st, 20X1, company Beta Software Ltd. owns a piece of equipment purchased for 50,000 lei, with an estimated useful life of 5 years and for which the double decline method of depreciation is used. At the end of financial year 20X2, the recoverable value of the equipment is 25,000 lei. What is the correct recording for evaluating the asset at the balance sheet moment in N?
a. Expenses with the revaluation = Equipment 5000 lei;
b. Expenses with impairment adjustments = Equipment 15,000 lei;
c. Expenses with impairment adjustments = Impairment adjustment of equipment 5000 lei;
d. Equipment = Impairment adjustment of equipment 15,000 lei;

9. During December 20X8, a company executes maintenance work needed to assure the normal functioning of a piece of equipment. The related expenses consist in services provided by a specialized third party in the amount of 1700 lei. What is the accounting entry that reflects the correct accounting treatment of the maintenance work?

a. Expenses with maintenance = Equipment 1700 lei;
b. Expenses with services = Accounts payable 1700 lei;
c. Expenses with services = Equipment 1700 lei;
d. Equipment = Accounts payable 1700 lei.
10. During financial year 20X8, a company develops an upgrade project for a building, resulting in total costs of 10,000 lei. The upgrade will lead to a decrease of the monthly utilities costs. Which accounting entry reflects the correct accounting treatment of the upgrade project?
a. Expenses with maintenance = Accounts payable 10,000 lei;
b. Buildings = Accounts payable for non-current assets 10,000 lei;
c. Expenses with services = Buildings 10,000 lei;
d. Buildings = Revenues from the production of non-current assets 10,000 lei.

**Exercises:**

**Exercise 1**: *Initial recognition*. In financial year 20X1, company Beta Consulting Ltd. purchases a piece of equipment. The expenses related to the acquisition are the following: purchase price 80,000 lei, commercial discount 2000 lei, customs tax 5000 lei, delivery expenses 18,000 lei, engineers' fee related to the installation of the equipment 14,000 lei, marketing expenses for the promotion of finished goods 6000 lei. What is the acquisition cost of the equipment?

**Exercise 2**: *Subsequent expenditure*. On January 1st, 20X1, company ALFA SA holds a piece of equipment, with a purchase price of 500,000 lei and an accumulated depreciation in the amount of 200,000 lei. The remaining useful life is 5 years and the depreciation method used by the company is the straight-line method.

During December 20X1, the company undertakes maintenance work needed in order to assure the normal functioning conditions of the asset. The related expenses are the following:

- Consumption of raw materials 500 lei;
- Labour expenses 1500 lei;
- Services provided by a specialized third party 700 lei.

During December 20X21, the company develops an upgrade project for the asset. The related upgrades entail the following expenses:

- Consumption of consumable materials 25,000 lei;
- Labour expenses 50,000 lei;
- Energy consumption 12,000 lei;
- Equipment depreciation 5000 lei;
- Services provided by a specialized third party 70,000 lei.

The feasibility study attests that after the upgrade of the equipment, the useful life is extended by 3 years and cost savings on routine maintenance will be recorded. During the upgrade works, the depreciation is not interrupted. Knowing that the company applies IAS 16, present the accounting treatment of the transactions listed above for 20X1 and 20X2.

**Exercise 3**: On December 15th, 20X1, Bijou Ltd. purchases a vehicle under the following conditions: acquisition cost in the amount of 3000 CU, delivery fee 600 CU (applied by the same supplier), VAT 19%. On December 17th, 20X1, the supplier is paid. On December 31st, 20X1, the vehicle is put into operation. The useful life is estimated at 5 years. The residual value is estimated at 200 CU and the depreciation method used is the straight-line method. Present the accounting treatment of the vehicle if:

a. after 5 years—the vehicle is disposed;
b. after 4 years—the vehicle is sold at the selling price of 500 CU, VAT 19%.

**Exercise 4**: *Depreciation methods.* A company holds a piece of equipment purchased on December 31st, 20X1, at an acquisition price of 60,000 lei. The company's management estimates a useful life of 5 years. Determine the annual depreciation to be recognised from 20X1 to 20X5 if the company uses the following depreciation method:

a. Straight-line method;
b. Diminishing balance method—fixed ratio and variable base;
c. Diminishing balance method—variable ratio and fixed base;
d. Accelerated method.

**Exercise 5**: *Number of units depreciation.* For an agreement that stipulates the supply of 270,000 pieces of finished goods within 3 years, a company uses specific equipment which was manufactured by the company at the production cost of 180,000 lei. The due date of the deliveries is the following:

- First year—54,000 pieces;
- Second year—81,000 pieces;
- Third year—135,000 pieces.

The equipment is disposed at the end of the contract. What is the amount of the annual depreciation?

**Exercise 6**: *Revaluation model.* A company holds a building purchased at an acquisition cost of 200,000 lei and its accumulated depreciation is in amount of 50,000 lei. At the end of the financial year, the company decides to revaluate the building at a fair value of 450,000 lei, established by experts. Present the accounting treatment of the revaluation according to IAS 16, taking into account the following methods:

a. Revaluation of the gross carrying amount and of the accumulated depreciation;
b. Revaluation of the net carrying amount.

**Exercise 7**: *Cost model—impairment of non-current assets.* At the beginning of financial year 20X1, Top Engines Ltd. purchased a piece of equipment at the acquisition cost of 500,000 lei, VAT 19%. The useful life is estimated at 5 years and the depreciation method used is the straight-line method. At the end of financial year 20X1, there are circumstances that indicate a decrease of the equipment's value. The fair value minus the costs of disposal is 280,000 lei. The forecast of cash-flows expected to be obtained from using the equipment throughout the remaining useful life is represented below (using a discount rate of 15%):

| Financial year | 20X2 | 20X3 | 20X4 | 20X5 | Value in use |
|---|---|---|---|---|---|
| Cash-flow | 55,000 | 175,000 | 150,000 | 80,000 | |
| Discount factor $(1/(1+0.15)^t)$ | 0.870 | 0.756 | 0.658 | 0.572 | |
| Present value of future cash-flows (discounted cash-flow) = Cash flow × discount factor | 47,850 | 132,300 | 98,700 | 45,760 | 324,610 |

At the end of 20X2, the value in use of the asset is 290,000 lei and the fair value minus the costs of disposal is 320,000 lei. What will be the disclosed value of the equipment in the Balance Sheet at the end of 20X1 and 20X2, pursuant to IAS 16 and IAS 36? Present the corresponding accounting treatment.

**Exercise 8**: A company holds a piece of equipment purchased on January 1st, 20X1, at an acquisition price of 50,000 lei. The company's management estimates a useful life of 5 years. What is the annual depreciation amount if the company uses the straight-line method? Journalise the acquisition and the depreciation for the first year and calculate the carrying amount of the machine at the end of the first 2 years of use. How will these transactions affect the financial statements of the two years of use?

**Exercise 9**: A company purchases a ventilation system at an acquisition price of 500,000 lei. According to its technical book, the equipment is guaranteed 200,000 rotations. The rotations in the early years of operation are: 20X1—12,000 rotations, 20X2—15,000 rotations, 20X3—21,000 rotations. Present the accounting treatment of the asset pursuant to IAS 16 for the first 3 years of use.

**Exercise 10**: An entity holds a vehicle purchased on December 31st, 20X1, at an acquisition price of 100,000 lei, for which a residual value in the amount of 10,000 lei was estimated. The company's management estimated a useful life of 8 years. Determine the annual depreciation by applying each one of the below depreciation methods:

a. Straight-line method;
b. Diminishing balance method—using the following versions:
 • double decline method;
 • with diminishing coefficient;
 • sum of years' digits;
c. Accelerated depreciation method.

**Exercise 11**: At the beginning of financial year 20X1, a company purchases a piece of equipment in the amount of 100,000 lei and incurs delivery expenses in the amount of 20,000 lei. The asset will be used consistently over 5 years and the residual value is estimated at 20,000 lei. On December 31st, 20X2, the equipment is revalued at a fair value of 120,000 lei. On December 31st, 20X2, the equipment's fair value is estimated at 70,000 lei.

Journalise the transactions related to the accounting treatment of the equipment for 20X1 and 20X2 (the revaluation will be recorded by eliminating the accumulated depreciation against the gross carrying amount of the asset—revaluation of the net carrying amount). What is the value of the equipment disclosed in the statement of financial position at the end of each financial year?

**Case study.** *The accounting treatment of non-current assets*

On January 1st, 20X1, the clothing manufacturer Top Fashion Ltd owes 15 pieces of production equipment initially purchased at the total acquisition price of 250,000 lei. Their accumulated depreciation at the same date is 50,000 lei and their remaining useful life is estimated at 10 years. Also, the company holds a building representing its headquarters, which was purchased at the acquisition cost of 1,000,000 lei and has an accumulated depreciation of 250,000 lei. The building's remaining useful life is 20 years and its residual value is estimated at 50,000 lei. The company applies the straight-line method of depreciation for all its non-current assets. The trial balance of the entity shows the following opening account balances on January 1st, 20X1:

- Accounts receivable 15,000 lei;
- Finished goods 18,000 lei;
- Merchandise 12,500 lei;
- Accounts payable 25,000 lei;
- Salaries payable 14,000 lei;
- Raw materials 36,000 lei;
- Cash at bank 50,000 lei;
- Equipment 250,000 lei;
- Accumulated depreciation of equipment 50,000 lei;
- Buildings 1,000,000 lei;
- Accumulated depreciation of buildings 250,000 lei
- VAT payable 13,500 lei;
- Sundry creditors 90,000 lei.

During financial year 20X1, Top Fashion Ltd. conducts the following transactions (19% VAT is applied to all purchases and sales):

  a. on January 1st, the company purchases a piece of equipment for 5000 lei, with a 2% trade discount and delivery expenses of 500

lei; managers estimate a useful life of 10 years using the straight-line method;
b. on January 31st, the equipment supplier is fully paid via bank transfer;
c. on July 1st, the entity acquires a vehicle for the delivery of produced goods, the acquisition cost is 180,000 lei and the estimated residual value is 30,000 lei. The company estimates a 5 year useful life with a straight-line method of depreciation;
d. on August 1st, the vehicle supplier is partially paid via bank transfer in the amount of 30,000 lei which was due at this date;
e. on December 31st, the company records the annual depreciation of all non-current assets;
f. on December 31st, the company revaluates its building at the fair value of 800,000 lei;
g. on December 31st, the fair value minus costs to sell all of the entity's equipment is amounts to 150,000 lei and the value in use is estimated at 175,050 lei;
h. on December 31st, 20X2, the company records the annual depreciation of all non-current assets;
i. on December 31st, 20X2, the recoverable value of the vehicle is estimated at 190,000 lei;
j. on December 31st, 20X3, the company records the annual depreciation of all non-current assets;
k. on December 31st, 20X3, the recoverable value of the company's equipment is in amount of 180,000 lei;
l. on December the 31st, 20X3, the fair value of the building is 600,000 lei.

*Requirements:*

1. Journalise all of the above transactions of Top Fashion Ltd. during 20X1 to 20X3, considering the adequate accounting treatment of non-current assets;
2. Determine the closing account balances on December 31st, 20X1, of all of the accounts involved and then prepare both balance sheet and income statement at the end of financial year N.
3. Present the impact of the accounting treatment of non-current assets in the company's financial statements for 20X2 and 20X3.

CHAPTER 7

# Liabilities, Receivables and Other Related Items

*Adriana Duțescu and Lavinia Olimid*

*Learning objectives:*

- *Understanding and assessing different categories of liabilities and receivables*
- *Understanding the relevant techniques of classification and measurement for liabilities and receivables*
- *Understanding the importance of different categories of liabilities and receivables in decision-making process*
- *Assessing the influence of liabilities and receivables in financial statements*

## 7.1 Introduction

This chapter will focus on liabilities and other obligations, generated by companies' transactions with suppliers, clients, employees, governmental agencies, associates, investors, creditors and other stakeholders and the claims related to operations and investments.

The "mirror" effect of a liability is a receivable. For example, when companies purchase inventories on account, a liability (account payable) emerges, as the source of financing the inventory; when the company is the seller of the inventory, then a receivable (account receivable) will be disclosed, to represent a claim, the right to cash-in the appropriate amount. The way we depict liabilities could be extrapolated to

© The Author(s) 2019
A. Duțescu, *Financial Accounting*,
https://doi.org/10.1007/978-3-030-29485-4_7

receivables (classification, disclosure, measurement), with some differentiation to be highlighted further.

A *liability* consists of an obligation to an outside party arising from past transactions or events for the settlement of which cash or other assets are needed (IFRS Conceptual framework, par. 4.46).

There are different ways to classify liabilities, based on different criteria:

- *by nature* criteria, that splits liabilities into *financial* and *operating*;
- *by settlement date* criteria, that generates *current & non-current liabilities*;
- *by source of funds*: that depicts *debt capital & equity capital*.

## 7.2 Classification of Liabilities and Receivables

The Balance Sheet disclosure of liabilities is based upon the classification of "current" vs "non-current liabilities" (that applies also to assets), originated in the IAS/IFRS framework but also used by the US GAAP and the Romanian accounting framework. A **current liability** is an obligation due in 12 months' time that (IAS 1, proposed amendments):

- is expected to be settled in the normal operation cycle;
- is primarily for trading purposes;
- does not have an unconditional right at the end of the reporting period to defer the settlement of the liability for at least twelve months after the reporting period.

All the other liabilities are classified as **long-term** or **non-current liabilities**.

A **receivable** is a claim to an outside party, as a result of past events, from which future economic benefits are expected to flow in the form of cash or other assets. Receivables are meeting the assets' definition (see Chapter 3) and the current assets' characteristics: the expectation to be realized in the normal operating cycle of the entity, within 12 months (IAS 1, par. 1.66).

Entities and individuals in connection with liabilities are named *creditors* and the entities that should settle (pay for) the liabilities are called *debtors*.

The following examples of liabilities might be seen in company's Balance Sheet:

a) **Current liabilities**:
- account payables or trade payables, emerging from the acquisition of inventories and services on account;
- note payables: trade liabilities settled via promissory notes e.g. cheques or other similar trading notes;
- salary payable and other contributions payable; liabilities related to employees' activities within the company and the appropriate contributions;
- tax payables (e.g. TVA payable, Income tax payable etc.): amount due for different categories of taxes;
- bank overdrafts: short-term bank loans used to finance the current activity of the business;
- other payables on short term i.e. to shareholders (dividends payable), to associates or joint-ventures (associates payables etc.).

b) **Long-term liabilities**:

- Other payables/Long-term payables: liabilities due in more than 12 months i.e. to the real-estate provider, for the equipment/car provider, liabilities to the lessor in leasing contracts;
- Interest bearing loans/long-term bank payables: bank credits with medium and long-term maturity;
- Associates payables, third-party transactions etc.;
- Deferred income tax liability: related to deferred taxation generating a liability.

The accounting bookkeeping system should provide all necessary details of each category and subcategory of liabilities and receivables, which impact the business activity of the year.

## 7.3 Measurement and Valuation

The core principle used for both current liabilities and long-term liabilities is measured at the amount to be paid at maturity.

For receivables, current or long-term, the measurement principle is based upon the value to be received at maturity.

There are two different ways to evaluate liabilities, depending on their maturity:

a) at *historical cost* or *nominal value*, for current liabilities: i.e. a 10,000 lei package of bananas, bought from a fruits and vegetables distributor will generate a 10,000 lei liability/account payable until its maturity, say in 2 months' time;
b) At *present value of future cash-flows* (*discounted cash-flows*) for long-term liabilities: i.e. a 10,000 lei bond, 3 years maturity and 10%/year interest should be disclosed at its present value by the end of each year (see the Chapter 9 for more details).

## 7.4 Current Liabilities and Receivables

In previous chapters we had explained that the Balance Sheet's classification of assets and liabilities is based upon the "current" vs "non-current perspective", which is another way to analyse these items. Sometimes the same type of liability is disclosed both on the "non-current" and "current" sections of the Balance Sheet, because an entity might have bank loans with long maturities (non-current liabilities) and also bank loans with short maturities (current liabilities). Therefore, depending on their maturity, different liabilities may be found in one of the two sections of the Balance Sheet or in both.

For example, the 2017 OMV Petrom Consolidated Balance Sheet discloses the following categories of liabilities (from the 2017 OMV Petrom Annual report):

Non-current liabilities:

- Provisions for pensions and similar obligations;
- Interest-bearing debts;
- Provisions for decommissioning and restoration obligations;
- Other provisions;
- Other financial liabilities;
- Other liabilities.

Current liabilities:

- Trade payables;
- Interest-bearing debts;
- Income tax liabilities;
- Other provisions and decommissioning;
- Other financial liabilities;
- Other liabilities.

One important classification of liabilities (and receivables) is based on their nature: *operating liabilities vs financial liabilities*. An *operating liability* is an obligation arising from the company's operations and main activities, for example account payables or salary payables. A *financial liability* (or receivable) is incurred due to a financial flow, for example a bank loan to finance an investment or an interest payable related to a bank loan. This "by nature" approach is important when disclosing the Balance Sheet subcategories of liabilities.

Most of the operating liabilities are current, but there are also exemptions, as it was previously exemplified. Another example relates to Romanian hospitals, that have an average of 250 days' time to pay their medicine suppliers. Therefore, the specific Account Payable could be classified as long-term. A Real-estate contract over 3 years, for example, where the debt is incurred by the beneficiary, should be classified long-term as well.

Financial liabilities (or receivables) emerge from financial flows in or out of the company, including events such as: bank loans received or granted, foreign exchange conversion rate differences leasing payables etc. Sometimes the term 'financial transactions' refers to **all** transactions (including those from daily activities of companies) which change the value of assets, liabilities and the company's equity. In this book, we shall refer to 'financial events' as being events which give rise to financial flows and result in liabilities or receivables.

### 7.4.1 Trade Liabilities and Receivables

Chapter 5 **Inventories** provides a complex set of examples and cases related to the acquisition of inventories and the specific trade liabilities involved. The same chapter depicts also examples of inventory sales and the respective trade receivables.

To fulfil the "operating liability" case, we provide another example that involves a **note payable**. A note payable, in form of bills of exchange, promissory notes, cheques etc., is a way to finance the assets & services' acquisition or borrow money. It is expected that the note payable will incur an interest related to the period of payment.

**Example 1**: Company ABC purchased raw coco beans of 10,000 lei on October 1st, 20X7, from its traditional supplier and issued a note payable for the amount. The specific interest expense to this note payable is 10%/year. The payment is due on September 30th, 20X8. The financial year closes on December 31st.

The acquisition of raw coco beans on October 1st, 20X7 is recorded as follows:

| 10,000 lei | Raw materials | = | Note payable | 10,000 lei |
|---|---|---|---|---|

The interest expense accrues on a monthly basis, as follows (this journal entry is repetitive every month, until maturity) 10,000 lei * 10% * 1/12:

| 83.33 lei | Interest expense | = | Interest payable | 83.33 lei |
|---|---|---|---|---|

By the end of 20X7 the interest is accrued for three months, therefore the ABC Company will disclose a total interest expense (item of Profit & Loss Account), equal to the total interest payable (item of Balance Sheet) of 250 lei (83.33 lei * 3 months).

For the year 20X8 an amount of 750 lei of interest expense and interest payable is accrued.

The payment on September 20X8 is disclosing the following entry:

| 11,000 lei | % | = | Bank account | 11,000 lei |
|---|---|---|---|---|
| 10,000 lei | Note payable | | | |
| 1000 lei | Interest payable | | | |

For the seller, these transactions based upon a note receivable are recorded in the following journal entries:

The sale of coco beans on October 1st, 20X7, with a 20% profit margin is disclosed as follows:

| 10,000 lei | Note receivable | = | Revenue from sales | 10,000 lei |
|---|---|---|---|---|
| 8000 lei | Cost of goods sold | = | Inventories | 8000 lei |

The interest revenue accrues on a monthly basis, as follows (this journal entry is repetitive every month until maturity) 10,000 lei * 10% * 1/12:

| 83.33 lei | Interest receivable | = | Interest revenue | 83.33 lei |
|---|---|---|---|---|

By the end of 20X7, the interest revenue is accrued for three months, therefore, the selling Company will disclose a total interest revenue (item of Profit & Loss Account), equal with a total interest receivable (item of Balance Sheet) of 250 lei.

For the year 20X8 an amount of 750 lei of interest revenue and interest receivable is accrued.

The receipt of cash on September 20X8 discloses the following entry:

| 11,000 lei | Bank account | = | % | 11,000 lei |
|---|---|---|---|---|
|  |  |  | Note receivable | 10,000 lei |
|  |  |  | Interest receivable | 1000 lei |

Another important issue related to operation is the **bad debt case**. A bad debt entails a client having financial difficulties and facing a material risk of default, in connection to a delay of payment or diminution of the amount owed. Starting with January 1st, 2018, the analysis of a bad debt should be focused upon the requirements of **IFRS 9 Financial instruments**, based on which companies should recognize the "impairment of financial assets in the amount of *expected credit loss*" (IFRS 9, par. 5.5.3–5.5.5). This is also called **"loss allowance"**. In other words, there is a future assumption of the probability of default of all financial assets, accounts receivables included, that can be classified as one of the following two categories: a) the expected credit loss of the claim is assumed for the first 12 months or b) the expected credit loss is for the lifetime of the receivable.

There is also a *simplified approach*, preferred by companies, when it comes to trade receivables, that relies only on the expected credit loss for the lifetime of the receivable. In this case, a provision matrix might be developed based on *default rate percentage* applied to the *group of financial assets*. One can use a classification based on product or service type, geographical segments, distribution channel, currency or aging to group the accounts receivables. The default rates may be assessed based upon the historical sales experience and the past defaults and should be adjusted to be forward-looking.

**Example 2**: The ABC Company should assess the impairment loss of its account receivables for 20X9, December 31st. ABC's commercial policy is to allow a 30 day period for collection of receivables (this means that there is no significant financial component—interest—related to the receivable). The receivables balance is related to a single product (for simplification).

The aging structure of trade receivables as of December 31st, 20X9 and the default rates are in Table 7.1.

The most difficult assessment is determining the appropriate default rate of each category. For an in-depth explanation of this process, refer to Chapter 9, Financial instruments.

**Table 7.1** Aging structure of trade receivables

| Aging period | Amounts (lei) (1) | Default rates (% of expected credit losses) (2) | Bad debt (loss allowance) (lei) (3= 1 * 2) |
|---|---|---|---|
| 0–30 days | 10,000 | 2 | 200 |
| 31–60 days | 2000 | 4 | 80 |
| 61–90 days | 1000 | 15 | 150 |
| 91–180 days | 1200 | 25 | 300 |
| Over 180 days | 800 | 100 | 800 |
| Total | | | 1530 lei |

*Source* The authors

The journal entry is a simple one: by the end of the year the total amount should be recorded as the following:

| 1530 lei | Bad debts expense | = | Accounts receivables | 1530 lei |
|---|---|---|---|---|

**Foreign currency conversion rates and their impact on liabilities and receivables** is an important topic, related to trade receivables and trade liabilities. There is a specific standard dedicated to the topic, **IAS 21 The Effects of Changes in Foreign Exchange Rates** and we shall apply its main requirements.

There are two important concepts that IAS 21 highlights: the **functional currency** and the **presentation currency**. The **functional currency** is the currency that mainly influences the prices and costs of goods and services, the labor costs and other material costs. Additionally, the functional currency could be the one on the main funds to finance the business or the currency of cash-ins (receipts) of the company. The **presentation currency** is the currency in which the company presents its financial statements and may differ from the functional currency. Due to the volatility of the rate of exchange between the functional currency and the presentation currency, companies are facing volatility in their Profit & Loss Account and Balance Sheet.

The following is an example of the impact foreign exchange conversion rates have on financial statements:

**Example 3**: Company ABC, located in Romania, sells IT services to a German client of 1000 euros, on December 10th, 20X6. The German client paid on January 17th, 20X7 as the contract requires.

On December 10th, 20X6 the exchange rate was 4.57 lei/euro, on December 31st, 20X6, it was 4.66 lei/euro and on January 7th, 20X7 it was 4.60 lei/euro.

The presentation currency is "lei" and the functional currency is "euro"; therefore, ABC Company should convert its euros transaction into lei, at the selling moment, at the balance sheet moment, and at the cash-in moment.

**Solution**:
On December 10th, 20X6 the ABC Company (the seller) records the sale in its books as follows: 1000 euro of sale at 4.57 lei/euro

| 4570 lei | Account receivable | = | Revenues from sale | 4570 lei |
|---|---|---|---|---|

On December 31th, 20X6 there is a potential gain in lei because the exchange rate has increased to 4.66 lei/euro. The claim now amounts to 4660 lei, compared to 4570 lei. The foreign exchange conversion has therefore created a difference of 90 lei:

| 90 lei | Account receivable | = | Gains from foreign exchange conversion | 90 lei |
|---|---|---|---|---|

On January 17th, 20X7 the ABC Company receives 1000 euros equivalent to 4600 lei, 60 lei less than in December 31st, 20X6. Therefore, the entry is as follows:

| 4660 lei | % | | = | Account receivable | 4660 lei |
|---|---|---|---|---|---|
| 4600 lei | Bank account | | | | |
| 60 lei | Losses from foreign exchange conversion | | | | |

Another example relates to the ABC Company purchasing some consultancy services from a French supplier of 2000 euros, in September 21st, 20X7 and paying in instalments, ½ on October 1st, 20X7 and the other ½ on November 30th, 20X7. The rates of exchange were the following:

September 21st, 20X7: 4.50 lei/euro
October 1st, 20X7: 4.55 lei/euro
November 30th, 20X7: 4.49 lei/euro

On September 21st, 20X7, the service purchased was worth 9000 lei (2000 euro * 4.50 lei/euro)

| 9000 lei | Expenses with services | = | Account payable | 9000 lei |
|---|---|---|---|---|

On October 1st, 20X7 the first ½ in the amount of 1000 euro (at 4.55 lei/euro) was paid. A loss was incurred as a result of the foreign exchange conversion rate of 50 lei = 1000 * (4.55 lei/euro – 4.50 lei/euro)

| 4550 lei | % | | = | Bank account | 4550 lei |
|---|---|---|---|---|---|
| 4500 lei | Account payable | | | | |
| 50 lei | Losses from foreign exchange conversion | | | | |

On November 1st, 20X7 the second ½ in the amount of 1000 euro (at 4.49 lei/euro) was paid. In this case, there was a favourable foreign exchange conversion rate of 10 lei = 1000 * (4.50 lei/euro – 4.49 lei/euro).

| 4500 lei | Account payable | = | % | 4500 lei |
|---|---|---|---|---|
| | | | Bank account | 4490 lei |
| | | | Gains from foreign exchange conversion | 10 lei |

Things change when there are *non-monetary* assets or liabilities in a foreign currency, as opposed to the *monetary* items (account receivables, account payables) previously explained. For example, a company paid 1 million euro for a plot of land in Austria and the presentation currency of the company is the Romanian "lei". The plot of land should be disclosed at its rate of exchange in the moment of acquisition, assuming here it was 4.60 lei/euro. Therefore, 4,600,000 lei is the acquisition cost of the land and this amount remains unchanged at the year end, no matter the volatility of the rate of exchange. Only when the revaluation model is used for land the difference on rates of exchange between the acquisition and the revaluation moment should be accounted for.

### 7.4.2 Employees Benefits and Other Related Issues

Another important category of liability relates to employees and depicts, on one hand, the cost of their work for the company (employer) and, on the other hand, how much the company has to pay for this "resource". The main document relating to employees' benefits is the payroll ("stat de plata" in Romanian).

There is a distinction between different categories of employees' benefits, such as (based on **IAS 19 Employees' benefits**):

- short-term benefits, in form of salaries and wages;
- long-term benefits, e.g. pension funds, share option plans, exit benefits etc.

We shall focus only on short-term benefits for the moment, with examples related to salaries and wages and all the effects in the financial statements.

**Example 4**: Company ABC provides the following data related to its employees, for the month of May 20X8 (this example is based upon the Romanian tax code and labour code which came into force in 2018, but the computation steps and principles can be replicated worldwide):

Employees' data extract—May 20X8

| Item | Amount |
| --- | --- |
| Contractual amounts | 10,000 lei |
| Overtime | 6000 lei |
| Additional benefits (performance bonuses) | 4000 lei |
| Employee's contribution to Social Security Fund (SSF) | 25% |
| Employee's contribution to Health Care Fund (HCF) | 10% |
| Salary tax | 10% |
| Employer's contribution to labour insurance (LI) | 2.25% |

What are the effects in the annual financial statements related to salaries?

**Solution**: Firstly, we shall provide the payroll computations and then disclosure process (Table 7.2).

**Step 1**: Disclose the gross salary amount in May 20X8:

| 20,000 lei | Expenses with salaries | = | Salaries payable | 20,000 lei |
| --- | --- | --- | --- | --- |

**Step 2**: Disclose the employee's contributions and salary tax in May 20X8:

**Table 7.2** Payroll extract—May 20X8

| No. | Item | Amount (lei) |
|---|---|---|
| 1 | Contractual amounts | 10,000 |
| 2 | Overtime | 6000 |
| 3 | Additional benefits (performance bonuses) | 4000 |
| 4 | **Gross salary amount (1 + 2 + 3)** | **20,000** |
| 5 | Employee's contribution to Social Security Fund (F) (25% * gross salary) | 5000 |
| 6 | Employee's contribution to Health Care Fund (HCF) (10% * gross salary) | 2000 |
| 7 | Salary tax (10% * (gross salary − employee's contribution to SSF and HCF)) = (20,000 lei − (5000 lei + 2000 lei)) * 10% | 1300 |
| 8. | Net salary, payable to the employee (gross salary − all contributions and taxes) | 11,700 |
| 9. | Employer's contribution to labour insurance-LI (2.25% * gross salary) | 450 |

*Source* The authors

| 8300 lei | Salaries payable | = | % | | 8300 lei |
|---|---|---|---|---|---|
| | | | Employee's contribution to SSF | | 5000 lei |
| | | | Employees' contribution to HCF | | 2000 lei |
| | | | Salary tax payable | | 1300 lei |

**Step 3**: Disclose the company's contribution to labour insurance in May 20X8:

| 450 lei | Other expenses | = | Employer's contribution to LI | 450 lei |
|---|---|---|---|---|

**Step. 4**: Disclose the payment of contributions, taxes and net salary in June 20X8:

| 20,450 lei | % | | = | "Bank account" | 20,450 lei |
|---|---|---|---|---|---|
| 11,700 lei | Salaries payable | | | | |
| 5000 lei | Employees contribution to SSF | | | | |
| 2000 lei | Employees contribution to HCF | | | | |
| 1300 lei | Salary tax payable | | | | |
| 450 lei | Employer's contribution to Labour insurance | | | | |

The conclusions of this example are:

- The total cost of labour is 20,450 lei, consisting of the gross salary expense plus the expenses related to the employer's contributions; this constitutes the total amount which the company should spend on its employees. This is an operating expense, in connection to the specific liabilities.
- The total employer contributions and salary tax is 8300 lei and represents liabilities until payed (41.5% of the gross salary);
- The net salary amount of 11,300 lei represents a liability for the company (the employer) until payed (56.5% of the gross salary amount);
- All payments, amounting to a total of 20,450 lei, should also be disclosed in the Statement of cash-flow of the year as operating cash-flow.

### 7.4.3 Value Added Tax (VAT)

The **Value Added Tax (VAT)** is an indirect tax related to the consumption of goods and services and it is added to the sale's price. It is taxing the value added by the product or service through its business cycle. Based on the tax rules (Tax Code) of the business environment, the VAT is computed by applying a certain percentage to the price of goods or services. All European Union members apply the VAT but each country has its own percentages for different categories or goods and services and certain exemptions. Specific examples of transactions involving the VAT were provided in Chapters 5 Inventories and 6 Non-current Assets. We shall now further show the procedure of the VAT adjustment by the end of the month or term.

**Example 5**: ABC Company S.R.L. had acquired in May 20X7 merchandise of 100,000 lei, VAT 19%, total acquisition cost of 119,000 lei (100,000 lei + 19,000 lei VAT). During the same month, merchandise was sold with a 10% profit margin and 19% VAT, the total price charged to customers being 130,900 lei (100,000 lei cost + 10% profit margin = 110,000 lei selling price; 130,900 lei = 110,000 lei selling price + 20,900 lei VAT).

At the end of May the account "VAT deductible" (also called "Input VAT"), has a debit balance of 19,000 lei and the account "VAT collectable" has a balance of 20,900 lei. The two accounts should be offsetted and:

a) When "VAT deductible" is lower than "VAT collectable" (also called "Output VAT"), the difference is payable to the tax authorities (what has been collected from clients is greater than what has been payed to suppliers) and there is a "VAT payable" as balance;
b) When the "VAT deductible" is higher than "VAT collectable", the difference is to be received from the tax authorities (what has been collected from clients is lower than what has been payed to suppliers) and there is a "VAT receivable" as balance.

In our example, the first case applies (VAT deductible < VAT collectable), therefore the settlement of VAT shall be recorded in the following journal entry:

| 20,900 lei | VAT collectable | = | % | 20,900 lei |
|---|---|---|---|---|
|  |  |  | VAT deductable | 19,000 lei |
|  |  |  | VAT payable | 1900 lei |

Then, the VAT payable is settled and the following journal entry should the recorded:

| 1900 lei | VAT payable | = | Bank account | 1900 lei |
|---|---|---|---|---|

**Example 6**: In May, 2017, the ABC Company S.R.L. has acquired merchandise in the amount of 100,000 lei, VAT 19%, total acquisition cost of 110,000 lei (100,000 lei + 19,000 lei VAT). During the same month, 80% of the merchandise was sold with a 10% profit margin and 19% VAT, the total price charged to customers being 104,720 lei (80,000 lei cost + 10% profit margin = 88,000 lei selling price; 104,720 lei = 88,000 lei selling price + 16,720 lei the VAT). In this example, the second case applies (VAT deductible > VAT collectable) and a VAT receivable should be recorded as follows:

| 19,000 lei | % | = | VAT deductible | 19,000 lei |
|---|---|---|---|---|
| 16,720 lei | VAT collectable |  |  |  |
| 2280 lei | VAT receivable |  |  |  |

When the amount is received from tax authorities the journal entry should be recorded as follows:

| 2280 lei | Bank account | = | VAT receivable | 2280 lei |

This indirect tax should not be confused with the sales tax (applied in the US and other countries). Even though the sales tax is also based on the price of goods and services, difference lies in the payment obligation. The sales tax is collected only by the retailer and paid by the end customer, whereas the VAT is progressively paid through the value-chain of the product/service.

### 7.4.4 Other Current Liabilities and Receivables

Other current liabilities (and receivables) might arise in connection with the companies' relationship to the shareholders, associates and joint ventures.

For example, when dividends are distributed from the annual profit, this should be disclosed as a current liability of the company.

**Example 7**: Let's assume that a 100,000 lei is distributed to dividends from the 1 million lei annual profit; the journal entry is:

| 100,000 lei | Retained Earnings | = | Dividends payable | 100,000 lei |

Another example is when a parent company lends 2 million lei for a period of 10 months to one of its subsidiaries. This should be disclosed as a receivable:

| 2,000,000 lei | Loans to subsidiary (Other receivables) | = | Cash in bank (Bank account) | 2,000,000 lei |

## 7.5 NON-CURRENT LIABILITIES

Long-term liabilities, also called non-current liabilities, are obligations with a maturity greater than one year. Bank loans payables, liabilities to other companies or provisions fall into this category. Provisions are explained later on, alongside with the resemblances and differences between them and liabilities.

An important business aspect should be noted in connection with bank loans and bonds: whenever a company needs money, it may take out a bank loan or issue securities (bonds) to be sold and then redeemed at a maturity date.

***Classification of bonds***: mortgage bond, secured bond, debenture bond, sinking fund bond, serial bond, callable bond, zero-coupon bond, convertible bond, subordinated bond.

***Features of bonds are***:

- Book/face value;
- Issue value (price);
- Redemption value;
- Bond premium/discount;
- Maturity date;
- Interest rate.

An important aspect of financial liabilities is their valuation for Balance Sheet purpose. Non-current liabilities are presented at their present value, at the Balance Sheet moment. The present value computation is described as follows:

$$PV = FV/(1+i)^n$$

where:

$PV$ = present value
$FV$ = future value of payment
$i$ = interest rate
$n$ = number of periods

**Example 8**: A 50,000$ bond with a 5 years maturity, issued at 20% discount, a 10% annual interest and 17% effective interest rate (EIR) is measured at amortized cost by the issuer. The bonds will be redeemed after 5 years with a premium of $2926. The bondholders pay $40,000 when buying the bonds ($50,000 * 80%). The computations related to the interest expense should be based on the effective interest rate (the rate on the market of 17%) and the annual payments are based on the 10% at nominal value of the bond ($50,000). The following computations are provided (Table 7.3):

The issued bonds are recorded at the inception as follows:

| $40,000 | Bank account | = | Bonds payables (long-term) | $40,000 |

**Table 7.3** Long-term bond

| Year | Opening balance | Interest expense (17% EIR) | Cash payments (At 10%) | Closing balance |
|---|---|---|---|---|
| 1 | $40,000 | 6800 | 5000 | 41,800 |
| 2 | $41,800 | 7106 | 5000 | 43,906 |
| 3 | $43,906 | 7464 | 5000 | 46,370 |
| 4 | $46,370 | 7883 | 5000 | 49,253 |
| 5 | $49,253 | 8373 | 5000 | 52,626 |
| Total | | 37,626 | 25,000 | |

*Source* The authors

The annual interest for the 1st year will generate the following journal entry (every year the accrual of interest expense and the annual instalment will be recorded, based on Table 7.3):

| $6800 | Interest expense | = | % | $6800 |
|---|---|---|---|---|
| | | | Bank account | $5000 |
| | | | Bonds payables | $1800 |

At the maturity date the bondholders will receive 52,626$:

| $52,626 | Bonds payables | = | Bank account | $52,626 |
|---|---|---|---|---|

The total financial cost with the interest for the bond issuer is $37,626 (disclosed in the P&L Account) and the overall amount paid was $77,626 ($25,000 of interest + $52,626 at redemption), disclosed in the Statement of Cash-Flow.

## 7.6 Leasing

Another important aspect related to liabilities are leasing contracts. Starting with January 1st, 2019 the **IFRS 16 Leasing** becomes mandatory for leasing contracts. The "old" classification into "operating" and "financial (capital) leasing" is still useful but the context has changed. According to IFRS 16, a leasing contract gives the **lessee** (the beneficiary) "the right to control the use of an identified asset for a period of time in exchange for the consideration" (IFRS 16, par. 9).

The **lessee** is the company that has the "right-to-use" the asset and the **lessor** provides this "right-to-use" (in most of the cases is the legal owner of the asset). The right-to-use the asset is defined as the right to use an underlying asset, a right which belongs to the lessee.

As stated before, there are **operating leasing** contracts and **financial leasing** contracts. A financial leasing contract is the one that:

- Contains the right to transfer the ownership of the asset to the lessee, at the end of the term of the lease;
- the lessee has an option to purchase the asset at a "bargain" price;
- the term of the lease is for the majority of the economic life of the asset;
- at the inception of the contract the present value of the lease payments is equal or substantially the same as the fair value of the asset;
- the asset is of a specialized nature, enabling its use by the lessee, without any change;
- there is a compensation to the lessor, paid by the lessee if any losses from cancellation would occur.

All the other contracts are operating leasing contracts. Another exemption from the previous classification relates to contracts with a duration lower than 12 months or contracts with "low value" assets (e.g. tablets, telephones etc.).

The financial leasing contract is the classical example of the application of the principle **"substance over form"**, meaning that the economic substance of an event will prevail over its legal format. Simpler said, the lessee will be the one to disclose the asset in its Balance Sheet during the leasing contract, as if the asset would belong to the lessee, even though by the end of the contract the asset might be returned to the lessor.

**Example 9**: A company leases a piece of equipment with a usage life of 6 years and the contract period is 5 years. The fair value of the equipment is $10,000 and annual payments in the amount of $3000 are due. The implicit interest rate is 15%. In the interest of simplicity, we shall assume that the residual value is zero.

Table 7.4 shows the annual computation of the interest, payments and ending balances of the leasing liability.

The accounting information flow is shown in the following board, for the lessee and the lessor.

Table 7.4 Financial leasing contract

| Years | Opening balance ($) (1) | Interest (15%) (2) | Annual payments ($) (3) | Closing balance ($) (4=1+2−3) |
|---|---|---|---|---|
| 1 | 10,000 | 1500 | 3000 | 8500 |
| 2 | 8500 | 1275 | 3000 | 6775 |
| 3 | 6775 | 1016 | 3000 | 4791 |
| 4 | 4791 | 719 | 3000 | 2510 |
| 5 | 2510 | 490 | 3000 | – |
| Total |  | 5000 | 15,000 |  |

*Source* The authors

The **lessee** will present the asset in its financial statements, as if the asset belongs to it, including the asset's annual depreciation (let's assume the depreciation is straight-line, over the 5 years of the contract) (Table 7.5).

The lessor should provide the following set of transactions (Table 7.6).

## 7.7 Provisions

Provisions are perhaps one of the most misunderstood item presented in financial statements. Regulations and textbooks write about provisions for litigation and warranties, provisions for obsolete stocks and bad debts, provisions for income tax and so on. For accounting purposes, a provision is thus defined as a liability affected by uncertainty ("**Provision is** a liability of uncertain timing or amount"—IAS 37, par. 10). Uncertainty refers to the amount of the liability or to its timing. When faced with a transaction or event that may cause a provision, the reader should resort to the conceptual framework.

The **IAS 37 Provisions, Contingent Liabilities and Contingent Assets** provides information on when a provision should be recognized: "if, and only if a present obligation (legal or constructive) has arisen as a result of a past event (the obligating event), payment is probable ('more likely than not'), and the amount can be estimated reliably [IAS 37.14]".

There are several types of provisions. One possible classification is in connection to the Balance Sheet effect:

**Table 7.5** Journal entries of the lessee, in a financial leasing contract

| Year | Transactions | Lessee |
|---|---|---|
| 1 | a) Inception of the contract<br>b) The interest cost accrued<br>c) Payment of the annuity<br>d) Annual depreciation<br>($10,000/5 years = $2000/year) | $10,000 Right-of-use-asset = Leasing payable $10,000<br>$1500 Interest expense = Leasing payable $1500<br>$3000 Leasing payable = Bank account $3000<br>$2000 Expense with depreciation = Accumul. depreciation $2000<br>*Note: by the end of the year the lessee has an "asset" of $8000 in its balance sheet ($10,000- $2000), a $1500 interest expense in its P&L Account and a $3000 payment* |
| 2 | a) The interest cost accrued<br>b) Payment of the annuity<br>c) Annual depreciation | $1275 Interest expense = Leasing payable $1275<br>$3000 Leasing payable = Bank account $3000<br>$2000 Expense with depreciation = Accumul. depreciation $2000 |
| 3 | a) The interest cost accrued<br>b) Payment of the annuity<br>c) Annual depreciation | $1016 Interest expense = Leasing payable $1016<br>$3000 Leasing payable = Bank account $3000<br>$2000 Expense with depreciation = Accumul. depreciation $2000 |
| 4 | a) The interest cost accrued<br>b) Payment of the annuity<br>c) Annual depreciation | $719 Interest expense = Leasing payable $719<br>$3000 Leasing payable = Bank account $3000<br>$2000 Expense with depreciation = Accumul. depreciation $2000 |
| 5 | a) The interest cost accrued<br>b) Payment of the annuity<br>c) Annual depreciation | $490 Interest expense = Leasing payable $490<br>$3000 Leasing payable = Bank account $3000<br>$2000 Expense with depreciation = Accumul. depreciation $2000 |

*Source* The authors

**Table 7.6** Journal entries for the lessor, in a financial leasing contract

| Years | Transactions | Lessee |
|---|---|---|
| 1 | a) Inception of the contract<br>b) The interest revenue accrued<br>c) Cash-in of the annuity | $10,000 Leasing receivable = Asset $10,000<br>$1500 Leasing receivable = Interest revenue $1500<br>$3000 Bank account = Leasing receivable $3000<br>Note: *by the end of the year the lessor had a receivable of $10,000 in its balance sheet, a $1500 interest revenue in its P&L Account and a $3000 receipt in cash* |
| 2 | a) The interest revenue accrued<br>b) Cash-in of the annuity | $1275 Leasing receivable = Interest revenue $1275<br>$3000 Bank account = Leasing receivable $3000 |
| 3 | a) The interest revenue accrued<br>b) Cash-in of the annuity ($2500/year) | $1016 Leasing receivable = Interest revenue $1016<br>$3000 Bank account = Leasing receivable $3000 |
| 4 | a) The interest revenue accrued<br>b) Cash-in of the annuity | $719 Leasing receivable = Interest revenue $719<br>$3000 Bank account = Leasing receivable $3000 |
| 5 | a) The interest revenue accrued<br>b) Cash-in of the annuity | $490 Leasing receivable = Interest revenue $490<br>$3000 Bank account = Leasing receivable $3000 |

*Source* The authors

- Provisions for asset impairment (a "contra account"—an account that corrects the amount of a specific assets, for which the provisions have been disclosed, for example provisions for bad debts);
- Provisions for risks & charges (a liability account).

The obligation that generates a provision may be a legal one (the consequence of a law or contract) or a constructive one (resulting from company policies). Examples may be the provisions set up for litigation and tax investigations in progress, or for warranty costs but also for clean-up costs following the enactment of anti-pollution legislation. The obligation may be unilaterally assumed (a constructive obligation), when an enterprise publicly accepts responsibilities that third parties expect it to fulfil. This is the case of a newly established optician that has advertised his decision to reimburse dissatisfied customers. No law or contract binds the enterprise to do so, but the public expects it to keep its promise. As it is probable that the price of some services must be reimbursed, the enterprise recognizes a provision based on past experience.

When an enterprise has a present obligation as a result of a past event, but when either the outflow of economic benefits is not probable, or the amount of the obligation is not measurable, the obligation should be treated as a **contingent liability**. Contingent liabilities are not recognized in financial statements, but if their probability is not remote, they are disclosed in the explanatory notes.

From the accounting point of view, managing a provision will involve an *expense account to be debited* and a *provision account to be credited*. Whenever we have to diminish or cancel provisions, the provision account will be debited and a revenue account will be credited.

**Example 10**: The following transactions and events have affected Sharp Technologies S.A. pior to December 31st, 20X7. The management of the company authorizes the financial statements for issue on March 15th, 20X8.

a) The company has accidentally polluted a neighbouring property. The management estimates clean-up costs at 300,000 lei. Current legislation requires immediate clean-up of polluted sites. The company holds an insurance policy covering such incidents for up to 80% of actual costs, but the company is aware that the recovery of their value from the insurer is laborious.

**Solution**: The company has a legal obligation to clean up the neighbouring property and an outflow of economic benefits is probable. Therefore, a provision should be recognized for the amount of 300,000 lei. The amount receivable from the insurer should be treated as a contingent asset (explained later), as its receipt is uncertain. The journal entry is as follows:

| 300,000 lei | Expense with provision | = | Provision for Clean-up Costs | 300,000 lei |

b) The company sells industrial equipment with a warranty period of 12 months. Estimated warranty costs in 2018 amount to 200,000 lei.

**Solution**: At the end of the year, the company has a legal obligation to repair the equipment sold during the year. Although not every item sold will require repairs, there is a high probability that some warranty costs will be incurred. A provision should then be recognized for the best estimate of these costs, that is, for 200,000 lei.

| 200,000 lei | Expense with provision | = | Provision for warranties | 200,000 lei |
|---|---|---|---|---|

c) On February 15th, 20X5 the Office for Patents and Trademarks has granted the company the patent for its new aluminium casting technology. Some potential customers have already shown their interest in this breakthrough in the defence industry. The company estimates revenues of 800,000 lei in the coming year.

**Solution**: This grant from the Office for Patents and Trademarks is material; therefore, the company should disclose a contingent asset in the notes. Future revenues are not allowed in the financial statements, but such an event is considered a contingent asset and disclosed in the notes, which informs the stakeholders.

d) On a meeting held in November, 20X7, the Board of Directors has decided to discontinue the chemical division of the company. In the following month, the company terminated contracts with suppliers of chemical materials and sent a letter to every employee in the division announcing the close-down scheduled for March 1st of the following year. Compensations payable to employees and other restructuring costs amount to 500,000 lei.

At the end of the financial year 20X7, the company has a constructive obligation towards its personnel and third parties as it has begun to implement the restructuring plan. It is highly probable that resources will leave the enterprise to settle this obligation and thus the company should recognize a provision for restructuring of 500,000 lei.

| 500,000 lei | Expense with provision | = | Provision for discontinued operations | 500,000 lei |
|---|---|---|---|---|

e) The company is a defendant in two court cases concerning product defaults. The plaintiffs, General S.R.L. and KUT S.A., seek damages of 50,000 lei and 100,000 lei respectively. The company's legal advisors estimate that there is a high probability to lose the case against General S.R.L., but a strong chance to win against KUT S.A.

**Solution**: Based on existing evidence, the company has a legal obligation in the General S.A. case, but has no obligation in the KUT S.R.L case. The probability to pay damages in the first case is high, in the second case remote. The company will recognize a provision of 50,000 lei in the first case; it will neither recognize a provision, nor disclose a contingent liability in the second case, as there is a remote probability that it will have to pay damages to KUT S.A.

| 50,000 lei | Expense with provision | = | Provision for litigations | 50,000 lei |

Provisions are in place until either the risk event takes place or the timing (for warranties for instance) is off. Consequently, the provisions are reversed/cancelled.

In Example a) above, the company should set up a provision for clean-up costs at the end of the year 20X7 for the estimated amount of 300,000 lei.

Now, assume that in 20X8, the company pays 310,000 lei plus 19% VAT to a business specialized in decontamination. The disclosure of the service bought is:

| 368,900 lei | % | = | Other payables | 368,900 lei |
| 310,000 lei | Other Services Expense | | | |
| 58,900 lei | VAT Deductible | | | |

The provision previous recognized is reversed/cancelled:

| 300,000 lei | Provision for Clean-up Costs | = | Revenue from Provisions | 300,000 lei |

When the insurer announces to the company that it will reimburse the clean-up costs, the company recognizes an asset (a receivable) and the corresponding revenue (248,000 lei = 310,000 lei * 80%):

| 248,000 lei | Other Debtors | = | Other Operating Revenue | 248,000 lei |

Provisions and contingent liabilities are often misunderstood and used as synonyms. This is an error and should be better understood by looking at the following example.

**Example 11**: Rolls Royce (both group and company) enters into significant long-term contingent obligations: guarantees for the indebtedness of other companies within its group, which are considered to be insurance arrangements. In this respect, the Company treats the guarantee contract as a contingent liability until such time as it becomes probable that the Company will be required to make a payment under the guarantee. On December 31st, 2017, these guarantees amounted to £2930 m (2016: £2735 m) (RR 2017 Annual Report, note 5, pg. 174).

The opposite of a **contingent liability** is a **contingent asset**, that is, a possible asset determined by future events, again not totally controlled by the enterprise. A contingent asset is not recognized in the financial statements; if the inflow of economic benefits is probable, then it is disclosed in the notes. An example of a contingent asset is an insurance policy that a company is likely to recover.

**Example 12**: Oil Transport S.A. operates gas pipelines guarded by a private security company. In December, 20X8, the company has made a claim against an employee of the security company for alleged negligent acts which have led to perpetrators causing damages in the amount of 40,000 lei. On December 31st, 20X8, it is disputed whether Oil Transport S.A. has a right to receive compensation from the security company.

**Solution**: a contingent asset should be disclosed in the annual report, if this is considered to be material.

## 7.8 Conclusions

The following summary questions and their answers will provide a brief conclusion of this chapter.

### Chapter summary questions:

| | |
|---|---|
| 1. What is a liability? | A **liability** consists of an obligation to an outside party, arising from past transactions or events for the settlement of which cash or other assets are needed. |

| | |
|---|---|
| 2. What is a claim (receivable)? | A **claim (receivable)** is the opposite of a liability and represents the right to receive an amount of money or another asset from the business partner. |
| 3. How do we classify liabilities and receivables, for Balance Sheet disclosure? | Both liabilities and claims should be classified in "**current**" (under 1 year) and "**non-current**" (over 1 year), for balance sheet purpose, based upon their maturity. |
| 4. What is the measurement technique for non-current liabilities? | Non-current liabilities are measured at the present value of future cash-flows (discounted cash-flow technique). |
| 5. What are the most important concepts related to employees' salaries and their effect in the financial statements? | The **gross salary** amount is the sum of all employee's benefits from a job, before any deduction to various contributions to funds or taxes<br>**Employee's contributions** consist of all deductions from the gross salary amount to various funds or taxes, such as Social Security Fund, Health Care Fund, Unemployment Fund and Salary tax, owed by each employee<br>**Employer's contributions** mean additional company costs with employees or companies' contributions to various funds and taxes, related to its employees<br>**Net salary** is in fact the amount of money that the employee receives every month and it is computed based on the gross salary amount out of which all employees' contributions & salary tax are deducted. |
| 6. What generates the monthly/quarterly VAT adjustment? | When "VAT deductible" is lower than "VAT collectable" the difference is payable to the tax authorities and it is a **VAT payable**<br>When the "VAT deductible" is higher than "VAT collectable" the difference is to be received from the tax authorities and it is a **VAT receivable**. |

| | |
|---|---|
| 7. What are the major effects of a financial leasing contract? | The **lessee** (the beneficiary) records the asset ("right-to-use asset") in its balance sheet, depreciates it and acts as if the asset belongs to it (substance over form concept). The financial cost is based upon the interest, payable to the lessor<br>The **lessor** (the legal owner) is entitled to receivables, through the contract period. |
| 8. What is a provision? Which are the effects in the financial statements? | **Provisions** are legal or constructive obligations to future payments, which are uncertain in respect of their timing or amount<br>A provision will give rise to an expense in the P&L Account and a provision (liability category) or a decrease of the asset account, in the Balance Sheet<br>When the provision is reversed/cancelled, a revenue will be disclosed, alongside with the cancellation of the provision. |

**Quizzes (only one correct answer):**

1. Which of the following are estimated liabilities?
   a. Account payables
   b. Salary payables
   c. Income tax payable
   d. Product warranties
2. The note payable relates to a liability for which the unknown relates to:
   a. The payable amount
   b. The nominal value
   c. Beneficiary of the amount
   d. Creditor
3. The total cost with employees is based on:
   a. Gross salary
   b. Net salary
   c. Gross salary and employer's contribution
   d. Employees' and employer's contribution

4. When an acquisition of goods is in a foreign currency, a loss from foreign currency occurs when:
   a. The functional currency increases in relationship to the presentation currency
   b. The functional currency decreases in relationship to the presentation currency
   c. The functional currency equals the presentation currency
   d. Non-applicable
5. A long-term bank loan shall be measured by the debtor by the end of each year at the:
   a. Nominal value
   b. Market value
   c. Present value of future cash flows
   d. Future value
6. When a good has a warranty period, the seller should estimate and record a:
   a. Loss
   b. Discount
   c. Provision
   d. Bonus
7. In a financial leasing contract, the asset is disclosed in the financial statements of the:
   a. Lessor
   b. Lessee
   c. Owner
   d. Intermediate company
8. A current year's distribution of $12,000 dividends (dividends were distributed from last year's profit) will influence:
   a. Operating cash-flow
   b. Current liabilities
   c. Assets
   d. None
9. A company paid $200,000 as dividends. An amount of $20,000 is still owed to shareholders as distributed dividends. The effects in the annual financial statements end of the year are:
   a. A financing cash out-flow of $200,000 and a $20,000 of current liabilities in the balance sheet
   b. An investing cash out-flow of $200,000 and a $220,000 of current liabilities in the balance sheet

c. A financing cash out-flow of $200,000 and a $220,000 of current liabilities in the balance sheet
   d. A financing cash in-flow of $200,000 and a $220,000 of current assets in the balance sheet
10. If a company signs a contract with a strategic client, that will generate an increase in the turnover of 25% next year, then the company should:
    a. Disclose nothing
    b. Disclose a provision
    c. Disclose a contingent asset
    d. Disclose a contingent liability

**Exercises**:

**Exercise 1**: Company BETA borrows on January 1st, 20X6 from the bank 1,100,000 euro to purchase a building, at an annual interest rate of 10% for any unpaid balance, on 5 years. The loan is to be repaid in equal areas, at the end of each accounting period. The interest is to be paid at the end of each accounting period. Provide the effects in the annual statements related to this loan.

**Exercise 2**: Company ZETA, located in US, purchased goods from a German company of 100,000 euro on December 22nd, 20X7. An amount of 3000 euro was paid on December 27th, the rest being due on January 4th, 20X8. The rate of exchange were the following:

December 22nd, 20X7: 1.15 $/euro;
December 31st, 20X7: 1.18 $/euro;
January 4th, 20X8: 1.14 $/euro.

Provide the journal entries and the effects in the annual statements of these transactions for the American company.

**Exercise 3**: The following information refers to Company ABC payroll of May 2017: gross salary amount 100,000 lei, employees' contribution to Social Security Fund 15%, employees' contribution to Health Care Fund 10%, employees' contribution to Unemployment Fund 5%, salary tax 10%,, employer's contribution to Social Security Fund 5%, employer's contribution to health care Fund 2% and employer's contribution to Unemployment Fund 1%, 2000 lei fines to employees and 1000 lei bank installments of some employees. Provide the effects in the monthly statements of the previous information; what is the overall employment cost for ABC?

**Exercise 4**: Company ABC is a lessee within a financial leasing contract, the following data being provided: the fair value of the leased equipment is $20,000, the contractual period is 36 months, the annual rate of interest is 10% (annual lease payments are based on 1/3 of the fair value of the equipment) and the residual value is $2000, the estimated utility life of the equipment is 4 years and the double—decline method is considered appropriate for the depreciation. There is high certainty that the lessee will not purchase the equipment in the end of the contract. Explain the effects in the financial statements (balance sheet, income statement and statement of cash-flow) for first year of the contract, for ABC. Which are the most important pros and cons of a financial leasing contract for the lessee (provide business arguments)?

**Exercise 5**: a) Provide the effects in the annual financial statements of A if a fire destroyed one warehouse that had a net book value of $500,000; b) A lawsuit was filed against the business that claimed $50,000 in punitive damages and $100,000 for personal injury; the suit was not settled as for December 31st, current year, but the company's attorney is convinced that the insurance would pay 75% of any award; c) Several dissident shareholders intended to sue the company for rejection of a merger offer; the company's attorney felt any such suit would be without merit.

**Exercise 6**: Company ABC has incurred a 140,530 lei as VAT deductable and 134,444 lei as VAT collectable for the month of May 2018. Provide the effects of the VAT adjustment for May 2018.

**Exercise 7**: Company XYZ issued 100,000 euro bonds with a 10% discount, an 8% annual interest, a 115 effective interest rate and a 5 years maturity on January 2nd, 20X4. There are 5 annual payments of the interest and a repayment of the 101,832 euro to the bondholders at the end of the 5 years. Provide the effects in the annual financial statements of this bond loan (and journal entries).

**Exercise 8**: Company BAC produces and sells washing machines, with 1 year warranty. During 2017 the turnover was 10 mil euro (corresponding to an average of 15,500 washing machines). Based on the history track 10% of the washing machines will require minor repairments of 50 euro/piece and 0.5% will require replacement, that will cost 200 euro/piece. Provide the effects in the annual financial statements.

**Exercise 9**: The Company AAA is distributing dividends from the previous year's annual profit of 100,000 lei, based upon the decision of the Annual Shareholders' meeting. The dividend tax is 20%. Provide the effects in the financial statements of the year, knowing that the payment is due in the following 4 months.

**Exercise 10**: Delta Company enters into a long-term agreement with a major hypermarket chain, to sell its meat products, on December 14th, 20X7. The first delivery will take place in January 3rd, 20X8 for am amount of 100,000 lei. Which are the implications in the annual financial statements?

# CHAPTER 8

# Equity

*Adriana Duțescu*

*Learning objectives:*

- *Understanding and using different equity elements for business decisions*
- *Understanding and using the capital of the business and related items*
- *Understanding and using retained earnings and profit & loss of the year*
- *Analysing the profit distribution*

## 8.1 INTRODUCTION

Enterprises are financed throughout two major sources: equity from owners (shareholders) and debts. In this chapter we shall study the components of the equity section of the Balance Sheet, namely:

1. Capital;
2. Share premium (also called additional-paid-in-capital);
3. Legal reserve;
4. Revaluation reserve;
5. Other reserves;
6. Profit or loss for the year;
7. Retained earnings.

## 8.2 Share Capital

The Memorandum and the Articles of Association (in Romanian "contract de societate" and "statut") represent the birth certificate of a company and states the names of the founders, the name, object and headquarters of the company, the procedures for the company's management and organisation, capital subscription amounts and dates, special procedures, etc. A company gains legal personality upon its registration within the Trade Registrar ("Oficiul Comertului"). The share capital of the enterprise is raised upon its incorporation by capital contributions in cash only or in cash and in kind. The current minimum capital requirement in Romania is 200 lei for a limited liability company (S.R.L.) and 90,000 lei for a share company (S.A.). The shares in a share company can be transferred with the annual approval of the General Shareholders Meeting ("Adunarea Generală a Acționarilor" in Romanian). The value of share capital of a listed company (also called "public companies" in the US) is computed as follows:

$$\text{Share Capital} = \text{Shares issued} \times \text{Nominal value/share}$$

There are different stages related to shares (also called "stock"): "issued shares", in connection to shares that have been issued, "outstanding shares", representing shares currently issued and held by shareholders and the basis for share capital computation (as stated in the previous formula) and "treasury shares", that are the company's own shares purchased from the Stock Exchange, for various purposes (see the following paragraphs for more examples).

Investors become shareholders by buying shares which entitle them to dividends, voting rights, rights to receive their capital share at liquidation or withdrawals for the company and pre-emption rights. Based upon their characteristics, there are two major categories of shares in public (in Romanian "companii listate") companies: ordinary shares (also called "common stock") and preference shares (also called "preferred stock").

**Ordinary shares** give shareholders the right to dividend payments and a residual claim on the company's assets. This means that, in the event of bankruptcy, ordinary shareholders' claims are taken into consideration after the creditors and the preference shareholders have received the amounts owed or promised to them. Shareholders' rights are expressed in the Annual General Meeting. On this occasion, shareholders elect the members of the Board of Directors and the auditors, approve the financial statements and make other important decisions, such as: changes of economic activity, changes in the size of the share capital, approval of mergers and acquisitions, issue of debentures etc.

The nominal value (also called "par value" or "face value") is the amount printed on the face of the share. The book value of the share is derived by dividing the capital of the business to the number of outstanding shares.

**Preference shares** carry a special right: the specific dividend (preferred dividend) is paid before any other profit distribution and sometimes even at a fixed amount, no matter if the company incurs a profit or a loss. Preference shareholders have all of the ordinary shareholders' rights, if it is not stated otherwise in the contract. Preference shares may be converted into ordinary shares with the approval of the Annual General Meeting and are considered to be at the border of ordinary shares and long-term debts, because of the obligation to annually pay preference dividends.

Treasury shares are shares which a public company has bought back. This may occur for various reasons. One of these reasons could be managements' desire to increase the market price of shares or the reported earnings per share.[1] Management may also want to prevent a hostile take-over bid and, in this way, prevent the "aggressor" to obtain voting power. It is also possible that the capital of the company has overgrown and the company plans to reduce share capital by buying back and cancelling distributed shares. Such shares could also be distributed to employees. But as a company cannot own itself, the International Financial Reporting Standards[2] require that these shares be presented as a deduction from equity (IAS 32, par. 33). The buy-back of shares is strictly regulated in every jurisdiction. Romanian Company Law imposes a maximum threshold of 10% of total shares issued and a maximum duration of 18 months for the buy-back operation.

### 8.2.1 Contribution to Capital

According to Romanian Company Law, capital is contributed in a two-phases process:

- the subscription;
- the actual payment.

---

[1] Net profit less dividend of preference shares divided by the number of outstanding ordinary shares.

[2] IAS 32: Financial Instruments: presentation.

The general rule is that upon set-up, every shareholder will pay at least 30% of the subscribed capital, with the balance payable within 12 months from registration. The subscription is the owner's promise to contribute to the capital of the company and, from the company's accounting point of view, the right to receive this contribution. The payment takes place on the day the owners bring their contribution in cash or in kind. In this moment, the company's right to receive the contribution ceases. The following examples will explain this procedure.

**Example 1**: On January 1st, 20X4, ABC SRL, a private limited liability company, is set-up by two close friends. The subscribed capital amounts to 10,000 lei, of which Mr. Ion subscribed 7000 lei in cash and Mr. Petru subscribed 3000 lei, out of which 2000 lei in cash and 1000 lei as a used computer, valued by an expert. The payment is made on January 31st, 20X4. Provide the journal entries.

**Solution**: The subscription generates a claim for the company to receive the promised amounts and the recognition of the capital; therefore, the journal entry will be:

| 10,000 lei | Shareholders receivable | = | Share capital subscribed and unpaid | 10,000 lei |
|---|---|---|---|---|

The actual payment will generate two journal entries: one for the contributions that are brought (in cash and in kind) and the second for the "capital conversion" (the "capital subscribed and unpaid" is converted into "capital subscribed and paid"):

| 10,000 lei | % | = | Shareholders receivable | 10,000 lei |
|---|---|---|---|---|
| 9000 lei | Bank account | | | |
| 1000 lei | Non-current assets | | | |

| 10,000 lei | Share capital subscribed and unpaid | = | Share capital subscribed and paid | 10,000 lei |
|---|---|---|---|---|

Sometimes the capital is subscribed in foreign currency. The principle is the same as in the case of contributions in lei, with the only difference being that between subscription and payment an exchange difference may appear. According to Romanian regulations, this exchange difference is not treated as a gain or a loss, but is transferred to other reserves.

**Example 2**: Company Flash SA is set-up by three associates in January 20X4. The 10,000 euro capital is subscribed when the exchange rate is 3.20 lei/euro. The actual payment takes place when the exchange rate is 3.30 lei/euro. Provide the journal entries.

**Solution**: The subscription of the capital at 3.20 lei/euro:

| 32,000 lei | Shareholders receivable | = | Share capital subscribed and unpaid | 32,000 lei |
|---|---|---|---|---|

The payment at 3.30 Lei/euro:

| 33,000 lei | Bank account | = | % | 33,000 lei |
|---|---|---|---|---|
| | | | Shareholders receivable | 32,000 lei |
| | | | Other revenues | 1000 lei |

The transfer of capital:

| 32,000 lei | Share capital subscribed and unpaid | = | Share capital subscribed and paid | 32,000 lei |
|---|---|---|---|---|

### 8.2.2 Increase and Decrease of Capital

The capital of an entity may be increased when an expansion is envisioned and internal resources are insufficient. The operation may be realized via:

- increase in number of shares, keeping the nominal value unchanged;
- increase in nominal value of shares, without changing the number of shares;
- capitalization of reserves (with the exception of legal reserves);
- capitalizations of the net profit of the year or retained earnings;
- conversion of debenture loans and other liabilities into shares and
- combinations of the above.

When new shares are issued for cash the company will generate them at an issue price, different from their nominal value. The nominal value of both old and new shares must be the same, as the rights of old and new shareholders are identical. However, the issue price of the new shares depends on the company market value which, for a growing entity, is usually higher than their nominal value. **The share premium** (also called "additional-paid-in-capital", "paid-in surplus") is an equity item often found in companies' Balance Sheets and refers to the amount of shareholders' contributions that exceeds the nominal value of shares. For legal reasons (but without economic substance) accountants separate the share capital of the company (the nominal value of the shares) from the excess amount paid by the shareholders (share premium).

The new shares issued for cash require a down payment of a certain percentage of their nominal value, on the subscription date. The balance is payable within a required period from the date of publication of the General Meeting's decision in the Official Journal. The shares rewarding contributions in kind follow the same procedure. In all cases, the share premium must be entirely paid upon subscription.

The share capital of public companies may be decreased when significant losses have been incurred, that cannot be absorbed by existing reserves or future profits. The share capital may also be reduced when it is overstated, compared to the company's commercial activity. The reduction of the share capital is rather a sensitive operation. The creditors are particularly interested in maintaining the capital unchanged as a guarantee for their loans. Therefore, there is a publication requirement in the Official Journal and an interval of some months in which creditors may oppose; limitations also apply when the company has outstanding debenture loans.

Some of the techniques for reduction of capital are:

- a decrease in the number of shares, keeping the nominal value unchanged;
- a decrease in the nominal value of shares, without changing the number of shares;
- an acquisition of own shares followed by cancellation;
- a cancellation of shareholders receivable;
- a payback to shareholders.

**Example 3**: Company ABC SA has the following items of equity at June 30th, 20X5:

- Share capital 100,000 lei, represented by 25,000 shares of 4 lei/share;
- Legal reserve 5000 lei;
- Retained earnings 20,000 lei.

The Annual General Meeting decides the increase of capital, aiming at expanding the company's activity in a new market. Therefore, a number of 1000 new shares are issued at 5 lei per share, the book-value remaining the same (4 lei/share); consequently, an amount of 1 lei/share is the share premium. Provide the journal entries.

**Solution**: The subscription of the new shares on June 30th, 20X5:

| 5000 lei | Shareholders receivable | = | % | | 5000 lei |
|---|---|---|---|---|---|
| | | | Share capital subscribed and unpaid | | 4000 lei |
| | | | Share premium | | 1000 lei |

The payment of the new shares on June 30th:

| 5000 lei | Bank account | = | Shareholders receivable | 5000 lei |
|---|---|---|---|---|

The transfer of the capital:

| 4000 lei | Share capital subscribed and unpaid | = | Share capital subscribed and paid | 4000 lei |
|---|---|---|---|---|

**Example 4**: On December 31st, 20X3 company DEF SA has the following capital structure:

- Share capital 25,000 lei, consisting of 5000 shares of 5 lei each;
- Legal reserve 5000 lei;
- Retained earnings 15,000 lei;
- Net profit for the year 2000 lei.

The Annual General Meeting decided the increase of the share capital by issuing 3400 shares as the capital increase throughout the retained earnings and net profit for the year's capitalisation. The new shares are given to current shareholders, proportionally to their current contribution to the capital of the business.

**Solution**: The journal entry is:

| 17,000 lei | % | | = | Share capital subscribed and paid | 17,000 lei |
|---|---|---|---|---|---|
| 15,000 lei | Retained earnings | | | | 15,000 lei |
| 2000 lei | P&L Account | | | | 2000 lei |

**Example 5**: CleanGas SA has been founded to take advantage of a new technology to produce biogas out of used cooking oil. The subscription took place on January 5th, 20X2, through public offering and required a down payment of 50% with the balance payable within six months. At the end of the subscription period, the account "Shareholders' receivable" showed a debit balance of 12,000 lei, representing unpaid shares. The Annual General Meeting decided the cancellation of the receivable and therefore the reduction of the share capital.

**Solution**: The appropriate journal entry is:

| 12,000 lei | Share capital subscribed and unpaid | = | Shareholders' receivable | 12,000 lei |
|---|---|---|---|---|

**Example 6**: Traffic SRL is a carrier that provides relocation services to companies moving headquarters. A slowdown of the business activity in the area has left a part of the company's truck fleet idle for several months. A team of consultants suggest that the company has overgrown its market and should down-scale. The Annual General Meeting decides to reduce the share capital of the company by paying back the shareholders one fourth of the subscribed and paid capital, that is 20,000 lei.

**Solution**: The journal entry is:
(a) Capital down-size:

| 20,000 lei | Share capital subscribed and paid | = | Shareholders' receivable | 20,000 lei |
|---|---|---|---|---|

(b) Amount paid to shareholders:

| 20,000 lei | Shareholders' receivable | = | Bank account | 20,000 lei |
|---|---|---|---|---|

## 8.3 Legal Reserve and Other Reserves

In Romania and in other Roman law countries the mandatory distribution of profit to legal reserves is a measure designed to protect creditors. The Anglo-Saxon accounting systems assume that creditors' interests are protected via asset valuation and profit measurement rules. This means that profit is fairly determined, and dividends are distributed from real profits and are not disguised reimbursements of capital. As we have previously seen, the reduction of capital through acquisition of own shares or payback to shareholders is strictly regulated.

Under Romanian Companies Act, at least 5% of the profits should be appropriated (distributed) to the legal reserve until it reaches a minimum of 20% of the share capital. This distribution is treated as a deductible item for tax calculations.

**Example 7**: Credential SRL was established on December 1st, 20X3. The net profit for the year 20X3 amounts to 10,000 lei. On May 31st, 20X4, the Board proposes the following appropriation from the net profit:

- 5% to the legal reserve;
- 40% for dividends;
- the balance is carried forward.

**Solution**: The journal entry is:

| 10,000 lei | Profit appropriation account | = | % | 10,000 lei |
|---|---|---|---|---|
|  |  |  | Legal reserve | 500 lei |
|  |  |  | Dividends payable | 4000 lei |
|  |  |  | Retained earnings | 5500 lei |

The legal reserve is never used to increase the share capital but only to absorb future losses, if other sources are not available. If the ratio of legal reserve to share capital has fallen under 0.2:1, new appropriations to the legal reserve must be made.

**Example 8**: Swing SA has incurred a series of losses starting with 20X4. The Retained Earnings account balance is a debit of 100,000 lei at December 31st, 20X4. The company has 100,000 outstanding shares of 8 lei/share nominal value and a legal reserve of 16,000 lei. The Board of Directors proposes the use of the legal reserve and a reduction of share capital with 40,000 lei (5000 share * 8 lei/share) to cover a part of the loss.

**Solution**: The Journal entry is:

| 56,000 lei | % | = | Retained earnings | 56,000 lei |
|---|---|---|---|---|
| 40,000 lei | Share capital subscribed and paid |  |  | 40,000 lei |
| 16,000 lei | Legal reserve |  |  | 16,000 lei |

**Example 9**: The Annual General Meeting of Agenda SA decides to purchase 5000 ordinary shares (2 lei nominal value), out of the total 60,000 shares outstanding, in order to alleviate the company's vulnerability in front of a major competitor. The purchase will take place during the next two months. The minimum and maximum purchase prices approved by the General Meeting are 4 lei and 6 lei respectively. The management of Agenda SA takes advantage of a momentary drop in share prices and buys back the shares at 4.7 lei each. Provide the appropriate journal entries.

**Solution**: The shares are shown at acquisition cost, regardless their nominal value (23,500 lei = 5000 shares * 4.7 lei/share):

| 23,500 lei | Treasury shares | = | Bank account | 23,500 lei |
|---|---|---|---|---|

This amount shall be disclosed as a reduction in the share capital of the business, for balance sheet purpose:

| Share capital | 120,000 lei (60,000 shares * 2 lei/share) |
|---|---|
| – Treasury share | – 23,500 lei |
| **Capital** | **96,500 lei** |

A company can also set up non-mandatory reserves based on the provisions of its Articles of Association, with the aim of keeping profits in the business in order to finance its development. The set-up of such a reserve is accounted for similarly to the legal reserve. It may be converted into share capital, if needed.

**Example 10**: The Articles of Association of NewTech SA include a disclosure for the establishment of a reserve for future growth. Allocations to this reserve are to be made annually at a rate of 10% of net profits. On December 31st, 20X3, the net profit of the company amounts to 300,000 lei.

| 30,000 lei | Profit appropriation account | = | Other reserves | 30,000 lei |
|---|---|---|---|---|

## 8.4 Net Profit or Loss for the Year and Retained Earnings

**Retained earnings** means part of the net profit of the entity, which has not yet been distributed and paid as dividends, or the net loss has not yet been covered, and retained by the company. The decision to either distribute the retained earnings or to cover the retained loss is taken in the future meetings of shareholders, next years.

The "Retained earnings" account may have a credit or a debit final balance, showing accumulated profits (credit balance) or accumulated losses (debit balance) from previous years.

When accounting for the net profit's distribution, the critical information is whether this has taken place before or after the Balance Sheet date. If the net profit was distributed before the Balance Sheet date, this is an event of the expired year, with all respective consequences such as the presentation of a liability for dividends.

The next important moment is the date when the financial statements are approved for issue. According to **IAS 10 Events after the Reporting Period**, this is the date when the financial statements are authorised for issue and public disclosure. If dividends and other profit's distributions are declared after the Balance Sheet date but before the date when the financial statements were approved for issue, a liability for dividends should not be recognised. A presentation in the notes should be made instead, but an appropriation within equity is also acceptable.

Profits are distributed to various destinations, such as: covering previous losses, reserves (legal or other reserves), distribution of dividends, capital increase. Dividends are only distributed from the business's profits.

**Example 11**: The Profit and Loss Account of TeleCO SA has a credit balance of 100,000 lei after having collected all revenues and expenses of the financial year 20X4. On December 31st, 20X4, management proposed the following appropriation of the net profit:

- 20,000 lei to increase capital;
- 30,000 lei for dividends (dividend tax 5%);
- For the balance—50,000 lei—a decision to be carried forward was made.

In February 20X5, the Annual General Meeting formally agreed to the profit distribution proposed by the management.

On December 31st, 20X4:

| 100,000 lei | Profit appropriation account | = | % | 100,000 lei |
|---|---|---|---|---|
| | | | Share capital subscribed and paid | 20,000 lei |
| | | | Retained earnings | 50,000 lei |
| | | | Dividends payable | 30,000 lei |

*Note* In international business practice, there is no Profit Appropriation Account and the distribution is provided directly from the Profit & Loss Account

Based upon Romanian regulations, the net profit for the year has an informative role in the Balance Sheet, as it is shown together with its counterpart, the "Profit Distribution Account". The balances of these two accounts amounts to zero.

| Net profit for the year | 100,000 lei |
|---|---|
| Profit distribution account | (100,000) lei |

In February 20X5, the Annual General Meeting approved the final distribution of the net profit:

| 100,000 lei | Profit and loss for the year | = | Profit appropriation account | 100,000 lei |
|---|---|---|---|---|

During 20X5, dividends were paid:

| 30,000 lei | Dividends payable | = | % | 30,000 lei |
|---|---|---|---|---|
| | | | Bank account | 28,500 lei |
| | | | Dividend tax payable | 1500 lei |

If the Board of Directors had decided to distribute profits after December the 31st, 20X4, no accounting entry would have been made on December the 31st, 20X4. A note explaining the distribution of profits may be required. All accounting entries would be made during the year 2015.

**Example 12**: Because of the decreasing number of passengers in the airline industry, AviaLine SA incurred a 400,000 lei loss in the financial year, which ended on December 31st, 20X3. At the same date, the company had 100,000 shares of 20 lei nominal value each, a legal reserve of 40,000 lei and retained earnings amounting to 500,000 lei. The management estimated that the business conditions would improve in 20X4; therefore they proposed to cover the loss from past profits.

On December 31st, 20X3:

| 400,000 lei | Retained earnings | = | Profit and loss for the year | 400,000 lei |

The "Retained Earnings" account remains with a credit balance of 100,000 lei.

**Example 13**: Due to a volatile chemicals market, Allias SRL has incurred a 90,000 lei loss in the financial year which ended on December 31st, 20X5. The company had the following equity structure on December 31st, 20X5:

| Share capital | 50,000 lei |
| Legal reserve | 10,000 lei |
| Other reserves | 20,000 lei |
| Retained earnings | 80,000 lei |
| Profit and loss for the year | (90,000) lei |

The management proposed to cover the loss from accumulated profits and other reserves.

In 20X6 the journal entry are:

| 90,000 lei | Retained earnings | = | Profit and loss for the year | 90,000 lei |
| 10,000 lei | Other reserves | = | Retained earnings | 10,000 lei |

## 8.5 Revaluation Reserve

The revaluation reserve, also called the revaluation surplus, is used to account for the increases or decreases in the fair value of property, plant and equipment in time, as it is stated in the **IAS 16 Property, Plant and Equipment** and **IAS 38 Intangible Assets** (specific examples are provided in Chapter 7 Non-current Assets). For most non-current assets, the fair value is synonymous with their market value. For specialised items, the depreciated replacement cost or utility value may be used instead.

The **IAS 16 Property, Plant and Equipment** requires that the transfer to Retained Earnings is made only when the revaluation surplus is realised. This is realised when the asset reaches the end of its useful life, at the latest upon its disposal.

**Example 14**: Company YCO SA has undertaken a revaluation of a plot of land in the northern part of Bucharest and of a building located in the City centre. An independent surveyor presented the company with the following evaluation report (all amounts are in lei):

| Non-current asset | Cost | Accumulated depreciation | Net book value | Fair value | Revaluation differences |
|---|---|---|---|---|---|
| Land | 50,000,000 | – | 50,000,000 | 90,000,000 | 40,000,000 |
| Building | 100,000,000 | 20,000,000 | 80,000,000 | 120,000,000 | 40,000,000 |

Set-up of a reserve for the revaluation of land:

| 40,000,000 lei | Land | = | Revaluation reserve | 40,000,000 lei |
|---|---|---|---|---|

For the building, eliminate the accumulated depreciation to revaluation date:

| 20,000,000 lei | Accumulated depreciation | = | Buildings | 20,000,000 lei |
|---|---|---|---|---|

Then increase the cost of the building to the market value:

| 40,000,000 lei | Buildings | = | Revaluation reserve | 40,000,000 lei |
|---|---|---|---|---|

**Example 15**: The management of YCO SA decided to sell the revalued building in the above example, two years after it had been revalued. The straight-line depreciation rate of 5% was used before the revaluation and a rate of 6.25% after the revaluation. The change of the depreciation rate is necessary because the remaining useful life has changed from 20 years to 16 years. It appears from the evaluation report that the revaluation has taken place four years after the purchase of the building. The

new rate will be applied to the revalued amount of 120,000,000 lei. When the building is sold the revaluation reserve can be transferred to Retained earnings:

| 40,000,000 lei | Revaluation reserve | = | Retained earnings | 40,000,000 lei |
|---|---|---|---|---|

## 8.6 Conclusions

The following summary questions serve as chapter conclusion. We encourage you to practice and also make use of the specific answers provided:

### Chapter summary questions:

| | |
|---|---|
| 1. What is the meaning of capital (own capital or share capital)? | **Capital** (own capital or share capital) is the owner's contribution to the business, in cash or in kind. From the company's point of view this is classified as an equity item. |
| 2. What is the difference between an ordinary share and a preference share? | An **ordinary share** (common share) is the basic equity instrument of a share company, which gives holders voting rights, dividend rights and rights to the residual economic value of the company. **Preference shares** provide the shareholders with preference rights, such as preference dividends, which are distributed before the ones due to ordinary shareholders, in some cases even regardless of the profit or loss of the year. |
| 3. What are "treasury shares"? | **Treasury shares** are the company's own shares. They are repurchased by the entity due to various reasons: to increase the market price of shares or the reported earnings per share, to prevent a hostile take-over bid and/or to be distributed to employees. Treasury shares are netted-off from the capital of the business. |
| 4. When does capital of the business decline? | The business declines, either due to previous losses or when a crucial stakeholder withdraws from the business without a replacement. |

| | |
|---|---|
| 5. What is a share premium? | A **share premium** is an additional amount of money paid by the shareholders, over the nominal value of shares. |
| 6. What is a legal reserve and what is its scope? | A **legal reserve** is a compulsory reserve emerging for the profit distribution up to certain limits and is meant to cover future losses. |
| 7. Provide examples of other reserves and their purpose | Other reserves may refer to **statutory reserves**, due from the net profit of the business and provided because of the provisions of the Association Act of the Company <br> A revaluation reserve is generated by the increase in the fair value of a non-current asset and is due when this asset is measured based upon the revaluation policy. |

**Quizzes (only one correct answer):**

1. During the year, Semper Investments has $60,000 in revenues, 40,000$ in expenses, 10,000$ in issuance of stock, 3000$ in dividend payments and 15,000$ in payments on account payable. The stockholders' equity changes by:
   A. +27,000$
   B. +42,000$
   C. +12,000$
   D. −27,000$

2. A business entity had capital in the amount of 10,000$, with 1000 common shares issued. An increase of capital occurred in 2012 and 100 new shares were issued and sold with a 12$/ share market price. The effects in the annual balance sheet of capital increase are:
   A. increase of business capital with 1000$ and increase in cash with 1200$
   B. increase of capital with 1200$ and increase in cash with 1200$
   C. increase of capital with 1000$ and increase liabilities with 1200$
   D. increase of capital with 1000$ and decrease in cash with 1000$

3. The entry to record a shareholder investment of 600$ into the business would be:

| A) Dr. Dividends | 600$ | Cr. Cash | 600$ |
| B) Dr. Cash | 600$ | Cr. Dividends | 600$ |
| C) Dr. Cash | 600$ | Cr. Service revenue | 600$ |
| D) Dr. Cash | 600$ | Cr. Share Capital | 600$ |

4. A purchase of own share (treasury shares) will:
   A. Increase a liability and increase the equity
   B. Increase an asset and decrease another asset
   C. Increase an asset and increase equity
   D. Decrease an asset and decrease a liability
5. A dividend distribution will:
   A. Decrease the profit and increase a liability
   B. Increase an asset and increase a liability
   C. Decrease a liability and decrease an asset
   D. Increase an asset and increase an equity
6. A previous loss covered by the annual profit will:
   A. Debit profit and loss and credit retained earnings
   B. Credit profit and loss and debit retained earnings
   C. Debit cash and credit retained earnings
   D. Credit cash and debit retained earnings
7. The legal reserve's source is:
   A. The net profit
   B. The net asset amount
   C. Provision amount
   D. Cash amount
8. The entry to record an owner withdrawals from a business of 1000$ is:

| A) Dr. Share Capital | 1000$ | Cr. Cash | 1000$ |
| B) Dr. Cash | 1000$ | Cr. Dividends | 1000$ |
| C) Dr. Cash | 1000$ | Cr. Service revenue | 1000$ |
| D) Dr. Cash | 1000$ | Cr. Share Capital | 1000$ |

9. A revaluation reserve for a building of 10 million lei shall generate:
   A. A debiting amount in the Building account and a crediting amount in the Revaluation reserves account, of 10 million lei

B. A crediting amount in the Building account and a debiting amount in the Revaluation reserves account, of 10 million lei
C. A debiting amount in the Bank account and a crediting amount in the revaluation reserves account, of 10 million lei
D. A debiting amount in the Profit & Loss Account and a crediting amount in the revaluation reserves account, of 10 million lei

10. Capital subscribed is:
A. Capital paid
B. Capital postponed
C. Capital promised to be paid
D. Total equity of the business

**Exercises:**

**Exercise 1.** On January 1st, 20X5 the private company XYZ SA is founded by three shareholders. The subscribed capital amounts to 100,000 lei and is divided into 100 shares of 1000 lei each. Shareholder X subscribes 50 shares in cash. Shareholder Y subscribes 20 shares of which 10 are paid in cash and brings a car for the balance. Shareholder Z subscribes 30 shares of which 20 shares are paid in cash and 10 shares represent the value of raw materials contributed. The cash contributions are paid at the end of January and the contribution in kind is made upon subscription. Provide the journal entries and the effects in the annual financial statements for the capital contribution to Company XYZ SA.

**Exercise 2.** Chatel SRL was established on November 1st, 20X3 with a share capital of 5000 dollars. On the subscription date the exchange rate was 4 lei/US$, while on the payment day, November 6th, the exchange rate was 4.1 lei/US$ according to the capital deposit note issued by the bank. The company has paid 3000 lei for lawyers' fees and 1190 lei (VAT included) to the Trade Registrar for the registration tax. The company has not undertaken any commercial activity until December 31st, 20X3. The closing exchange rate is 4.15 lei/US$. Draft the company's Balance Sheet on December 31st, 20X3.

**Exercise 3.** Altis SA has closed the financial year with a net loss of 210,000 lei. The shareholders' equity consists of: share capital 100,000 lei, legal reserve 20,000 lei, other reserves 5000 lei, retained earnings 80,000 lei. What options does the company have for covering the loss and what is their accounting treatment?

**Exercise 4.** On December 31st, 20X6, Valmont SRL's net profit amounts to 250,000 lei. The management proposes the following profit's distributions: 20% to legal reserve, 40% to dividends with the balance carried forward. On February, the 10th, 20X6, the General Meeting approves the distribution of the net profit. Provide the journal entries for these events.

**Exercise 5.** Company ABC SA owns a building acquired for 100 million lei with an estimated useful life of 10 years and no residual value. The straight-line method of depreciation is used. At the end of the fourth year the fair value of the building is 90 million lei according to a chartered surveyor hired for its revaluation.

Required:

1. Compute the revaluation difference and account for the revaluation.
2. Assume the building is sold at the end of the year 8. Compute the net book value of the building.
3. Discuss the accounting treatment of the revaluation reserve during the useful life of the asset and on its disposal.

CHAPTER 9

# Financial Instruments

*Adriana Duțescu*

*Learning objectives:*

- *Understanding the importance of financial instruments and their role*
- *Understanding and applying the classification of financial instruments*
- *Understanding and using the recognition and derecognition of financial instruments*
- *Understanding and applying the accounting effects of the expected loss impairment model*
- *Understanding and applying the derivative financial instruments and hedge accounting*
- *Links with other management tools*

## 9.1 Importance and Scope

In the last eighty years a profound, rapid and irreversible revolution emerged in the capital market area. A set of correlated events gave rise to the situation: the globalization of traditional capital markets, financial innovations and fintech business models. The increasing volatility of capital markets has created new hedge needs, covered by new derivative instruments and complex hedge methods.

The International Accounting Standard Board elaborated and published several International Accounting Standards/International Financial

Reporting Standards to cover the topic of financial instruments: **IAS 32 Financial Instruments: Disclosure and Presentation, IFRS 7 Financial Instruments: Disclosure, IFRS 9 Financial Instruments** (incorporating the former IAS 39).

This chapter will cover several important topics, such as:

a. Definitions;
b. Classification of financial instruments;
c. Recognition and valuation of financial instruments;
d. Impairment of financial instruments; and
e. Hedge accounting.

## 9.2 Definitions

IAS 32 provides the basic definitions which help identify a financial instrument. A **financial instrument** is a contract that gives rise simultaneously to a financial asset of one enterprise and a financial liability or equity instrument of another enterprise (IAS 32). Financial assets consist of "cash, contractual rights to receive cash or another financial asset or equity instruments" issued by other enterprises. Financial liabilities are contractual obligations to transfer cash or other financial assets or "to exchange financial instruments with another enterprise under conditions that are potentially unfavourable." Equity instruments are contracts that demonstrate a residual interest in the net assets of an enterprise (IAS 32, par. 11).

As it can be concluded, items such as **Account receivables** and **Account payables** (alongside with "Other receivables" and "Other payables") are financial instruments and should be understood and analysed according to the principles and models enforced by the specific IAS/IFRS.

Table 9.1 provides an overview of the main financial instruments:

To illustrate the previous note let's assume that a company enters into an agreement pursuant to which it has to pay the difference in the interest rate between 3% and ROBOR[1] if ROBOR is higher than 3%, or is allowed to receive the difference in the interest rate between 3% and ROBOR, otherwise. The notional amount is 1,000,000 lei. At the end of June, 20X7, ROBOR is 2% and at the end of July of the same year, ROBOR increased to 5%.

---

[1] ROBOR means the average interest rate that the Romanian banks are using for inter-banking loans in lei (the national currency).

Table 9.1  Financial instruments—examples

| Financial assets | Financial liabilities | Equity instruments |
|---|---|---|
| • Cash<br>• Cash equivalents (such as bank deposits);<br>• Accounts receivable (such as trade receivables and others)<br>• Loans issued;<br>• Bonds purchased;<br>• Owned equity instruments issued by another entity;<br>• Derivatives | • Accounts payable;<br>• Notes payable;<br>• Loans received;<br>• Bonds issued;<br>• Derivatives | • Own ordinary shares issued |

*Source* The authors

*Note* Not necessarily all of the financial assets and liabilities presented above are handled by IAS 32 and IFRS 9. Some of them are handled by other standards, despite their nature as financial instruments (i.g accounts receivable, or accounts payable or receivables as a result of a lease agreement)

Notice that derivatives may be both liabilities and assets, depending on their nature and on the impact on the entity

In the end of June, 20X7, the company has a right to receive the difference of the interest rate between 3% and ROBOR (which is 1% at 1,000,000 lei = 10,000 lei). As such, the company presents an asset (a financial asset) in the Statement of Financial Position.

In the end of July, 20X7, the company is required to pay the difference in the interest rate between 3% and ROBOR (which is 2% at 1,000,000 lei = 20,000 lei). As such, the company presents an asset (a financial asset) in the statement of its financial position.

**Classical and Derivative Financial Instruments**
**Classical (primary) financial instruments** refer to shares and bonds. A share is an equity instrument, while a bond is a liability instrument. As we explained in chapter eight, companies may issue ordinary shares and/ or preference shares that grant additional rights. Treasury shares represent a company's own shares, acquired in order to decrease the capital, to obtain shares useful in future acquisitions, for share-based payment plans,[2] conversion of bonds into shares or to increase the shares' price.

From the buyer's perspective, shares and bonds are assets. However, the financial instrument should be referred to either as an "equity instrument"—the shares—or as a "debt instrument"—as a bond, for example.

[2] IFRS 2 *Share-based payments* is covering in detail this topic.

Some authors use "marketable securities" when referring to financial instruments purchased with the intention of earning a short-term gain, as opposed to "investments" when the intention is to keep a continuing interest in the capital of the issuer (Stickney et al. 2010).

Equity investments can be classified as follows:

- **non-controllable interest** (also called **minority investments**)—refers to the portion of ordinary shares acquired by an investor in order to earn dividends or capital gains, but because of its insignificant influence on the control of the issuing company, this share package is considered to be of minor importance. The general accepted practice would assume that there is a capital share of under 20%;
- **significant investment**—refers to shares acquired by an investor, shares that grant a significant influence over the issuer's activities. The investor may significantly influence policy-making, based on their voting power; a more than 20% but lower than 50% capital contribution may indicate a significant investment. The accounting method to consolidate the financial statements of the group is referred to as the **"equity method"**; the company that issued shares is considered to be "an associate" of the buyer;
- **majority investment** refers to shares purchased by an investor which grant a controlling influence over the company, both at the policy-making level and at the operational level. A majority investment is considered to own more than 50% of the issuing company capital. The accounting method to consolidate the financial statements of the group is referred to as the **"(fully) consolidation method."**

**Bonds** are liability instruments that give rise to the issuer's obligation to settle the liability at a maturity date and to pay an interest. In order to raise funding, companies may have the choice between initiating a bank loan or a bond loan. Both methods feature a principal amount, an interest rate, a maturity date and possibly collaterals. However, bond loans may be more suitable as lower costs are generally involved. Bonds may exhibit a discount or premium value, which is, the difference between what one pays for the bond and the value one will obtain at the maturity date. For example, if a 10% annual interest (market/effective interest is 16%) of a 1000 lei nominal value bond is issued for 826 lei, the discount is 174 lei. The presence of the discount shows that the effective cost for the issuer is actually higher than the stated one (the effective interest rate is higher than the nominal interest rate). More examples are provided in Chapter 7.

Companies also issue complex financial instruments, such as convertible bond loans, a classical bond payable with an embedded conversion option into ordinary shares (see the comments and examples for compound financial instruments).

**Derivative financial instruments** are instruments such as future, forward, option and swap contracts, all being linked to a primary instrument, called the *underlying instrument*. The value of a derivative changes in response to developments of the *underlying instrument*.[3] The buyer is generally required to only make a small initial investment and he/she can settle the contract or withdraw from it before its maturity date.

**Future and forward contracts** are agreements to buy or sell assets (such as oil, gold, foreign currencies etc.) in the future, at stated prices. Futures are standardised instruments traded on established exchanges such as the Chicago Board of Trade, Euronext Brussels, etc. Forwards, however, trade over the counter, within a network of dealers who customise the terms of the contract to suit the investors' needs.

**An option contract** gives the holder the right, but not the obligation, to buy (call option) or sell (put option) an *underlying instrument* before the option's expiration date. The option for the issuer or writer means that there is a corresponding obligation to sell (call option) or to buy (put option). For example, assuming a future increase in share prices, an investor purchases a call option on shares, at a fixed price. If the share price evolution is unfavourable, the investor's exposure is limited to the option price. A holder of equity instruments (shares) may wish to purchase a put option, which is a right to sell the shares at a specified price. If the market price of shares falls below this price, he/she will exercise the option; if the price stays above the contractual price, he will let the option expire. Options trade over the counter and in exchanges.

The parties involved in a **swap contract** periodically exchange payments based on the price of securities, commodities, exchange rates, interest rates and other *underlying instruments*. One of the most common swaps is the exchange of fixed interest payments for floating interest payments or vice versa, to take advantage of lower rates. Swaps trade over the counter and in Stock Exchanges. Another over the counter derivative, the interest rate cap, offers payments to the issuer of floating rate loans, whenever the underlying interest rate exceeds the specified strike rate (the cap rate). Issuers of floating rate loans use interest rate caps for protection against increases in short term interest rates. Conversely,

---

[3] A financial instrument on which the value of a derivative depends (IAS 32).

holders of floating rate bonds use interest rate floors for protection against declines in short-term interest rates. The holder will receive a payment when the underlying interest rate falls below a specified strike rate (the floor rate).

## 9.3 Classification of Financial Instruments

Financial instruments are classified, based on their substance, as **equity** or **liability**, from the perspective of the issuer. If an **obligation** to repay cash or exchange financial instruments exists, then it must be classified as a liability. If redeemable preference shares provide for redemption of a fixed amount or on a fixed date then they must be classified as a liability, as there is an obligation to repay. There is another special category of financial instruments, **derivatives**, that follows the appropriate rules of recognition and derecognition.

**Example 1**: ABC Company needs to raise extra funding to support its new power plant. Therefore 10,000 bonds at a 100 euro/bond are issued, with a three-year maturity and a 10% annual interest. The issuer, the ABC Company, shall disclose a financial liability in the Balance Sheet and should follow the specific measurement requirements of the appropriate IFRS. On the other hand, the bondholder shall disclose the acquired bonds in its annual reports, as a financial asset.

This classification, based on IFRS 9 requirements, is simpler that the former one (provided by IAS 39) and should be correlated with the recognition rules enforced by the same IFRS.

## 9.4 Recognition and Valuation

The **initial recognition** of financial instruments is effective from the moment the enterprise becomes a party to the contractual provisions of the financial instrument.

**Financial liabilities** are initially measured at **fair value** (the same principles apply to the corresponding **financial assets** from the buyer's perspective). Depending on the business model, financial instruments can follow different **measurement models**:

- **the amortised cost model**, if the financial instrument is held solely to collect cash-flows related to the principal and interest; the transaction costs should be withdrawn from the carrying amount;

- **the fair value through other comprehensive income model**, if the financial instrument is held to collect cash-flows related to the principal and interest or for selling; the transaction costs should be withdrawn from the carrying amount;
- **the fair value through profit and loss model**, if the financial instrument does not fall under the previous two categories; the transaction costs are expensed to the Profit and Loss Account.

**Equity instruments** are recognised at **fair value through other comprehensive income**, if they are not held for trading and this is irrevocable or at **fair value through profit and loss**. For the first category, the transaction costs are embedded in the value of the instrument, for the second category, the transaction costs are expensed to the P&L Account.

**Example 2**: The ABC Company takes a 10 million lei bank loan at a 10% annual interest rate, with equal principal payments in a 4-year period. Provide the specific journal entries and amounts.

**Solution**: The following journal entries and measurements should be disclosed:

| ABC Company (the debtor) | The Bank (the creditor) |
|---|---|
| 1. Receiving the loan (financial asset at amortised cost) | 1. Granting the loan (financial liability at amortised cost) |
| 10 mil lei Bank account = Long-term loan 10 mil | 10 mil lei Long-term receivables = Bank Account 10 mil |
| 2. Payment of the first arrear and interest | 2. Receipt of the first arrear and interest |
| 1.25 mil lei % = Bank Account 1.25 mil lei | 1.25 mil lei Bank Account = % 1.25 mil lei |
| 1 mil lei Interest expense | Interest revenue 1 mil lei |
| 0.25 mil lei L.T. Loan | L.T. Receivable 0.25 mil lei |

**Example 3**: Erasmus S.A. issues 100,000 lei, 10% debenture bonds, for three years, 20X4–20X7. After taking the current situation on the debenture market into account, the company's broker sets the interest rate at 12%. The issue price is calculated by discounting all interest payments and the repayment of capital at the effective rate of interest (12%).

Issue price: $10,000/1.12 + 10,000/1.12^2 + 10,000/1.12^3 + 10,000/1.12^4 + 100,000/1.12^4 = 93,925$ lei

Discount: $100,000 - 93,925 = 6075$ lei

The amortised cost over the years is presented in the table below:

| Date | Interest payment | Interest expense | Amortised discount | Amortised cost |
|---|---|---|---|---|
| 0 | $1 = 100{,}000 * 10\%$ | $2 = 4 * 12\%$ | $3 = 2 - 1$ | $4_i = 4_{i-1} + 3$ |
| 1 Jan. 20X4 | | | | 93,925 |
| 31 Dec. 20X4 | 10,000 | 11,271 | 1271 | 95,196 |
| 31 Dec. 20X5 | 10,000 | 11,424 | 1424 | 96,619 |
| 31 Dec. 20X6 | 10,000 | 11,594 | 1594 | 98,214 |
| 31 Dec. 20X7 | 10,000 | 11,785 | 1785 | 100,000 |

**Solution**: Erasmus S.A. accounts for the issued debenture as follows (first year 20X4):

a) the subscription:

| 100,000 lei | % | = | Debenture loan payable | 100,000 lei |
|---|---|---|---|---|
| 93,925 lei | Other debtors | | | |
| 6075 lei | Debenture discount | | | |

b) the receipt of cash:

| 93,925 lei | Cash | = | Other debtors | 93,925 lei |
|---|---|---|---|---|

c) the accrual of the interest liability for the first year:

| 11,271 lei | Interest expense | = | % | 11,271 lei |
|---|---|---|---|---|
| | | | Debenture interest payable | 10,000 lei |
| | | | Debenture discount | 1271 lei |

d) the payment of annual interest:

| 10,000 lei | Debenture interest payable | = | Cash | 10,000 lei |
|---|---|---|---|---|

The sequence c) and d) is repeated every year. On 1 January 20X8, Erasmus S.A. repays the loan:

| 100,000 lei | Debenture loan payable | = | Cash | 100,000 lei |
|---|---|---|---|---|

**Example 4**: The X Corporation issues 1000 bonds with a nominal value of 1000 $/bond, with a 5% interest rate, payable in 2 instalments. The redemption date is in 2 years. The X Corporation also trades bonds on a short-term basis. By the end of the issue year, the market interest rate is 8%. How should the X Corporation disclose this financial instrument in its annual report?

**Solution**: This financial liability should be measured at fair value through profit and loss, because it is traded on a short-term basis. Therefore, the liability should be re-evaluated for the reporting date, at its fair value. Let's assume that the fair value of the bond cannot be reasonably observed from an active market and the fair value is based upon the discounted cash-flows of the instrument, at the effective interest rate (market rate):

|  | Cash-flows ($)<br>(1) | Discount rate<br>(2) | Present value<br>(3)= (1) * (2) |
|---|---|---|---|
| Year 1 (interest) | 1 mil * 0.05 = 0.05 mil | 1/(1.08) | 0.046 mil |
| Year 2 (interest + principal) | 1 mil $ + 0.05 mil = 1.05 mil | 1/(1.08)$^2$ | 0.900 mil |
| Total |  |  | 0.946 mil |

By the end of the first year, the financial liability should be remeasured at its fair value, 0.946 million $, meaning that a 0.054 million $ revenue/gain (1 mil $ − 0.946 mil $) should be disclosed in the P&L Account

| 0.054 mil $ | Financial liability (bond) | = | Profit and loss | 0.054 mil $ |
|---|---|---|---|---|

A special case concerns the initial recognition and valuation of complex (compound) financial instruments, such as a **convertible bond**, from the perspective of the issuer. Suppose that a company issues bonds that are convertible at any time into its shares at a stated price, with a fixed interest rate and a specified maturity date. IAS 32 requires the issuer of the financial instrument, which contains both a liability and an equity item, to split the proceeds obtained into a loan and a written call option on the issuer's shares. This can be done either by measuring the liability component and assigning the residual amount to the equity component or by measuring the two components separately. The IAS 32 favour the first method. We explain the first method below.

**Example 5**: Assume that the Silver S.A. issued convertible bonds in the amount of 50,000 lei at an 8% interest rate with a maturity of three years, 20X1–20X3. Interest is payable in annual instalments. Every bond (nominal value of 100 lei) may be converted into 50 ordinary shares. At the time of the bond issue, the interest rate for a similar loan was 10%.

The present value of the liability component, using a discount rate of 10% is based on the following computations:

|  | *lei* |
|---|---|
| Nominal value of the loan | 50,000 |
| Present value of the loan, payable after three years | 37,566* |
| Present value of three annual interest payments of 4000 lei each | 9947** |
| Total value of liability component (37,566 lei + 9947 lei) | 47,513 |
| Residual equity component (50,000 lei − 47,513 lei) | 2487 |

$$37{,}566^* = 50{,}000 \text{ lei} /(1+0.1)^3$$

$$9947^{**} = \sum 4000 /(1+0.1)^3$$

The journal entry that separately recognises the two components is:

| 50,000 lei | Bank account | = | %<br>Bonds payable<br>Other equity | 50,000 lei<br>47,513 lei<br>2487 lei |
|---|---|---|---|---|

Another way of providing funds for investments and operating activities is the bank loan. Depending on their maturity, bank loans (this is also true for bond loans) can be classified into short-term (less than one year), medium (one to five years) and long term (more than five years) loans. Short term loans are reported as current liabilities in the Balance Sheet, while medium and long term loans are non-current liabilities.

**Example 6**: On January 1st, 20X4, the GlassWare S.A. borrowed 100,000 lei from Trade International Bank at a 12% annual interest rate. The loan is payed in four equal annual instalments, starting on December 31st, 20X4. Provide the computations of arrears and interest and the journal entries.

**Solution:**
Let's assume the following formula of P:

Table 9.2  Loan amortisation table

| Years | Instalment | Opening balance | Interest | Capital payment | Closing balance |
|---|---|---|---|---|---|
| 0 | 1 | 2 | 3 = 2 * 12% | 4 = 1 − 3 | 5 = 2 − 4 |
| 31 Dec. 20X4 | 32,923 | 100,000 | 12,000 | 20,923 | 79,077 |
| 31 Dec. 20X5 | 32,923 | 79,077 | 9489 | 23,434 | 55,643 |
| 31 Dec. 20X6 | 32,923 | 55,643 | 6677 | 26,246 | 29,397 |
| 31 Dec. 20X7 | 32,923 | 29,397 | 3527 | 29,397 | 0 |

*Source* The authors

$P = C*(1 - v)/[v(1 - v^n)]$, where P is the amount of an instalment, v the discount factor $v = 1/(1+i)$, C is the capital borrowed, i the annual interest rate and n the number of annual payments.

At a 12% interest rate, the instalment is: P = 32,923.4 lei (Table 9.2).

a) The receipt of the loan on January 1st, 20X4:

| 100,000 lei | Cash | = | Bank loan payable | 100,000 lei |
|---|---|---|---|---|

c) Payment of capital and interest on December 31st, 20X4:

| 32,923 lei | % | = | Cash | 32,923 lei |
|---|---|---|---|---|
| 20,923 lei | Bank loan payable | | | |
| 12,000 lei | Interest expense | | | |

Entry b) is repeated with appropriate amounts on December 31st, 20X5, 20X6 and 20X7.

## 9.5  Impairment of Financial Assets

IFRS 9 has created an important change in the way financial instruments are impaired. Before IFRS 9, financial instruments were impaired only when the trigger event had occurred and the effect on the instrument was provided; this was known as the "incurred loss model". IFRS

9 comes with a totally new concept of the **"expected loss model"**, which forces all entities dealing with financial instruments to predict future losses related to those instruments and not wait for default to happen. Expected credit losses represent the weighted average of credit losses, related to risks of occurring defaults (IFRS 9).

The so called "loss allowance model" must be developed for debt instruments at amortised cost or at fair value through other comprehensive income.

There is a *three-stage model* approach:

- Stage 1: includes **performing financial instruments**, with low credit risk, for which a *12 month expected credit losses*[4] estimate must be made;
- Stage 2: relates to **underperforming credits**, with a significant increase of the *credit risk*,[5] for which expected credit losses are estimated for the entire lifetime of the credit;
- Stage 3: includes **non-performing credits** (impaired credits[6]), with objective evidence of impairment, for which expected credit losses are estimated for the entire life time of the credit.

This three-stage model is very specific to the business model and strategies applied in each company and is based upon statistics and econometric methods.

**Example 7**: Company P provides a five-year loan of 100,000 lei to Company S, with an 8% coupon rate and a principal payment at maturity, the same market rate at that time. The interest is received at the end of each year. By the end of year 4, Company S is encountering significant financial difficulties (the market rate is 10%). Company P estimates that no further interest payments will be received and only 50,000 lei from the principal will be paid back. How should this case be approached?

---

[4] 12 month expected credit losses represents the expected credit losses that result from default events possible in 12 month after the reporting date (IFRS 9, appendix A).

[5] Credit risk is considered for payments with more than 30 days overdue and is defined as the risk that one party to a financial instrument will cause a financial loss to the other party, by failing to discharge an obligation.

[6] Impaired credits are the ones with significant financial difficulties of the borrower, default contracts, it is probable that the borrower will enter into bankruptcy.

**Solution**: If there is significant evidence about material financial difficulties of Company S, the credit must be considered impaired. Expected credit losses are the difference between the asset's gross carrying amount and the present value of expected future cash-flows, discounted to the original market interest rate:

PV = 50,000 lei/1.08 = 46,296 lei
Expected credit loss = 100,000 − 46,296 = 53,703 lei

The interest for an impaired credit loan must be calculated on the net carrying amount of 46,296 lei (gross amount − expected impairment loss). For the next year, an amount of 3703 lei (46,296 lei * 8%) should be recognised in the P&L.

## 9.6 Hedge Accounting

Transactions with financial instruments entail various risks that management should try to mitigate. Some of these risks require an enterprise to present its risk management policies concerning price risk, credit risk (failure of the other party to perform contractual obligations), liquidity risk (the enterprise lacks funds to meet contractual obligations) and cash flow risk (unexpected cash flows associated with financial instruments). Price risk compounds currency risk (e.g. financial instruments denominated in foreign currencies, such as forwards), interest rate risk (e.g. changes in interest rates have an effect on the fair value of financial instruments, such as fixed rate bonds) and market risk (e.g. changes in market prices have an effect on the fair value financial instruments, such as the release of unfavourable macroeconomic data).

Enterprises may hedge against certain risks in an asymmetrical or in a symmetrical way.[7] Asymmetrical hedges act similarly to insurances,[8] eliminating potential losses, but allowing potential gains, such as the purchase of an interest rate cap by the issuer of a floating rate loan or the purchase of a put option by a holder of shares. Symmetrical hedges may be secured using non-derivatives (natural hedges), but also by using derivatives. A typical natural hedge is obtained by matching foreign currency debtors and creditors: in the event of a depreciation of the foreign currency, losses made on debtors are offset by gains made on creditors.

---

[7] Lien (2005).
[8] Lien (2005).

A derivative can be designated to act as a hedging instrument if its fair value or cash flows follow an opposite pattern than those of the hedged item.

Hedge accounting is therefore an accounting technique aimed at insulating the profit and loss account when symmetrical hedges are used. Hedge accounting is optional. The hedged item may be an asset, liability, firm commitment or a highly probable future transaction. The hedging instrument may be a derivative or, less frequently, another financial asset or liability. The reader should note that there are particular accounting techniques for three hedging relationships: fair value hedging, cash flow hedging and the hedging of an investment in a foreign entity. Before moving on to the mechanism of hedge accounting, we will explain the first two hedging relationships.

Fair value hedging provides protection against changes in the fair value of a recognised asset or liability, changes which will otherwise affect the net profit figure. The changes in the fair value of the hedged item are offset by the opposite changes in the fair value of the hedging instrument and are both taken to the profit and loss account. The holder of a fixed rate bond retains a fair value risk: the market price of fixed rate bonds falls when interest rates rise and vice versa.[9] The enterprise could enter into a fixed to floating interest rate swap, where it pays a fixed rate amount and receives a floating rate amount. The enterprise has therefore made up for the loss in fair value by getting higher interest payments. The issuer of a fixed rate loan also have a fair value exposure: as interest rates fall, the value of existing bonds increases. If the enterprise wishes to repay the loan without incurring a loss, it enters into a fixed to floating interest rate swap: in return for receiving fixed rate payments under the swap, the enterprise will make payments based on a floating rate.

Cash flow hedging hedges risks associated with asset or liability induced cash-flows or a foreseen transaction. The gain or the loss on the hedging instrument is recognised directly in the statement of changes of equity. An enterprise holding a floating rate portfolio should seek to protect itself from a decrease in short term interest rates. The enterprise thus enters into a floating to fixed interest rate swap, making floating payments (which hedge the floating receipts from the assets) and receiving fixed payments. Additionally, an enterprise issuing a floating rate loan

---

[9] Other companies will issue more favorable loans and investors will give up lower rate securities, thus depressing their market price.

incurs a cash flow risk, should interest rates rise in the short term. To hedge this risk, it purchases a floating to fixed interest rate swap. Under this contract, the enterprise makes fixed rate payments and receives floating rate payments that hedge the floating interest expense on the loan.

**Example 8**: On January 1st, 20X4, ABRA S.A. issues bonds in the amount of 12,000 lei with a 10% interest rate, with a maturity of two years, 20X4–20X6. ABRA's management wishes to hedge the fair value exposure and enters into a fixed to floating interest rate swap which costs 500 lei. Practically, the swap contract involves a payment (or a receipt) to (or from) the swap partner of an amount equal to 12,000 * (10% − r) lei, when short term interest rates rise above or fall below 10% (r is the short term interest rate). On December 31st, 20X4, the market interest rate is 8%. Provide the specific journal entries.

**Solution:**
The relevant journal entries are:

- on the acquisition of the swap contract:

| 500 lei | Swap contract | = | Cash | 500 lei |
|---|---|---|---|---|

- accrue the interest on the loan: 12,000,000 * 10% = 1200 lei

| 1200 lei | Interest expense | = | Loan interest payable | 1200 lei |
|---|---|---|---|---|

- account for the swap: 12,000 * (10% − 8%) = 240 lei

| 240 lei | Swap contract | = | Revenue from derivatives | 240 lei |
|---|---|---|---|---|

ABRA S.A. will receive an amount of 240 lei at the end of 20X4 from the swap partner and the profit and loss account will show a net interest expense of 11,760 lei (12,000 lei − 240 lei).

## 9.7 Conclusions

The following summary question provide an important conclusion of this chapter. The answers may help you in this respect:

## Chapter summary questions:

| | |
|---|---|
| 1. What is a financial instrument? | A **financial instrument** is a contract that gives rise simultaneously to a financial asset of one enterprise and a financial liability or equity instrument of another enterprise. |
| 2. Provide examples of financial liabilities, financial assets and equity instruments | Examples of **financial liabilities** are:<br>• bonds issued;<br>• loans to be paid;<br>• account payables<br>Examples of **financial assets** are:<br>• shares and bonds bought,<br>• loans granted<br>Examples of **equity instruments** are:<br>• shares. |
| 3. What valuation models are used for financial instruments? What are the accounting effects of each? | The following valuation models apply:<br>• **amortised cost**—the financial instrument should be valuated at each reporting date at its amortised cost and should be reviewed for impairment;<br>• **fair value through other comprehensive income**: any gain or loss should be disclosed in other comprehensive income and reviewed for impairment;<br>• **fair value through profit and loss**: any gain or loss should be disclosed in the P&L Account (no impairment review). |
| 4. What is an impaired financial instrument and how is the impairment assessed? | An impaired financial instrument (mainly loans but not exclusively) is a financial instrument which faces a quality deterioration over time. The expected credit loss model applies in three stages:<br>• Stage 1: includes **performing financial instruments**, for which a *12 month expected credit loss is assessed*;<br>• Stage 2: includes **underperforming credits**, for which expected credit losses are estimated for the entire life time of the credit;<br>• Stage 3: includes **non-performing credits** (impaired credits), which provides objective evidence of impairment, for which expected credit losses are estimated for the entire life time of the credit. |
| 5. What does hedging mean and which accounting perspectives of hedging must be considered? | **Hedging** means to mitigate risk. There are three main types of hedging: **fair value hedging, cash-flow hedging, net investment in foreign operation hedging**. In accounting, hedging is disclosed as important information about risk management activities based on financial instruments. |

**Quizzes (only one correct answer)**

1. Which of the following items are not financial instruments?
   a. Shares
   b. Bonds
   c. Account payables
   d. Equipment
2. A bank loan granted by a bank should be recognised at:
   a. Fair value
   b. Nominal value
   c. Amortised cost
   d. Present value
3. A bond, with a maturity of 3 years and an interest rate at 10%, bought by an investor in order to gain short-term profit should be recognised in the annual report of the investor at:
   a. Nominal value
   b. Amortised cost
   c. Fair value
   d. Present value
4. A bank loan with a DPD (Days-Past-Due) of 30+ is classified in stage:
   a. Stage 1: performing financial instruments
   b. Stage 2: underperforming credits
   c. Stage 3: non-performing credits
   d. Stage 4: impaired credits
5. A 2:1 convertible bond is classified by the issuer as:
   a. A liability and equity instruments
   b. A liability instrument
   c. An equity instrument
   d. An asset instrument
6. Shares acquired for trading are classified as:
   a. Non-current assets
   b. Current assets
   c. Current liabilities
   d. Equity instruments
7. Shares of a subsidiary are classified by the parent company as:
   a. Current assets
   b. Non-current assets
   c. Liability instruments

d. Equity instruments
8. An interest swap contract is classified, by the buyer, as:
   a. An asset instrument
   b. A liability instrument
   c. An equity instrument
   d. A compound instrument
9. A risk related to foreign exchange rate volatility for export trading of a multinational company might be hedged through:
   a. Forward contracts
   b. Future contracts
   c. Warrant contract
   d. Not applicable
10. Are the account receivables subject to impairment testing?
    a. Yes
    b. No
    c. Sometimes
    d. Not applicable

## Exercises

**Exercise 1**: ABC Corporation issued 4 million preference shares for 1 euro/each, no dividends to be paid. These shares will be redeemed in 2 years by issuing 5.5 million common shares, amounting to 4 million euros. The exact number of common shares to be issued shall be determined at the redemption date, based upon their fair value at the moment. How should the ABC Corporation disclose these shares in its financial statements: as a liability or as an equity instrument? Provide comments.

**Exercise 2**: Company XYZ takes a 3 year bank loan of 120,000 lei, at a 5% annual interest and 3 instalment payments (40,000 lei each). The administrative costs of initiating the loan are not material. What is the valuation method Company XYZ shall use for this loan? What are the annual effects in its financial statements, related to this loan? How would the granting bank recognise this loan?

**Exercise 3**: On November 13th, 20X7, Company WWW purchased 100 Facebook shares at 120 $ each. The purpose is to sell them at a 10% capital gain. On December 31st, 20X6, the market price of FB shares was 115 $/share. On March 10th, 20X7, Company WWW sells all of its FB shares at 138 $/share. How does Company WWW classify these shares and what is the valuation method it must use? Provide the effects in the financial statements related to these shares on December 31st, 20X6 and March 10th, 20X7.

**Exercise 4**: Bank Morgan Inc provides a five year loan of 200,000 lei to the Company Boots, with a 7% annual interest rate (equal to the effective interest rate) and 5 equal instalments. The interest is received by the end of each year, as the instalment payment. By the end of year 3, the Company Boots encounters significant financial difficulties (the market rate is 10%). The Bank Morgan Inc. estimates that further interest payments will be received and only 50,000 lei from the principal will be paid back. Provide the annual analysis for Bank Morgan Inc for this impaired loan.

**Exercise 5**: In June, 20X6, the Company ABC enters into an option contract to buy 2000 shares of the Company XYZ at 10 lei/share on August, 10th, 20X6. The purchase price of the option is 0.8 lei/each. On August 10th, 20X6, the fair value of the option is 1 lei/each and the market price of the Company XYZ share is 7 lei/share. Should Company ABC exercise its option? Provide the effects on the annual financial statements of your solution.

## References

Lien, D., The Use and Abuse of the Hedging Effectiveness Measure. *International Review of Financial Analysis*, No. 14, 2005.

Stickney C.P., Weil, R., Schipper, K., Francis, J., Financial Accounting: An Introduction to Concepts, Methods and Uses, *Cengage Learning*, 2010.

CHAPTER 10

# Closing Procedures, Financial Statements and Financial Analysis

*Mădălina Dumitru and Adriana Duțescu*

*Learning objectives:*

- *Understanding and applying the closing procedures*
- *Understanding and applying the adjustments and estimates*
- *Understanding the importance of the financial statements*
- *Training the ability to prepare the financial statements*
- *Understanding and applying the main financial ratios*
- *Understanding and applying horizontal analysis, vertical analysis and benchmarking analysis*
- *Using ratios to support management decisions*

## 10.1 CLOSING PROCEDURES

The objective of financial reporting is to provide financial information that is useful to the decision-making process of various stakeholders. In order to accomplish this objective, the financial statements must present the assets, liabilities, owner's equity, expenses and revenues at their correct values. Sometimes, before the preparation of the financial statements, some closing procedures must be made.

The closing procedures can be structured as it follows:

- Establish the trial balance before the physical checking of inventory;
- Provide the general account inventory of the assets and liabilities;
- Register the adjustments;

- Provide the trial balance after the inventory count;
- Determine the profit or loss, profit distribution and loss financing;
- Provide the final trial balance, at the Balance Sheet date.

**The trial balance before the physical checking of inventory** includes all the assets, liabilities, owner's equity, expenses and revenues, as they result after the registration in accounting of all the transactions which occur during the year.

**The general account inventory of the assets and liabilities** represents the closure procedures during which a team of employees establishes the net realisable value of the assets and liabilities at the Balance Sheet date. The net realisable value is determined by the inventory team through direct observation (counting, measuring etc.) in the case of non-current assets, inventories and cash through confirmation from third parties (for the liabilities and receivables). The net realisable value on the inventory date is estimated according to the market price, the asset's usefulness and its place. The value established is called *inventory value*. The net realisable value is compared with the value from the trial balance before the account inventory (the cost value) and the differences are registered when needed. The differences can be classified as it follows:

- Quantitative differences, which might be:
  - Positive: the quantity established during the account inventory is higher than the quantity in the trial balance;
  - Negative: the quantity established during the account inventory is lower than the quantity in the trial balance;
  - All the quantitative differences are registered in accounting. Surpluses determined during the physical inventory are registered as entries in accounting, while shortages are registered as exits;
- Differences in value, which might be:
  - Positive: the net realisable value is higher than the cost value (the value in the trial balance);
  - Negative: the net realisable value is lower than the cost value;
  - Only the negative differences in value are registered in accounting. They are registered as impairments.

The net realisable value is the maximum of the fair value less costs to sell and the value in use.

**The adjustment transactions** refer to items or transactions such as: inventory, accruals and prepayments, interest, depreciation, bad debts and allowances for receivables/debtors. They are explained in detail in Sect. 10.2.

**The trial balance after the account inventory** is prepared after the adjustment transactions are recorded in accounting, based on specific journal entries. This approach is mainly used for establishing the profit or loss of the year.

**The profit or loss of the year** is established based on the accounting profit or loss. The accounting profit or loss amount is computed as the difference between the total revenues and the total expenses accrued during the year. The accounting profit or loss is the starting point for computing the taxable profit. The taxable profit is determined as the accounting profit or loss plus the non-deductible expenses minus the non-taxable revenues. Based on the tax profit, the income tax is computed and registered. The difference between the accounting profit or loss and the income tax represents the net profit or loss for the year. The net profit can be distributed to the following destinations: legal reserves, other types of reserves, retained earnings, dividends, etc. The loss can be covered from the retained earnings or other sources during the following year(s).

**The next step is to provide the final trial balance, at the Balance Sheet date**, as a preparation of the Balance Sheet and the other Financial Statements, after the net profit or loss of the year is computed. A detailed example of the connections between the flow of the accounting information, the trial balance and the financial statements is provided in Chapter 4.

## 10.2 Adjustments and Estimates

The main possible post-trial balance adjustments include:

- Inventory adjustments;
- Accruals and prepayments;
- Depreciation and amortisation;
- Bad debts and allowances for receivables/debtors.

All these adjustments have an impact on both the statement of profit or loss and on the statement of financial position.

## 10.2.1 Inventories Adjustments

The inventory adjustments can be positive or negative in value or in quantity. The minuses in value are recorded as impairments. **IAS 2 Inventories** require inventories to be included in the Statement of Financial Position (the other name for the Balance Sheet) at the lower value of cost and net realisable value. It is necessary to compute the closing inventory figure before processing the adjustment. The impairment is the difference between the cost and the net realisable value.

**Example 1**: After the account inventory at the company SVD, the following anomalies were established (Table 10.1).

The cost before the account inventory of the raw materials B was 6945 lei (463 pieces at 15 lei per piece) and of the finished goods A was 1542 lei (10 pieces at 154.2 lei). It is estimated that the unitary selling expenses for the finished goods A could be 1 lei.

**Required:** Prepare the necessary adjustments at the end of the year.
**Solution**:
For raw materials A, there is a quantitative surplus of 460 lei to be recorded. The journal entry should be:

| 460 lei | Raw materials | = | Raw materials expenses | 460 lei |
|---|---|---|---|---|

For the finished goods B a quantitative shortage is recorded. The journal entry should be:

| 3500 lei | Differences in finished goods | = | Finished goods | 3500 lei |
|---|---|---|---|---|

**Table 10.1** Anomalies established

| Inventories | | Current price | Surpluses | | | Shortages | | |
|---|---|---|---|---|---|---|---|---|
| Code | Name | | Q | Price | Value | Q | Price | Value |
| 31 | Raw materials A | | 10 | 46 | 460 | | | |
| 32 | Raw materials B | 16 | | | | | | |
| 33 | Finished goods A | 155 | | | | | | |
| 34 | Finished goods B | | | | | 2 | 1750 | 3500 |

*Source* The authors

For raw materials B, nothing should be recorded, because of the principle "the lower of carrying amount and net realizable value". Thus, raw materials B will be disclosed in the balance sheet at the carrying amount (of 6945 lei).

The net realisable value for the finished goods A is to be computed.

Net realisable value for the finished goods A = Estimated selling price − Estimated selling expenses = 155 − 1 = 154 lei

The net realisable value is lower than the cost. In this case, an impairment should be recorded in accounting.

Impairment for the finished goods A = (154.2 − 154) * 10 pieces = 2 lei

The journal entry should be:

| 2 lei | Expenses with inventories impairments | = | Finished goods impairments | 2 lei |

### 10.2.2 Accruals and Prepayments

We apply the accruals concept according to IFRSs and Romanian Accounting Standards. This means that the Income Statement (or the Profit and Loss Account) has to include the expenses accrued in the period, whether or not they have been paid. If an expense was paid in advance or a revenue was collected in advance, but they refer to the future periods (financial years), they should be included in the Statement of Financial Position as a current asset or as a current liability, where applicable.

Unpaid balances relating to the period should be included in the Statement of Financial Position as current liabilities. Uncollected balances are presented as current assets in the statement of financial position.

**Example 2**:

The following transactions were registered during the year 20X8:

- Subscriptions of journals paid in 20X8 of 7000 lei, of which paid in advance for January, 20X9 of 1000 lei;
- Subsidies received from the Government: 10,000 lei, of which 30% apply to the year 20X9;
- Rent received in 20X8 in the amount of 20,000 lei, of which rent of 2500 lei was received in advance for January, 20X9.

Provide the journal entries.

**Solution:**
The journal entries are the following:

a) The subscription paid in advance:

| 7000 lei | % | = | Account Payables | 7000 lei |
|---|---|---|---|---|
| 6000 lei | Expenses with subscriptions | | | |
| 1000 lei | Prepaid expenses | | | |

b) Subsidies received from the Government:

| 10,000 lei | Bank account | = | % | 10,000 lei |
|---|---|---|---|---|
| | | | Revenues from subsidies | 7000 lei |
| | | | Deferred income | 3000 lei |

c) Rent received

| 20,000 lei | Bank account | = | % | 20,000 lei |
|---|---|---|---|---|
| | | | Revenues from rent | 17,500 lei |
| | | | Deferred income | 2500 lei |

The extracts from the Income Statement and the Statement of Financial Position are presented in Table 10.2.

**Table 10.2** Extract from the Financial Statements

| Income statement | Lei |
|---|---|
| Revenues from subsidies | 7000 |
| Revenues from rent | 17,500 |
| Expenses with subscriptions | (6000) |
| **Statement of financial position** | **Lei** |
| Current assets | |
| Prepayments | 1000 |
| Current liabilities | |
| Accruals and deferred income | 5500 |

*Source* The authors

### 10.2.3 Bad Debts and Allowance for Receivables/Debtors

Writing off a **bad debt** means transferring the balance of the receivables to the **Income Statement** as an expense, because the balance has proved irrecoverable. In this case, the entire value is recorded as an expense and nothing will be recovered from the customer.

There are cases in which the company estimates that it will partially recover the balance of the receivables. In this case, an **allowance for receivables/debtors** is set up in order to include a more realistic value for receivables in the Statement of Financial Position. The receivables are not written-off, as the balance is left in the Receivables Ledger and collection is expected. The collection procedures continue, but for Balance Sheet purposes the receivables are valued at the amount which is expected to be recovered.

**Example 3**:

The trial balance at the beginning of the year 20X8 is presented in Table 10.3.

This means that at the beginning of the year it was estimated that 10% of the value of the receivables would not be recovered. In this case, the Statement of Financial Position shows in Table 10.4.

Only the last figure (90,000 lei) will appear on the face of the Statement of Financial Position.

Let us say that at the end of the year 20X8 it is estimated that only 75% of the receivables will be collected. In this case, the allowance is increased to 25,000 lei (100,000 lei * 25%). Thus, the amount of the increase will be 15,000 lei (25,000 lei vs 10,000 lei). The journal entry will be:

| 15,000 lei | "Expenses with allowance for receivables" | = | "Allowance for receivables" | 15,000 lei |
|---|---|---|---|---|

Table 10.3  Extract from the Trial Balance

| Trial balance | Dr (lei) | Cr (lei) |
|---|---|---|
| Account receivables | 100,000 | |
| Allowance for receivables/debtors | | 10,000 |

*Source* The authors

**Table 10.4** Extract from the Statement of Financial Position

| Statement of financial position | Lei |
|---|---|
| Account receivables | 100,000 |
| Less: Allowance for receivables | 10,000 |
| **Account receivables for balance sheet disclosure** | **90,000** |

*Source* The authors

**Table 10.5** Extract from the Financial Statements

| Income statement | Lei |
|---|---|
| Expenses with allowance for receivables | 15,000 |
| **Statement of financial position** | **Lei** |
| Account receivables | 100,000 |
| Less: Allowance for receivables | 25,000 |
| **Account receivables for statement of financial position disclosure** | **75,000** |

*Source* The authors

This will impact the financial statements as shown in Table 10.5.

In some cases, a bad debt is recovered during future accounting periods. Let's assume that our company recovers the value of the account receivables in 20X9. In this case, the journal entries will be:

The cash collected:

| 100,000 lei | "Bank Account" | = | "Account receivables" | 100,000 lei |
|---|---|---|---|---|

Allowance for receivables is written off:

| 25,000 lei | "Allowance for receivables" | = | "Revenues from allowance for receivables" | 25,000 lei |
|---|---|---|---|---|

The extracts from the financial statements in 20X9 are in Table 10.6. Other specific examples are provided in Chapter 7.

### *10.2.4 Provisions*

Provisions are recognised in accordance with **IAS 37 Provisions, contingent liabilities and contingent assets**. They are recorded in the end

Table 10.6 Extract from the Financial Statements

| Income Statement | Lei |
|---|---|
| Revenues from allowance for receivables | 25,000 |
| **Statement of financial position** | **Lei** |
| Account receivables | 0 |

*Source* The authors

of the accounting period, as estimates of possible payments in future periods, such as: penalties, warranties, litigations, etc. In order to record a provision, the following three conditions should be met:

- "an entity has a present obligation (legal or constructive) as a result of a past event;
- it is probable that an outflow of resources embodying economic benefits will be required to settle the obligation;
- an outflow of future economic benefits is to be expected in this circumstance; a reliable estimate can be made of the amount of the obligation" (IAS 37. par. 14).

**Example 4:**

Company SVD is extracting minerals from a country in which there is no legislation regarding the obligation to restore the site at the end of the operation. During the year 20X8, the government drafts legislation which will affect the company SVD. The accountants estimate that the company will have to pay 1,000,000 lei to restore the site at the end of its activity.

As all of the conditions required by IAS 37 are met, the company will have to register a provision in 20X8:

| 1,000,000 lei | Non-current asset | = | Provisions for risks and charges | 1,000,000 lei |
|---|---|---|---|---|

More examples on provision can be found in Chapter 7.

### 10.2.5 Exchange Differences

The exchange differences are differences which result from the volatilities in the exchange rate, between the date at which a transaction is recorded and the year-end or between the moment receivables or payables are recorded and the moment of cash-in or cash-out. Exchange differences can be positive or negative, as it follows:

- Positive exchange differences:
  - Assets and receivables: when an increase in the exchange rate between the moment in which the transaction was recorded and the end of the year occurred;
  - Liabilities: when a decrease in the exchange rate between the moment in which the transaction was registered and the end of the year occurred;
- Negative exchange differences:
  - Assets and receivables: when a decrease in the exchange rate between the moment in which the transaction was registered and the end of the year occurred;
  - Liabilities: when an increase in the exchange rate between the moment in which the transaction was registered and the end of the year occurred.

**Example 5:**

The Company SVD registered the following transactions in accounting:

a) It purchased a non-current asset from Germany on November 11th, 20X8. The cost of the asset was 10,000 EUR and the exchange rate was 4.69 lei/EUR;
b) It charged services to a company in Italy on December 20th, 20X8. The value of the services was 2000 EUR and the exchange rate was 4.65 lei/EUR;
c) At the end of the year, the company had 5000 EUR in its bank account. The exchange rate was 4.72 lei/EUR (at the computation of the carrying amount).

The exchange rate at the end of the year was 4.67 lei/EUR. We assume that the amount for the non-current asset was not paid and the value of the services was not collected before the end of the year.

**Required:** present the effect of these transactions on the financial statements at the end of the year.

## Solution:

a) Exchange rate differences for the liability
Exchange rate differences = 10,000 EUR * (4.69 − 4.67) = 200 lei
This is a favourable exchange rate difference because the exchange rate decreased between the moment of the registration of the liability and the end of the year. This means that less will be paid in lei than expected when the transaction was registered. The journal entry is as follows:

| 200 lei | Account Payables | = | Gains from foreign exchange differences | 200 lei |
|---|---|---|---|---|

The impact will be shown on the financial statements as in Table 10.7.

b) Exchange rate differences for the account receivables
Exchange rate differences = 2000 EUR * (4.67 − 4.65) = 40 lei
This is a favourable exchange rate difference because the exchange rate increased between the moment of the registration of the receivables and the end of the year. This means that we will collect more than we expected when we registered the transaction. The journal entry is as follows:

| 40 lei | Account receivables | = | Revenues from exchange differences | 40 lei |
|---|---|---|---|---|

The impact will be shown on the financial statements in Table 10.8.

c) Exchange rate differences for the cash in the bank
Exchange rate differences = 5000 * (4.72 − 4.67) = 250 lei.
This is an unfavourable exchange rate difference because the exchange rate decreased between the moment of the registration of the receivables and the end of the year. This means that we have less

**Table 10.7** Extract from the Financial Statements

| Income statement | Lei |
|---|---|
| Revenues from exchange differences | 200 |
| **Statement of financial position** | **Lei** |
| Account payables (10,000 * 4.67) | 46,700 |

*Source* The authors

**Table 10.8** Extract from the Financial Statements

| Income statement | Lei |
|---|---|
| Revenues from exchange differences | 40 |
| **Statement of financial position** | **Lei** |
| Account receivables (2000 * 4.67) | 9340 |

*Source* The authors

**Table 10.9** Extract from the Financial Statements

| Income statement | Lei |
|---|---|
| Losses from foreign exchange differences | 250 |
| **Statement of financial position** | **Lei** |
| Cash in bank (5000 * 4.67) | 23,350 |

*Source* The authors

money than we expected when we registered the transaction. The journal entry is as follows:

| 250 lei "Losses from foreign exchange differences" = "Bank Account" 250 lei |
|---|

The impact will be shown on the financial statements in Table 10.9.

## 10.3 The Final Statements and Financial Analysis

The financial analysis is an important business tool for all stakeholders, offering a concentrated and integrated image about how an entity performed (or has not performed) within a specific timeframe, compared to the industry, compared to the main competitors or in relation to other relevant benchmarks. Classical methods of financial analysis include horizontal analysis, vertical analysis and benchmark analysis.

One method commonly used is the horizontal analysis. Financial statements offer data and information for at least two subsequent years, therefore a **horizontal analysis** (or **time-series analysis**) might be provided (how much has the operating profit increased?; how high is the reduction in the cost of sales?; etc.). Horizontal analysis consists of computing the monetary unit amount of change from the base (early) period to the later period and dividing it by the base period amount. A percentage value is obtained.

**Vertical analysis** provides the link between different items of the same financial statement and the weight of each separate item into the total or into a specific item. For example, it shows the percentage of non-current assets into the total of the asset's value, or the percentage of gross margin in total revenues.

**Benchmarking analysis** represents the comparison of a business entity with its peers, with the average of the industry or to the settled business standards. This type of analysis offers the positioning of the company in relation to different benchmarks (the leader of the market, other competitors, etc.).

**Cross-sectional analysis** involves comparison of different firms' financial ratios at the same point in time.

In order to have an overall picture of a company, some would prefer a combination of different ratios to give a complete image of the business potential. Major areas of interest are expressed subsequently:

- *Liquidity ratios*—measure the firm's ability to satisfy short-term obligations as they come due;
- *Leverage (financing) ratios*—measure the firm's ability to pay its long-term debt;
- *Profitability ratios*—shows the firm's ability to generate profit from its activity;
- *Efficiency (activity) ratios*—measure the speed with which various accounts are converted into sales or cash or the efficiency of different layers of business;
- *Market ratios*—give insights on how investors value the firm.

### 10.3.1 Example of Ratio Analysis

Financial analysis is an important decision tool for creditors, investors, managers and the general public, expressing ways to evaluate companies, based on financial statements. Financial analysis involves methods of calculating and interpreting financial ratios, their analysis and firm's performance's assessment.

As there are so many variations in the methods of calculating ratios, it is extremely important to practice a useful and meaningful layout. The presentation format must include, at a minimum:

- the name of each ratio;
- the formula in words;
- the workings to show how the formula has been applied;
- the value of the ratio;
- a narrative comment.

In the following example, information is provided about a company which buys and sells television and video equipment. Data is given for the current year, in the first pair of columns and there are comparative figures for the previous year in the last pair of columns. Ratios are calculated for two years, as an indication of trends. Tentative comments are provided regarding the possible interpretation of the resulting figures.

**Example 6**:

The following financial statements should be analysed (Tables 10.10 and 10.11):

**Table 10.10** Income Statement for the year which ended on December 31st, 20X2 Peter (Television) plc

| Items | Year 20X2 | | Year 20X1 | |
|---|---|---|---|---|
| | Million lei | Million lei | Million lei | Million lei |
| Revenue | | 720 | | 600 |
| Cost of goods sold | | (432) | | (348) |
| Gross profit | | 288 | | 252 |
| Distribution costs | (72) | | (54) | |
| Administrative expenses | (87) | | (81) | |
| | | (159) | | (135) |
| Operating profit | | 129 | | 117 |
| Interest payable | | (24) | | (24) |
| Profit before taxation | | 105 | | 93 |
| Taxation | | 42 | | 37 |
| Profit for the period (for ordinary equity holders) | | 63 | | 56 |

*Source* The authors

**Table 10.11** Statement of the Financial Position as of December 31st, 20X2

| Items | Year 20X2 | | Year 20X1 | |
|---|---|---|---|---|
| | Million lei | Million lei | Million lei | Million lei |
| *Non-current (fixed) assets* | | | | |
| Real-estate and buildings | 600 | | 615 | |
| Plant and equipment | <u>555</u> | | <u>503</u> | |
| | 1155 | | 1118 | |
| *Current assets* | | | | |
| Inventories (stock) | 115 | | 82 | |
| Account receivables | 89 | | 61 | |
| Prepayments | 10 | | 9 | |
| Bank | <u>6</u> | | <u>46</u> | |
| | 220 | | 198 | |
| *Current liabilities* | | | | |
| Trade payables (creditors) | (45) | | (30) | |
| Taxation | (21) | | (19) | |
| Accruals | <u>(29)</u> | | <u>(25)</u> | |
| | (95) | | (74) | |
| Net current assets | 125 | | 124 | |
| | 1280 | | 1242 | |
| 6% debentures | | (<u>400</u>) | | (<u>400</u>) |
| | | <u><u>880</u></u> | | <u><u>842</u></u> |
| Ordinary shares of 1 lei each | | 500 | | 500 |
| Retained earnings | | <u>380</u> | | <u>342</u> |
| Share capital and reserves | | <u><u>880</u></u> | | <u><u>842</u></u> |

*Source* The authors

**Table 10.12** Notes to the Financial Statements: Reconciliation of movements in equity

|  | Million lei |
|---|---|
| Share capital and reserves at the end of year 1 | 842 |
| Less dividend paid in respect to year 1 | (25) |
| Add profit for year 2 | 63 |
| Share capital and reserves at the end of year 2 | 880 |

*Source* The authors

**Extract from directors' report**

The directors propose a dividend of 0.06 lei per share for the year 20X2 (Year 1: 0.05 lei) (Table 10.12).

**Share price information**

When investors evaluate the share price, they take the most up-to-date price available. In order to compare financial ratios, it is useful to take the share prices immediately after the announcement of the Financial Statements (that is at the end of February or beginning of March of each year). This represents the market's opinion before the accounting information has become out-dated. In our example, we will consider the market price on March 1st, as follows:

| Market price at 1 March Year 2 | 0.202 lei |
|---|---|
| Market price at 1 March Year 3 | 0.277 lei |

The following examples present this information in a set of ratio calculations for Peter (Television) plc, each example covers one of the main topics explained earlier. The calculations are given first for the more recent year 20X2, followed by the comparative figures for year 20X1. A commentary is provided for each exhibit.

## a) Liquidity and working capital ratios (Table 10.13)

**Table 10.13** Workings for liquidity and working capital ratios

| Ratio | | | Formula | | |
|---|---|---|---|---|---|
| 1. Current ratio | | | Current assets/Current liabilities | | |
| Year 20X2 | | | Year 20X1 | | |
| Solution | | Result | Solution | | Result |
| 220/95 | | 2.32 | 198/74 | | 2.68 |
| 2. Acid test | | | (Current assets − Inventories)/Current liabilities | | |
| Year 20X2 | | | Year 20X1 | | |
| Solution | | Result | Solution | | Result |
| (220 − 115)/95 | | 1.11 | (198 − 82)/74 | | 1.57 |
| 3. Inventory period | | | Average inventories (stock) held × 365 / Cost of goods sold | | |
| Year 20X2 | | | Year 20X1 | | |
| Solution | | Result | Solution | | Result |
| (115 + 82)/2 × 365/432 | | 83.2 days | (*82 + 82)/2 × 365/348 | | 86 days |
| 4. Account receivables' collection period (trade debtors) | | | Account receivables (trade debtors) × 365 / Credit sales (revenue) | | |
| Year 20X2 | | | Year 20X1 | | |
| Solution | | Result | Solution | | Result |
| 89 × 365/720 | | 45.12 days | 61 × 365/600 | | 37.11 days |
| 5. Account payables' payment period (trade creditors) | | | Trade payables (trade creditors) × 365 / Credit purchases | | |
| Year 20X2 | | | Year 20X1 | | |
| Solution | | Result | Solution | | Result |
| 45 × 365/(432 + 115 − 82) | | 35.32 days | 30 × 365/(348 + 82 − *82) | | 31.47 days |
| 6. Cash operating cycle | | | Inventory period + Customers collection period − Suppliers payment period | | |
| 20X2 | | | 20X1 | | |
| Solution | | Results | Solution | | Results |
| 83.2 days + 45.12 days − 35.32 days | | 93 days | 86 days + 37.11 days − 31.47 days | | 91.64 days |

*Note* *It is assumed that the opening inventories are the same as the closing inventories
*Source* The authors

**Comments: The current ratio** measures the ability of the current assets to cover the current liabilities. In other words, it represents the ability of current assets to be converted into cash to pay current liabilities on time. A high or increasing figure is good, but it should be further investigated whether this is due to the high levels of inventories or unused cash. The appropriate value is considered 2, but 1.5 is also accepted. The values should be judged considering the market in which the company is active and the business environment. For instance, a supermarket will have a low current ratio because it has a low level of account receivables and high levels of trade payables.

The **acid test** shows whether the company has sufficient receivables and cash to cover current liabilities. The appropriate value should be included in the range from 1 to 0.7. There are markets in which it is normal to obtain a lower figure (such as the supermarkets).

An increasing number of days for the **inventory period** year on year is usually a bad sign because it means that the inventories are sold less quickly and generate higher costs for the company. There are significant differences in the value of the ratio from one company to another. For instance, a bakery will have an inventory turnover period of 1–2 days, while a construction company will have a period expressed in months.

The **receivables collection period** should be compared with the number of days of money collection, established pursuant to the contracts and with the values for the previous year. A decreasing value is normally a good sign, meaning that cash is received quicker than it is in our example.

The **payables payment period** represents the number of days in which an invoice is paid. It represents a source of free finance funds. Thus, a high value is a good sign, as is the case in our example. The figure can also be compared with the receivables collection period.

Average values should be used for the inventories, receivables and payables for a greater accuracy.

**The cash operating cycle** represents the average number of days of a cash shortage. The longer this period is, the worse it is for the company because it must cover accumulating days of shortages from other financial sources.

For the company in the example, the current ratio has fallen over the period while the acid test ratio remains constant. The ratios appear to be relatively high and are probably still within acceptable ranges (although this needs to be confirmed by comparison with industry standards). One cause of the relatively high current ratio at the start and end of the period appears to be in the combination of the inventory period and the customers' collection period compared to the account payables' payment period. The period of credit taken by customers has increased and this should be investigated as a matter of urgency. There is a marginal decrease in the stock holding period, but it remains relatively lengthy compared to the creditors' payment period. The acid test adapts correspondingly because there is an increase in the number of customer days for payment and a similar increase in the number of supplier days for payment.

b) **Gearing (leverage) ratios (Table 10.14)**

Table 10.14 Workings for gearing (leverage) ratios

| Ratio | | | Formula | | |
|---|---|---|---|---|---|
| 1. Debt/equity ratio | | | (Long-term liabilities + Preference share capital × 100)/(Equity share capital + Reserves) | | |
| Year 20X2 | | | Year 20X1 | | |
| Solution | Result | | Solution | | Result |
| 400 × 100/880 | 45.45% | | 400 × 100/842 | | 47.51% |
| 2. Interest cover | | | Operating profit (before interest and tax)/Interest payable | | |
| Year 20X2 | | | Year 20X1 | | |
| Solution | Result | | Solution | | Result |
| 129/24 | 5.38 times | | 117/24 | | 4.88 times |
| 3. Debt/Total assets (gearing ratio) | | | Total debts/Total assets | | |
| Year 20X2 | | | Year 20X1 | | |
| Solution | Result | | Solution | | Result |
| 495/1375 | 0.36 | | 474/1316 | | 0.36 |

*Source* The authors

**Comments:** The **gearing ratio** shows the degree of risk associated with the company and the sensitivity of earnings and dividends to changes in profitability and activity level. High gearing indicates a greater insolvency risk for the company.

**The interest cover** shows the ability of the profit to cover the interest. A low figure can show that the company is having difficulties paying the interest and, thus, satisfying the needs of other stakeholders (such as the shareholders). The appropriate value is at least two, but it depends very much on the industry, business models and other variables.

**The debt** reflects the percentage of assets financed through debts. The higher the debt, the riskier the company is considered. In our example, this ratio is stable. For more details on this, a benchmark analysis should be provided.

Based on the previous example, the gearing in the Balance Sheet has remained almost constant and the interest cover has increased marginally. The relative stability of the position indicates that there is no cause for concern, but the ratios should be compared with those of similar companies in the industry.

c) **Profitability ratios (Table** 10.15**)**

**Table 10.15** Workings for profitability ratios

| Ratio | | | Formula | | |
|---|---|---|---|---|---|
| 1. Operating profit margin | | | (Operating profit (before interest and tax) × 100)/Sales (revenue) | | |
| Year 20X2 | | | Year 20X1 | | |
| Solution | | Result | Solution | | Result |
| 129 × 100/720 | | 17.92% | 117 × 100/600 | | 19.5% |
| 2. Gross profit margin | | | (Gross profit × 100%)/Sales (revenue) | | |
| Year 20X2 | | | Year 20X1 | | |
| Solution | | Result | Solution | | Result |
| 288 × 100/720 | | 40% | 252 × 100/600 | | 42% |
| 3. Total assets usage | | | Sales (revenue)/Total assets | | |
| Year 20X2 | | | Year 20X1 | | |
| Solution | | Result | Solution | | Result |
| 720/(1155 + 220) | | 0.52 times | 600/(1118 + 198) | | 0.46 times |

*Source* The authors

**Comments:** The **operating profit margin** should be constant from one year to another. It can be compared with the gross profit margin and with the previous year's figures. The type of costs (variable or fixed) should be considered.

The **total assets usage** shows how well the assets were used. The higher the figure, the better it is for the company.

The company in our case study experienced a slight decrease in the operating profit margin. The gross profit margin fell by a similar amount, which suggests that the price charged for goods and services is not keeping pace with costs increases. The company should look carefully at either increasing prices or how to more effectively control the costs of goods sold. Despite these figures, the values registered during the periods analysed remained at satisfactory levels. The total assets' usage improved during the analysed period.

d) **Efficiency (activity) ratios (Table 10.16)**

**Table 10.16** Workings for efficiency (activity) ratios

| Ratio | Formula | | | |
|---|---|---|---|---|
| 1. Return on shareholders' equity (ROE) | (Profit after tax for ordinary equity holders x 100)/(Share capital + Reserves) | | | |
| Year 20X2 | | | Year 20X1 | |
| Solution | Result | Solution | | Result |
| 63 × 100/880 | 7.16% | 56 × 100/842 | | 6.65% |
| 2. Return on capital employed (ROCE) | (Operating profit x 100)/(Total assets − Current liabilities) | | | |
| Year 20X2 | | Year 20X1 | | |
| Solution | Result | Solution | | Result |
| 129 * 100/1280 | 10.08% | 117 * 100/1242 | | 9.42% |
| 3. Non-current assets turnover | Sales (revenue)/Non-current assets | | | |
| Year 20X2 | | Year 20X1 | | |
| Solution | Result | Solution | | Result |
| 720/1155 | 0.62 times | 600/1118 | | 0.54 times |

*Source* The authors

**Comments:** The **return on capital employed** for the year should be compared to the previous year's figure, a target, the cost of borrowing (i.e. the interest rate) and the values obtained by other companies in the same industry. This will show how efficient a business was in using its resources.

The **non-current asset turnover** shows how well the assets were used. The higher the figure, the better it is for the company.

**The return on shareholders' equity** and **the return on capital employed** both show an improvement compared to the previous year. This is due to an improvement in the way the assets are used (total assets and non-current assets) which compensate the fall in the operating profit margin.

e) **Market (investor) ratios (or Stock Exchange ratios) (Table 10.17)**

Table 10.17 Workings for market (investor) ratios

| *Ratio* | | | *Formula* | | |
|---|---|---|---|---|---|
| **1. Earnings per share (EPS)** | | | Profit after tax for ordinary equity holders/Number of issued ordinary shares | | |
| Year 20X2 | | | Year 20X1 | | |
| Solution | | Result | Solution | | Result |
| 63/500 | | 0.126 lei | 56/500 | | 0.112 lei |
| **2. Price earnings ratio (PER)** | | | Share price/Earnings per share | | |
| Year 20X2 | | | Year 20X1 | | |
| Solution | | Result | Solution | | Result |
| 0.277/0.126 | | 2.1985 | 0.202/0.112 | | 1.8036 |
| **3. Dividend per share (DPS)** | | | Dividend of the period/Number of issued ordinary shares | | |
| Year 20X2 | | | Year 20X1 | | |
| Solution | | Result | Solution | | Result |
| 30/500 | | 0.06 lei | 25/500 | | 0.05 lei |
| **4. Dividend cover (pay-out ratio)** | | | Earnings per share/Dividend per share | | |
| Year 20X2 | | | Year 20X1 | | |
| Solution | | Result | Solution | | Result |
| 0.126/0.06 | | 2.1 times | 0.112/0.05 | | 2.24 times |
| **5. Dividend yield (DY)** | | | (Dividend per share x 100)/Share price | | |
| Year 20X2 | | | Year 20X1 | | |
| Solution | | Result | Solution | | Result |
| 0.06 * 100%/0.277 | | 2.17% | 0.05 * 100%/0.202 | | 2.48% |

*Source* The authors

**Comments: Earnings per share** means the level of the net profit on per share basis is sensitive to both the changes in net profits and capital, which occurred during the year. As such, it is considered by some analysists to be a better measure of the financial performance of the entity than the profit itself. Also, it is a key stock exchange ratio which can be used to compare companies. The EPS have increased over the period, indicating improved performance.

**The dividend cover** has fallen marginally but is still covered more than twice. This marginal decrease in the dividend cover is caused by the increase of the dividend per share from 0.05 lei to 0.06 lei. **The dividend yield** has fallen, despite the increased dividend per share, because the market price has risen. The fall in yield may not be significant if it reflects a general trend in the market where, possibly, all shares have risen in price over the year. To be able to go deeper into the ratios, analysis requires comparative figures from the industry and from the market as a whole.

In conclusion, after analysing the above ratios, one can say that the strategy of the company is sufficient and the company has a stable financial position.

## 10.4 Conclusions

The following summary questions are providing conclusions for the topics within this chapter:

**Chapter summary questions:**

| | |
|---|---|
| 1. What are closing procedures? | Closing procedures are:<br>• The establishment of the trial balance before the physical inventory;<br>• The general account inventory/year-end stock-take of the assets and liabilities;<br>• Records of the adjustments;<br>• The establishment of the trial balance after the inventory count;<br>• The determination of the profit or loss, profit distribution and loss financing;<br>• The establishment of the final trial balance, at the balance sheet date. |

| | | |
|---|---|---|
| 2. What are the main possible post-trial balance adjustments? | The main possible post-trial balance adjustments are:<br>• Inventory adjustments;<br>• Accruals and prepayments;<br>• Depreciation and amortisation;<br>• Bad debts and allowances from receivables/debtors. | |
| 3. How can the inventory adjustment be classified? | The inventory adjustments can be:<br>• Positive or negative;<br>• Quantitative differences or value differences. | |
| 4. Which inventory adjustments are registered in accounting? | All the quantitative differences are registered in accounting. The surpluses noticed at the inventory are registered as entries in accounting, while the shortages are registered as exits. Only the negative differences in value are registered in accounting. They are registered as impairments. | |
| 5. How can the ratios be classified? | The ratios can be classified as follows:<br>• Liquidity ratios;<br>• Leverage (financing) ratios;<br>• Profitability ratios;<br>• Efficiency (activity) ratios;<br>• Market ratios. | |
| 6. Which are the most important benchmarks? | The results obtained can be compared with a peer entity, leader of the market or industry averages. | |

## Quizzes (only one correct answer)

1. A company's inventories on December 1st, 20X4, were 15 pieces at 3 lei per piece. The following transactions were recorded:
   December 3: 5 pieces sold for 4.30 lei/piece
   December 8: 10 pieces bought for 3.50 lei/piece
   December 12: 8 pieces sold for 4.00 lei/piece
   On December 31st it is estimated that the pieces in stock will be sold for 4.2 lei/piece and the necessary expenses of the sale will be 0.45 lei/piece. If the company applies the FIFO, the carrying amount of the inventories on December 31st and the net realisable value are:

   | | Carrying amount | Net realisable value |
   |---|---|---|
   | a. | 31.5 | 48 |
   | b. | 36 | 50.4 |

|   | Carrying amount | Net realisable value |
|---|---|---|
| c. | 39 | 39 |
| d. | 41 | 45 |

2. The variation of raw materials during December is as follows: December 1st, 20X2, initial balance 50 pieces × 20 lei/piece; Inputs: December 4th, 20X2, 60 pieces × 22 lei/piece, December 18th, 20X2, 40 pieces × 19 lei/piece; Outputs: December 12th, 20X2 65 pieces, December 20th, 20X2, 50 pieces. The net realisable value established on December 31st, 20X2, for this type is 19.50 lei/piece. What is the value of the outputs on December 20th, 20X2, for this type of raw material and what is the value of the adjustment if the company uses FIFO:

|   | Value of the outputs | Value of the adjustment |
|---|---|---|
| a. | 960 | 17.50 |
| b. | 1085 | 0 |
| c. | 980 | 18.75 |
| d. | 1025 | 35 |

3. During the year 20X9, company A acquired a mine at a cost of 6,000,000 lei. In addition, when all the metal has been extracted (estimated five years' time), the company will face estimated costs for landscaping the area affected by the mining with a present value of 500,000 lei. How should the 500,000 future costs be recognized in the financial statements?
   a. Provision 500,000 lei and 500,000 lei capitalised as part of cost of mine
   b. Provision 500,000 lei and 500,000 lei as part of operating cost
   c. Accrual 100,000 lei per annum for next five years
   d. Should not be recognized as no cost has yet occurred
4. An entity has an average operating profit margin of 24% and an average asset turnover of 0.70. These values are similar to the averages of the industry. The entity is likely to be:
   a. An architectural practice
   b. A supermarket
   c. A real estate agent
   d. A manufacturer

5. Extracts from the financial statements of company A are as follows:

| Profit or loss statement | | Statement of financial position | |
|---|---|---|---|
| Items | Amounts | Items | Amounts |
| Sales | 500 | Owner's equity | 5000 |
| Gross profit | 350 | Reserves | 1000 |
| Operating profit | 250 | Retained earnings | 2000 |
| Finance costs | 20 | Loan notes | 1000 |
| Profit before tax | 230 | Current liabilities | 5000 |
| Income tax | 20 | Current assets | 4000 |

What is the current ratio?
a. 0.50
b. 0.80
c. 0.70
d. 1.00

6. Extracts from the financial statements of company A are as follows:

| Profit or loss statement | | Statement of financial position | |
|---|---|---|---|
| Items | Amounts | Items | Amounts |
| Sales | 500 | Owner's equity | 5000 |
| Gross profit | 350 | Reserves | 1000 |
| Operating profit | 250 | Retained earnings | 2000 |
| Finance costs | 20 | Loan notes | 1000 |
| Profit before tax | 230 | Current liabilities | 5000 |
| Income tax | 20 | Current assets | 4000 |

What is the gearing ratio?
a. 0.50
b. 1.25
c. 1.50
d. 1.00

7. Extracts from the financial statements of company A are as follows:

| Profit or loss statement | | Statement of financial position | |
|---|---|---|---|
| Items | Amounts | Items | Amounts |
| Sales | 500 | Owner's equity | 5000 |
| Gross profit | 350 | Reserves | 1000 |
| Operating profit | 250 | Retained earnings | 2000 |
| Finance costs | 20 | Loan notes | 1000 |

| Profit or loss statement | | Statement of financial position | |
|---|---|---|---|
| Items | Amounts | Items | Amounts |
| Profit before tax | 230 | Current liabilities | 5000 |
| Income tax | 20 | Current assets | 4000 |

What is the gross profit margin?
a. 50%
b. 71.43%
c. 65.71%
d. 70%

8. Extracts from the financial statements of company A are as follows:

| Profit or loss statement | | Statement of financial position | |
|---|---|---|---|
| Items | Amounts | Items | Amounts |
| Sales | 500 | Owner's equity | 5000 |
| Gross profit | 350 | Reserves | 1000 |
| Operating profit | 250 | Retained earnings | 2000 |
| Finance costs | 20 | Loan notes | 1000 |
| Profit before tax | 230 | Current liabilities | 5000 |
| Income tax | 20 | Current assets | 4000 |

What is the return on capital employed?
a. 2.78%
b. 2.63%
c. 2.33%
d. 3.13%

9. A company has a current ratio of 1.1 and an acid test of 0.4. If the company purchases inventory on credit, what will the effect of these ratios on the transaction?

| | Current ratio | Acid test |
|---|---|---|
| a. | Decrease | Increase |
| b. | Decrease | Decrease |
| c. | Increase | Decrease |
| d. | Increase | Increase |

10. We know the following information regarding an entity:
    - Suppliers at the end of the year: 350,000 lei
    - Purchases on credit 4,000,000 lei

What is the suppliers' payment period?
a. 32 days
b. 89 days
c. 56 days
d. 51 days

**Exercises**

**Exercise 1**: On January 1st, 20X0, E paid the Government of country C 2,000,000 lei for a five-year license to operate a mine. At the end of the license, E must restore the land to its natural state. This will cost a further 600,000 lei. These costs will be incurred on January 1st, 20X4. Explain how this expenditure is treated in the financial statements of E prepared in December 20X0.

**Exercise 2**: An entity computed the end of the year results. It includes the value of the inventories assessed at cost. After it computed the result, it discovered that an item of inventory with a cost of 8500 lei had a net realisable value of 9000 lei. Explain the effect on the financial statements of the entity.

**Exercise 3**: We know the following information on January 1st, 20X2:

Buildings: 1,000,000 lei
Accumulated depreciation: 200,000 lei

The buildings are depreciated using a straight-line method over a period of 50 years. Determine the value of the expenses with the depreciation and the net book value of the assets at the end of the year.

**Exercise 4**: After the general account inventory, we know the following figures for the inventories on December 31st, 20X7:

| No. | Inventory | Cost value | Recoverable value |
| --- | --- | --- | --- |
| 1 | A | 400,000 | 375,000 |
| 2 | B | 1,000,000 | 1,400,000 |
| 3 | C | 600,000 | 275,000 |
| Total | | 2,000,000 | 2,050,000 |

At the end of the year 20X8, the information regarding the three categories of inventories is as follows:

| No. | Inventory | Cost value | Recoverable value |
|---|---|---|---|
| 1 | A | 500,000 | 450,000 |
| 2 | B | 1,000,000 | 900,000 |
| 3 | C | 200,000 | 200,000 |
| Total | | 1,700,000 | 1,550,000 |

Compute the necessary adjustments for the inventories on December 31st, 20X8 and 20X9 and prepare the journal entries.

**Exercise 5**: Entity A has three customers. We know the following information on December 31st, 20X8:

| Account receivables | A | B | C |
|---|---|---|---|
| Initial value | 100,000 | 50,000 | 60,000 |
| Registered adjustment for bad debts | 15% | 0% | 10% |
| Estimated collection percentage on December 31st, 20X8 | 10% | 10% | 10% |

Compute the values at which the account receivables will be presented in the balance sheet prepared for the year 20X8 and prepare the journal entries for the necessary adjustment.

## Cases
### Case study 1

The trial balance before the account inventory is as follows:

| Item | Ending balance Debit | Credit |
|---|---|---|
| Owner's equity | | 1,800,000 |
| Long term bank credit | | 500,000 |
| Goodwill | 500,000 | |
| Lands | 300,000 | |
| Buildings | 1,250,000 | |
| Equipment | 298,800 | |
| Furniture | 107,800 | |
| Depreciation of buildings | | 62,500 |
| Depreciation of equipment | | 51,410 |
| Depreciation of furniture | | 10,780 |
| Merchandise | 408,500 | |
| Trade payables | | 655,597 |

| Item | Ending balance Debit | Credit |
|---|---|---|
| Account receivables | 312,402 | |
| Social security | | 39,108 |
| Cash in bank | 135,674 | |
| Cash in hand | 6234 | |
| Expenses with merchandise | 2,150,481 | |
| Expenses with repairs | 42,210 | |
| Expenses with other services received from suppliers | 77,615 | |
| Expenses with other taxes | 95,219 | |
| Expenses with salaries | 229,282 | |
| Expenses with social security | 152,855 | |
| Expenses with interest | 62,510 | |
| Other expenses | 24,114 | |
| Expenses with non-current items sold | 4250 | |
| Expenses with depreciation and adjustments | 124,690 | |
| Income tax expenses | 100,007 | |
| Revenues from merchandise sold | | 3,229,308 |
| Revenues from interest | | 4124 |
| Other revenues | | 14,816 |
| Revenues from non-current items sold | | 15,000 |
| Total | 6,382,643 | 6,382,643 |

During the account inventory, the following situations were noticed:

- The depreciation for the year was not registered. The buildings were depreciated on a straight-line method for 50 years. The useful life for the equipment is 10 years and for the furniture seven years. The equipment is depreciated using a reducing balance method. The furniture is depreciated on a straight-line method.
- There is one type of merchandise which remained unsold over the year. The company has ten pieces in stock. The cost value was 5 lei per piece and the net realisable value is 4 lei per piece.
- The company received on an invoice on December 1st for the insurance of the buildings for twelve months (including December). The value of the invoice was 1200 lei. The invoice was registered as expenses with other services received from suppliers.
- The company has one supplier from Germany. On December 31st, it had unpaid invoices of 1000 EUR. The exchange rate on the acquisition date was 4.6834 lei/EUR. The exchange rate at the end of the year was 4.6952 lei/EUR.

- The company has a customer who did not pay the invoices according to the contract. The total value of the invoices issued for this customer is 10,000 lei. The accountant estimates that only 75% of this value will be collected.
- The company has 10,000 EUR as cash in bank. This was registered using an exchange rate of 4.6458 lei/EUR.

Prepare the final trial balance and the financial statements for the year.

## Case study 2

The following financial statements relate to Hope plc:

**Income statement (profit and loss account)**
**For the year which ended on June 30th (Year 4)**

| Items | Million lei – 000s |
|---|---|
| Revenue | 3100 |
| Cost of sales | 1375 |
| Gross profit | 1725 |
| Administration and selling expenses | 1097 |
| Operating profit | 628 |
| Debenture interest | (42) |
| Profit before taxation | 586 |
| Taxation | (240) |
| Profit for equity holder | 346 |

The directors have recommended a dividend of 36.7 pence per share in respect of Year 4, to be paid following approval at the next annual general meeting.

**Balance sheet as of June 30th (Year 4)**

| Items | Million lei – 000s | Million lei – 000s | Million lei – 000s |
|---|---|---|---|
| Non-current (fixed assets) net of depreciation | | | 875 |
| Current assets: | | | |
| Stocks and work-in-progress | 310 | | |
| Account receivables | 770 | | |
| Cash | 100 | 1180 | |
| Less: Current liabilities | | | |
| Trade payables (creditors) | (150) | | |
| Other creditors and accruals | (470) | (620) | |

| Items | Million lei – 000s | Million lei – 000s | Million lei – 000s |
|---|---|---|---|
| Net current assets | | | 560 |
| Total assets minus current liabilities | | | 1435 |
| Non-current liabilities | | | |
| 6% debentures | | | (700) |
| Total net assets | | 735 | |
| Share capital and reserves | | | |
| Issued share capital 4500 ordinary shares of 25p nominal value | | | 225 |
| Retained earnings | | | 510 |
| | | 735 | |

## Required:

(a) Calculate ratios which measure
  (i) Liquidity and the use of working capital,
  (ii) Management performance and
  (iii) Gearing.
(b) Explain how each ratio would help to understand the financial position and results of the company
(c) The market price is currently 550 pence per share. Calculate ratios which are useful to investors

## Case study 3

The following financial statements relate to Charity plc:

**Profit and loss account for the year which ended on September 30th (Year 4)**

| Items | Million lei – 000s |
|---|---|
| Revenue | 2480 |
| Costs of sales | (1100) |
| Gross profit | 1380 |
| Administration and selling expenses | (678) |
| Operating profit | 702 |
| Debenture interest | (31) |
| Profit before taxation | 671 |
| Taxation | (154) |
| Profit for equity holders | 517 |

*Note* The directors have recommended a dividend of 11.4 pence per share in total in respect of Year 4, to be paid following approval at the next annual general meeting

## Balance sheet as of September 30th (Year 4)

| Items | Million lei – 000s | Million lei – 000s | Million lei – 000s |
|---|---|---|---|
| Non-current assets, net depreciation | | | 785 |
| Current assets: | | | |
| Inventories (stocks) | 341 | | |
| Account receivables (debtors) | 801 | | |
| Cash | 110 | 1252 | |
| Less: Current liabilities | | | |
| Trade payables (creditors) | (90) | | |
| Other payable and accruals | (654) | (744) | |
| Net current assets | | | 508 |
| Total assets minus current liabilities | | | 1293 |
| Non-current liabilities | | | |
| 7% debentures | | | (440) |
| Total net assets | | | 853 |
| Share capital and reserves | | | |
| Issued share capital (68,000 ordinary shares of 25p nominal value) | | | 340 |
| Retained earnings | | | 513 |
| | | | 853 |

## Required

(a) Calculate ratios which measure
   (i) Liquidity and the use of working capital,
   (ii) Management performance and
   (iii) Gearing.
(b) Explain how each ratio would help to understand the financial position and results of the company.
(c) The market price of one share is 40 million lei. Calculate ratios which will be of interest to investors.

CHAPTER 11

# Fundamentals of Taxation

*Mirela Păunescu and Adriana Duțescu*

*Learning objectives:*

- *Understanding the importance of taxation and its role*
- *Learning the factors impacting the taxation*
- *Understanding the different types of taxes and how they could impact a taxpayer*
- *Learning and differentiate between tax evasion and tax avoidance*
- *Understanding the different purposes of the accounting reporting and tax reporting*
- *Learning some of the situations when the taxable profit is different than the accounting profit.*

## 11.1 Introduction

In this chapter, we will briefly consider the purpose of taxation as well as its economic and social implications. We will then examine the specific Romanian taxation framework, demonstrate how tax is administered in Romania and analyse how the Romanian tax system interrelates with other tax jurisdictions, may they be from the EU or from third countries.

We will then look into the differences between accounting and taxation principles, explaining the (sometimes) complicated relationship between the financial statements, accounting flows and the tax system.

Finally, we shall discuss the difference between tax avoidance and tax evasion, underlining the importance of ethical behaviour of accountants and companies.

After reading this chapter, the reader should be able to discuss the foundations of the tax system.

## 11.2 The Importance of Taxes for the Businesses

Taxes are considered to be one of the most important matters in the life of the company or individual. Ones of the many reasons that justify the interest of both individuals and corporations in the topic are:

1. non-compliance risk is high and could lead to significant supplementary costs. In other words, any mistakes made by the taxpayers when (not)filing the tax statement, computing or paying the tax could lead to fines and penalties. Keep in mind that even if no charges are payable, taxpayers may still be required to file tax forms and may be fined if they fail to do so. Non-compliance can happen fast, for example, by misunderstanding the complex provisions of tax legislation. A small misunderstanding/misstatement could lead to a significant cost;
2. the cost generated by taxes is significant (unless the company is involved heavily in avoiding to pay taxes), therefore the taxpayer is interested in keeping it at the lowest possible level, while making sure that the tax law was obeyed;
3. there is a significant interest in finding alternative ways of lowering tax payables. Depending on the case, this could be considered tax avoidance or tax evasion (we'll explain later the difference between them);
4. there is a growing interest in tax optimization. For example, companies have access to different structures which may lower their taxes. However, this could also lead to the tax inspectors to tax the transactions in a more beneficial way for the Government, if they don't accept this as a valid structure;
5. taxpayers understand the tax opportunities and are motivated to take advantage of them, as the tax-break may be significant. For example, an entrepreneur could choose between trading as a sole trader or incorporating a business, the options being either to pay tax on profit or to pay income tax. The differences could be significant;
6. the consequences are immediate and usually disturbing. For example, in Romania, if the company doesn't pay its taxes, The National

Agency of Fiscal Administration (ANAF) could immediately block its bank accounts;
7. taxes involve cash-flow. Therefore, an effort should be considered by the subjects of taxation, both legal and physical persons.

There are also compliance costs to be taken into account. Compliance costs are endured by the taxpayers, the individuals or corporations who prepare tax returns and collect income tax or value-added tax. These costs are usually quite high. These costs become higher when more bureaucracy and volatility in the tax legislation is involved.

Taxes payable in a country may affect a company's strategy. For example, a group may decide to open a warehouse or a manufacturing plant in a country due to its fiscal stability, low tax rates or relaxed Internal Revenue Service. On the other hand, groups may avoid some countries or exit them when the tax costs are high, or the fiscal environment is unstable and makes the planning for the future subject to estimation.

The sustainability of a business may be impacted by the tax environment. If the company faces increased tax rates, then the business may become unstable.

## 11.3 The Function and Purpose of Taxation

**The taxation system** regulates the tax paid or payable by individuals and businesses to the government through public agencies, including the methods used by tax authorities to collect and control those taxes.

It is hard to believe that someone would pay taxes if no such obligation would exist. That's why national laws impose tax payment obligations on residents and non-residents who derive income in their state. The money raised by the tax payments is distributed by the government according to the budget plan and used to support various social, economic and national activities and functions, such as national defence costs, medical services, education staff salaries, social insurance and so on.

According to Romanian legislation, all individuals and businesses must pay taxes in Romania, as long as they earn income in Romania. The money collected (which become public funds) is mainly used by the government to finance public expenses and public investment.

An increase in governmental and public spending require an increase in funds, which could result in an increase in the tax rate. On the other hand, tax increases discourage investment. Increased spending also leaves less money for private investment. Reduction in private investments shrink the production of goods and services which, as a consequence, may lead to the elimination of employment opportunities. Therefore, finding the right level of taxation and spending is critical in a healthy economy.

**Taxpayer** refers to someone who's liable to pay a tax, even if that person/entity will not bear the cost in the end.

**Taxes** (in Romanian language "*taxe*") is money collected from taxpayers by public authorities to fund Government spending.

**Duties** (in Romanian language "*impozite*") denote the price paid for the services provided by the state (through its institutions) at the request of the individuals and companies. Usually duties are mandatory, and legislation forbids competitors from supplying that service. The payment is usually higher than the cost incurred to provide such a service. For example: taxes paid to obtain a permit to build or modernise a building.

**Contributions** are obligations of the taxpayer to the social funds (such as the social security fund or healthcare fund), payable and incurred by the individuals which may benefit from them or by companies which have a labour force.

A government's tax policy can be influenced by economic, social and environmental factors.

**a) Economic factors**

In economic terms, taxation represents a withdrawal from the economy. We pay taxes and, as a consequence, the money available to spend in the economy decreases. On the other hand, public expenditure represents a booster into it. As such, the government's net position in terms of taxation and expenditure (which could also be financed from other sources) has an impact on the economy (more precisely, on the level of economic activity) within a country.

The current income in the budget administrated by the government is composed of:

1. fiscal income (collected from taxes); and
2. non-fiscal income (from other income paid by public entities to the budget, such as the amounts paid by the National Romanian Bank or dividends paid by companies where the Romanian state is a shareholder). This also includes the capital income which represents amounts received as a result of selling assets belonging to the Romanian state or to public institutions.

Furthermore, the way the government spends money may have an effect on demand for particular types of goods. For example, if the Government is committed to developing public infrastructure, then the demand of all the goods and services specifically involved will increase (e.g. raw materials used in constructions, services supplied by engineers, etc.). If more money is allocated to education, health or national defence, the demand for the goods and services relevant to those industries will increase. Changing demand levels has an impact on employment levels within each sector (e.g. construction, public administration, etc.), as well as on the profitability of different private sector suppliers.

With the net spending or withdrawal left in the private sector, **the government may use tax policies to encourage or discourage certain types of activities**. For example, when the taxes are high, the money left for investment or other activities are lower, therefore some industries may be impacted (such as the banking or leisure industry).

The government, throughout its decision to adapt taxation, may **encourage**:

(a) **saving** for individuals, by offering tax incentives such as reduced tax rates on savings (interest) or/and tax relief on pension contributions (such as the 400-euro exemption from taxes providing that the individuals contribute to the private pension fund or private health insurance, in Romania);

(b) **donations to charities** (though there may already be an income tax deduction for charity, for example 2% in Romania);

(c) **entrepreneurs** who build their own business, through tax reliefs (as it was the case of Limited Liability Companies in Romania, incorporated by young investors and exempted from some social contributions);

(d) **investment in productive equipment** through capital allowances (as it is the case in Romania where the profit reinvested in some productive equipment is exempt from profit tax);

(e) **different types of activities** (such as research and development, exempt from income tax under certain conditions in Romania, construction services or services in the IT industry, for which various exceptions were introduced by legislation);

(f) **exports**, through the exemption of income from export activities from profit tax (as it was the case in Romania years ago).

It may **discourage**:

(a) **smoking** and the consumption of **alcoholic beverages**, through the excise taxes being placed on each type of product;
(b) **driving fuel-powered vehicles**, through raising fuel taxes;
(c) **imports**, by setting a high level of customs taxes;
(d) **consumption**, by setting a high level of tax on dividends or on VAT (this is not the case of Romania, where the tax on dividend is set at a minimum of 5% and the standard VAT rate is 19%);
(e) **pollution**, by imposing a high pollution tax on harmful activities or by offering incentives for the use of eco-friendly technologies. For example, individuals selectively collecting trash may receive a tax-break in certain Romanian cities.

We must keep in mind that the Government needs to raise money for spending in areas where there are no consumers on whom the necessary funds can be levied, such as defence, justice, education, or administrative costs (i.e. salaries of public servants and administration expenses). The level of amounts cashed in by the National Budget may increase as a result of increased level of tax, or by the increased number and categories of taxpayers, or both. This is a matter of government fiscal policy. For example, over the last 2 years, the Romanian government decided to decrease the personal income tax down to 10% from 16%, but also to impose new taxes on different industries (such as on banking, energy, telecom and gambling industries).

### b) Social factors

Social justice should stay at the heart of tax politics; the attitude towards the distribution of wealth is an example.

In a free market, some generate greater amounts of income and capital than others. Once wealth has been acquired, this discrepancy tends to grow through the reinvestment of the income received. This can lead to the rich becoming richer and the poor becoming poorer, with economic power becoming concentrated among a few people or entities.

Some believe that such discrepancies should be smoothed by **taxation policies aimed to redistribute income and wealth** away from the rich towards the poor. This is one of the key arguments in favour of using a progressive tax rate or setting high taxes on capital gains or assets, especially in real estate. Others believe that individuals should be motivated to work more and declare their income. That is an argument in favour of a digressive tax rate.

Sometimes the government uses tax reliefs to stimulate investment in a certain area, for example, where poverty is significant or where the unemployment rate is higher than average. These tax reliefs consist of exemptions from profit tax or income tax of salaries paid to people hired in those areas. For example, in Romania, companies hiring freshly graduated or unemployed people may benefit from different governmental subsidies.

Almost everyone would argue that taxation should be **equitable** or 'fair,' but there are many different views as to what is equitable. For example, some consider that it is fair to use the same tax rate regardless of the income level, but others consider that it is fair to use a progressive tax rate, increasing with the income. Some consider that a digressive deductible amount is fair, while others consider a flat one, regardless of the salary income or wealth, as being fair.

Nevertheless, an **efficient tax** is the one for which the costs of collection are lower than the tax paid. Regularly, Governments (throughout the Ministries of Finance, in some cases) publish figures for the administrative costs incurred by governmental departments, in operating the taxation systems.

### c) Environmental factors

Over the past few years, the taxation system has been rapidly and drastically adapted to accommodate environmental concerns which had been neglected, especially those regarding non-renewable sources of energy and global warming.

Examples of tax changes which have been introduced for environmental reasons are:

(a) the **packing tax**;
(b) the **local tax on cars** meant to encourage the manufacturing and purchase of low $CO_2$ emission cars and to reduce pollution caused by driving.

Without government intervention, there is no market incentive for consumers to account for environmental damage, since its impact is spread across many people and has little or no direct immediate cost to the polluter. Therefore, protection of the environment generally requires collective action, usually led by government.

Some of the benefits that environmental taxes provide[1] are:

---

[1] OECD, 2011, Environmental Taxation A Guide for Policy Makers; available online at https://www.oecd.org/env/tools-evaluation/48164926.pdf.

- the cost of the harm to others (also called an "externality") is internalized into market prices, which ensure that consumers and firms take these costs into account in their decisions;
- ongoing incentive to abate at all levels of emissions;
- improves competitiveness of low-emission alternatives;
- strong incentive to innovate.

## 11.4 Categories of Taxes

The Central Government earns revenues through a wide variety of taxes. There are different ways to classify taxes and, as a consequence, several categories of taxes:

- direct vs indirect taxes;
- revenue/income taxes vs property tax;
- taxes owed by legal persons (businesses) vs taxes owed by individuals (physical persons) etc.

The following paragraphs analyse several tax categories.

**a) Revenue tax**
**Revenue taxes** are those taxes based on income, as for example:

(a) **Income tax**,
(b) **Corporation tax**, and
(c) **Social security contributions**.

Some corporate taxes are based on profits, while others are computed on the gross income. As examples, the tax on profit is only payable if the taxpayers declares a profit and not a loss (the taxable profit, not the accounting one is used). The corporate tax may be payable on the income, regardless of whether the company is profitable or not, from the accounting point of view. As an example, the microenterprise regime in Romania requires small companies to pay a flat tax on their income (1% or 3%, depending on whether they have employees or not). This tax is payable even in the event that the company reports a loss and not a profit.

**b) Direct and indirect taxes**
**Direct taxes** are those charged directly on **income, gains and wealth**, whilst **indirect taxes** are those **paid by the consumer to the**

supplier and then by the supplier to the Government. Income tax, social insurance and corporation tax are direct taxes and **VAT and excises** are indirect taxes.

**Direct taxes** are based on income and profits (such as the **income tax**), or wealth (**local tax** on building, land or cars for instance such taxes are also known as property taxes) and **impact only those who have these resources**. Direct taxed are set for every taxpayer individually and the tax payers can observe the tax payable (as examples, an employee knows the salary tax paid in a month or the local tax payable for owning a car).

**Indirect taxes** are included in the prices of the goods and even if they can be determined, they are not usually well understood. For examples, when a private individual buys food, the price she pays includes the VAT. This tax can be computed, usually based on the price of goods and services. Indirect taxes paid by the consumer (such of VAT) **discourage spending** and encourage saving. Lower tax or no tax can be charged on essentials, such as food, medicine or others. In Romania, a lower VAT is imposed on food, medicine, and social buildings. Indirect taxes are included in the prices paid for goods and services by individuals and companies and, even if they can be determined, are not usually transparent. The accounting treatment of the VAT was provided in Chapters 5–7 and 9.

### c) Flat, progressive and digressive taxes

Based on the tax rates and characteristics, taxes may be:

**Flat taxes**: a flat tax rate is applied on the taxable base, regardless its value. In Romania, the tax system is based on a flat tax rate (10% for individuals and 16% for corporations). However, for small salaries, progressive taxes apply due to the personal allowances.

**Progressive taxes** are charged on wealth or income and are **directed to those who can afford to pay**. The proportion of the tax to be payed exponentially increases with income or profits. Personal allowances and the rates of taxation can be adjusted to ensure that those on very low incomes pay little or no tax. In Romania, there is no minimum wage exempt from salary tax, while other countries have such a level for exemption in place. Romania also implements the progressive tax in case of some local taxes, such as the tax for owning a car—the higher the engine's power, the higher the tax. Some taxes imposed on wealth are progressive, such as the taxes paid for the buildings owned. The more buildings one owns, the higher the tax.

**Digressive taxes**, which may be imposed on income or wealth, are a real advantage for richer people which benefit from lower tax rates while their income grows.

## 11.5 Taxes in Romania

The main taxes and their occurrence in Romania are set out in Table 11.1.

**a) Principal sources of revenue law and practice**

The Ministry of Finance is the Government's specialized public administration institution and is in charge of managing the public incomes and expenses as well as creating fiscal policy. In Romania, the taxation is administered by the National Agency for Fiscal Administration (in Romanian: *Agentia Nationala de Administrare Fiscala*, further referred as ANAF).

ANAF supervises and assures the compliance of taxpayers with their tax obligations, controls the lawfulness of the inputs and outputs of products during border crossing, identifies and limits the tax fraud and, therefore, tries to collect enough income tax as efficiently as possible to finance the economic and social programmes of the Government and the functioning of society as a whole.

As stated before, taxes are imposed by law. This entails Acts of Parliament and regulations laid down by Statutory Instruments.

ANAF also issues:

(a) **orders**, setting out how they intend to apply the law;
(b) a wide range of **explanatory leaflets**;

**Table 11.1** Main taxes in Romania

| Tax | Imposed on |
| --- | --- |
| Individual income tax | Individuals, acting on their own or in partnerships |
| Corporation tax | Companies |
| Social security contributions | Both individuals and companies |
| Value Added Tax | Businesses, both incorporated and unincorporated |
| Other tax—such as excises, local taxes and so on | Final consumers, owners of goods and so on |

*Source* The authors

The main legal framework on taxation is the **Fiscal Code** (also referred to as the Tax Code). The main tax principles stated by the Fiscal Code are:

a) **neutrality** of fiscal measures for various categories of investors, capital and forms of ownership; ensures equal conditions for investors and for Romanian and foreign capital;
b) **certitude of taxation**, by developing clear legal norms that do not lead to arbitrary interpretations; deadlines, manner and amounts payable must be clear for each taxpayer as they may influence financial and management decisions and their impact;
c) **fairness of taxation or fair taxation**—a principle that ensures that the tax burden has been established on the basis of the contributory power of each taxpayer (i.e., the size of the income or the property);
d) **efficiency of taxation**, by providing long-term stability of the Fiscal Code's provisions, so that such provisions do not lead to unfavourable retroactive effects, in comparison to the taxation in place on the date;
e) **predictability**—requires that any amendment or additional provision becomes effective from the first day of the following year, starting with January 1st, and shall remain unchanged at least during that year.

## b) Taxpayer's obligations

Tax obligations for the taxpayer are:

a) **to declare** the taxable goods and revenues, or, the taxes, fees, contributions and other amounts due to the budget;
b) **to compute and record** in the accounting and tax statements the taxes, fees, contributions and other amounts due to the budget;
c) **to pay** the taxes, fees, contributions and other amounts due to the budget by the legal deadline;
d) **to pay penalties** (called ancillary tax obligations) related to deferred payments of the taxes, fees, contributions and other amounts due;
e) **to compute, retain and record** the **taxes** and contributions which are paid;
f) to fulfil any **other obligations incumbent** on taxpayers, following the application of tax laws.

**Sanctions and penalties** are applied if the fiscal laws are broken.

## 11.6 The Interaction of the Romanian Tax System with That of Other Tax Jurisdictions

### 11.6.1 The European Union Jurisdiction

The European Union's membership produces a substantial effect on Romanian taxes, especially on the direct ones. The EU Member States jointly agreed to enact specific laws, known as '**Directives**,' which provide a common code of taxation in some particular areas of taxation.

The most known and discussed example is the **VAT**, as Romania is obliged to pass its laws according to the rules enforced by European legislation. The EU VAT Directives still allow for a certain amount of flexibility between Member States (such as using lower tax rates, taxing or not taxing some goods or services or setting taxation rates) but only in certain limits. There are only a few examples of EU Directives in the area of Direct Taxes that have a significant impact on national legislation. For example, such Directives refer to the cross-border dividend and interest payments.

However, under the EU treaties, Member States are also obliged to allow freedom of movement of workers, of capital and freedom to establish business operations within the EU. Such treaties have a '**direct effect**'. This means that any taxpayer who believes that the Romanian legislation conflicts with European legislation is entitled to claim that the Romanian tax provision is ineffective because it **breaches one or more of the freedoms** guaranteed under European laws. For example, if Romania would tax the dividends paid by a subsidiary to its parent in Spain (provided some conditions are met), this would be against the European law.

As a result of the European legislation, European citizens may not be discriminated in other Member States, unless there is a very strong public interest justification. For example, a French resident having to pay salary tax in Romania must pay the same tax as a Romanian resident.

European Regulations must be applied, in their entirety, in EU Member States; they apply directly and therefore must not be transposed into national legislation.

**EU Decisions** are another example of legislation which has a direct impact on Romanian legislation. Decisions are binding for those to whom it is addressed (e.g. an Member State or an individual company subject to the EU's jurisdiction) and is directly applicable.

### 11.6.2 Other Countries

Romania has entered double taxation avoidance treaties with various countries. These treaties contain rules which prevent income and profits being taxed twice and include non-discrimination provisions, preventing a foreign citizen from being treated more severely than a national citizen. Usually there are also rules which stipulate the exchange of information between different Revenue authorities, rules meant to insure that Member States can collect their taxes from their residents.

## 11.7 TAX AVOIDANCE AND TAX EVASION

Tax avoidance is the legal minimisation of tax liabilities, where as tax evasion is illegal.

**a) Tax evasion**
**Tax evasion refers to the conduct of paying too little tax or no tax at all, deliberately misleading the Tax Authority.** The following examples are provided:

(a) Hiding compulsory, material information (e.g., failing to notify ANAF that you are liable to pay tax, understating income or profits or not disclosing a relevant fact, e.g., that a business expenditure had a dual motive), or
(b) Sending deliberately false information (e.g., deducting expenses which have not been incurred or claiming capital allowances on a plant that has not been purchased).

Tax evasion is, of course, prohibited. Slight cases of tax evasion may be settled in court by imposing a penalty payment, while severe cases of tax evasion, not to mention those involving fraud, are subject to **criminal prosecutions** which may lead to **fines and/or imprisonment on conviction**. This may be the case of entities which deduct fictive expenses or fail to record all incurred income, as opposed to the case of individuals bringing cars from EU, using false Romanian VAT codes and then failing to pay the VAT in Romania, claiming VAT without a legal base and so on.

Other common examples of tax evasion are:

1. forbidding the tax authority access to the company's office in order to prevent tax audits;
2. using or issuing false fiscal documents;
3. fraudulently and deliberately, directly or in association, declaring or the intent to declare false taxes to obtain money from the public budget as a reimbursement;
4. hiding taxable assets or incomes;
5. not declaring all the taxable income or taxable transactions during the period;
6. recording fake expenses or transactions;
7. using alternative accounting evidence in order to fake the taxes payable;
8. avoiding tax audits by not truly declaring the business' offices;
9. hiding assets taken into possession by the tax authorities;

**b) Tax avoidance**

Tax avoidance is more difficult to define. In a very broad sense, it could include **any legal method of reducing your tax burden**, e.g. taking advantage of tax shelter opportunities explicitly offered by tax legislation. In a narrower sense (more commonly used), it refers to ingenious arrangements designed to produce unintended tax advantages for the taxpayer.

Conventionally, the response of the Ministry of Finance and ANAF has been to seek to mend the **loopholes** in the law as they are discovered. However, other loopholes are identified or created by the amendment. In general, there is a presumption that the effect of such changes should not be backdated. For example: in the case of Romanian individuals building and selling new houses and failing to pay VAT for their economic activity. Subsequently, the fiscal code was amended, and now it is clear that such a person is a taxable person and should register for VAT.

**c) The distinction between avoidance and evasion**

The distinction between tax evasion and tax avoidance is generally clear, since tax avoidance is an entirely legal activity and does not entail misleading Tax Authorities. However, nowadays, despite being legal, many consider that tax avoidance is not ethical, as both corporations and individuals should pay their fair share of taxes and should contribute to the development of society.

However, care should be taken when giving advice in some circumstances. For example, a taxpayer who does not report the income he or she received from outside of Romania because they wrongly believe that they have no other obligation in Romania may, as a result, be guilty of tax evasion.

An example of tax avoidance is illustrated below.

**Example 1**: A group of companies has 2 subsidiaries. One is incorporated in Heaven Land (Happy Ltd.) where the tax rate is 10% and the other is incorporated in Sorrow Land where the tax rate is 40% (Sad Ltd.). Happy sells goods to Sad. The price paid by Happy on the goods was 10,000,000 lei. The price Sad uses to sell these goods (after minor changes) on its local market is 30,000,000 lei. In Sorrow Land, similar goods are sold on the free market for 25,000,000 lei. Happy still has to decide the selling price for Sad. What would be a price that would optimize the group's finances? What would be a price that would keep the group out of trouble?

**Solution**: Let's assume that Happy sells the goods for 10,000,000 lei (so no mark-up is added), in the two countries the following figures will be reported (Table 11.2).

Let's assume now that Happy sells the goods for 30,000,000 lei, in the two countries the following figures will be reported (Table 11.3).

It is obvious from the above example that, if the Group moves its entire profit to Heaven Land, where the tax rate is lower than in Sorrow Land, the profit is optimized for the Group. However, the tax authorities from Sorrow Land will not be happy with such conduct.

In this example, we illustrated the concept of transfer pricing. **Transfer prices** are prices used between related parties (i.e. entities that,

**Table 11.2** Example 1-assumption 1

|  | Happy – 10% tax rate | Sad – 30% tax rate | Group |
|---|---|---|---|
| Acquisition cost | 10,000,000 | 10,000,000 |  |
| Selling price | 10,000,000 | 30,000,000 |  |
| Profit | 0 | 20,000,000 | 20,000,000 |
| Income tax | 0 | 6,000,000 | 6,000,000 |
| Net profit | 0 | 14,000,000 | 14,000,000 |
| Tax rate (tax/gross profit) | 0 | 30% | 30% |

*Source* The authors

**Table 11.3** Example 1-assumption 2

|  | Happy – 10% tax rate | Sad – 30% tax rate | Group |
|---|---|---|---|
| Acquisition cost | 10,000,000 | 10,000,000 |  |
| Selling price | 30,000,000 | 30,000,000 |  |
| Profit | 20,000,000 | 0 | 20,000,000 |
| Income tax | 2,000,000 | 0 | 2,000,000 |
| Net profit | 18,000,000 | 0 | 18,000,000 |
| Tax rate (tax/gross profit) | 10% | 0 | 10% |

*Source* The authors

**Table 11.4** Example 1-comparison

|  | Happy – 10% tax rate | Sad – 30% tax rate | Group |
|---|---|---|---|
| Acquisition cost | 10,000,000 | 25,000,000 |  |
| Selling price | 25,000,000 | 30,000,000 |  |
| Profit | 15,000,000 | 5,000,000 | 20,000,000 |
| Income tax | 1,500,000 | 1,500,000 | 3,000,000 |
| Net profit | 13,500,000 | 3,500,000 | 17,000,000 |
| Tax rate (tax/gross profit) | 10% | 30% | 15% |

*Source* The authors

directly or indirectly, are controlled by or could control others). For taxation purposes, **transfer pricing** refers to the rules and methods used for pricing transactions within and between entities under common ownership or control.

Due to the potential of cross-border controlled transactions to distort taxable income, tax authorities may and will adjust intragroup transfer prices that differ from what would have been charged by unrelated enterprises dealing at free market values (the arm's-length principle).

Transfer pricing rules allow tax authorities to adjust prices for multinational intragroup transactions. In other words, the tax auditors in Sorrow Land may substitute the profit tax as they'll compute the tax owed by Sad based on an acquisition cost equal to the market value of the goods.

Using the same data as in the previous example, let's assume that Happy sells the goods by using the arm's length principle. In each country the following figures will be reported (Table 11.4).

These tax adjustments are generally calculated using one or more of the transfer pricing methods specified in the Organization of Economic

Cooperation and Development (OECD) guidelines. The OECD is an intergovernmental economic organization, founded in 1961 to stimulate economic progress and world trade.

The OECD's mission is to promote policies that will improve the economic and social well-being of people around the world. One of their many projects refers to taxation. Within these projects, the Base erosion profit shifting (BEPS) is probably the most known.

**d) The need for an ethical and professional approach**

Paying taxes is a duty which all tax residents have. Tax is now considered a social responsibility. One important outcome of taxation is the public system of education, which is financed by the state and is expected to become more efficient. The better the education, the more skilled the work forced. The more money available to the Government, the more money is invested into the insurance system or healthcare system, for example. Tax avoidance not only shifts funds away from the economy but also undermines perceived social fairness. Knowledge of multinational groups successfully avoiding taxes is a strong demotivator for honest individuals to pay their own share of tax. Tax avoidance helps multinational, complex, rich groups gain a competitive advantage over enterprises that operate at a domestic level. When taxpayers perceive multinational corporations legally avoiding tax, this undermines voluntary compliance.

Usually, the tax advisers or accountants help the taxpayers in their interactions with ANAF and situations can arise where the accountant has concerns as to whether the taxpayer is being honest in providing the full and accurate information needed to file in the tax forms.

How the accountant deals with such situations is a matter of **professional judgment**, but the accountant is expected to obey its professional standards and Code of Ethics. The professional accountant must act honestly and objectively, with due care and diligence, and show the highest standards of integrity.

## 11.8 The Relationship Between Accounting and Taxation

Although taxes are computed based on the accounting information, there are significant differences between accounting and taxation. An expense recognised for accounting purposes is not necessarily recognised for tax purposes. Therefore, the taxable profit (which is the profit taxable for tax purposes) is different than the accounting profit.

Differences can be observed between the objective and users of tax forms, as opposed to financial statements. The general objective of financial reporting is to provide financial information about the reporting entity that is useful to existing and potential investors, lenders and other creditors in making decisions about providing resources to the entity. The purpose of the taxation is to help the tax authority collect taxes and audit the taxpayers, while the user is the Government or other public agencies.

The accounting principles have already been discussed in Chapter 2, whereas principles stated in fiscal regulations are totally different. Moreover, some of the accounting principles are disregarded occasionally or systematically. For example, tax allows the change of methods, without taking the accounting principle of consistency into consideration.

**Example 2**: A company uses the declining balance depreciation for the equipment used, according to its accounting principles. The old tax law allowed the company to deduct the depreciation computed based on this method. Starting with the beginning of the year, the tax law is amended and only the straight-line method is allowed for tax purposes. The remaining value of the assets is depreciated for tax purposes on the remaining period.

At the end of the previous year, the remaining values of assets are presented in Table 11.5. A new asset is bought on January 1st, for 100,000 lei. The company depreciates its assets by 30% per year, for reporting purposes, computed on the remaining value. The revenues recognised for the year are 800,000 lei. The tax rate we'll use is 16%.

Table 11.5  Example 2

|   | Value | Period (years) | Tax depreciation for the year | Accounting depreciation for the year |
|---|---|---|---|---|
| 1 | 2 | 3 | 4 = 2/3 | 5 = 2*30% |
| Existing assets | 600,000 | 6 | 100,000 | 180,000 |
| New asset | 100,000 | 10 | 10,000 | 30,000 |
| Total | 700,000 |  | 110,000 | 210,000 |

*Source* The authors

**Solution:**
The company recognises revenues of 800,000 lei and expenses of 210,000 lei for accounting purposes.

The accounting profit = 800,000 − 210,000 = 590,000

For tax purposes, the tax depreciation should be deducted from the revenue

The taxable profit = 800,000 − 110,000 = 990,000

Profit tax expense = 990,000 * 16% = 158,400 lei. This expense will be recorded as a profit tax expense in the company's accounting records.

With very limited examples, materiality is not a principle recognised for tax purposes. In other words, one could not escape the obligation to file tax forms on the grounds that their payable value is insignificant.

For tax purposes, both expenses and revenues are those registered as per the accounting journals, however some adjustments are made to the accounting profit as we can see below:

(*Source* The authors)

The easiest example to illustrate refers to charity expenses (donations). An entity is not prohibited from charity, however, for tax purposes, the expense is fully disallowed. When an entity computes the taxable profit, this will be different than the accounting profit.

**Example 3**: In accounting, a company recognises revenues of 300,000 lei and expenses of 200,000 lei, from which 50,000 lei is a charity expense, which is disallowed pursuant to the Romanian Fiscal Code.

The accounting profit = 300,000 − 200,000 = 100,000
The taxable profit = Accounting profit + Disallowed expenses = 100,000 + 50,000 = 150,000

Profit tax expense = 150,000 * 16% = 24,000 lei. This expense will be recorded as a profit tax expense in the company's accounting records.

Estimation methods for tax purposes may differ from those for reporting purposes. For example, for tax purposes, the company must depreciate the non-current assets based on a period stated in the fiscal legislation. For accounting purposes, based on the economic substance, the useful life over which the asset is depreciated, should depend on the company's intention to use and sell the asset.

**Example 4**: A company uses estimates a of 6 years useful life for its assets, as accounting policy, while for tax purposes the law imposes a period of 10 years. The assets should be depreciated by using the straight-line method.

The revenues recognised for the year are 600,000 lei (Table 11.6).

For accounting purposes, the company recognises revenues of 600,000 lei and expenses of 100,000 lei (600, 000 lei/6 years).

Table 11.6  Example 4

|   | Value | Period for GAAP (years) | Period for tax (years) | Tax depreciation for the year | Accounting depreciation for the year |
|---|---|---|---|---|---|
| 1 | 2 | 3 |   | 4 = 2/3 | 5 = 2 * 30% |
| Existing assets | 600,000 | 6 | 10 | 60,000 | 100,000 |

*Source* The authors

The accounting profit = 600,000 − 100,000 = 500,000
For tax purposes, the tax depreciation should be deducted from the revenue
The taxable profit = 600,000 − 60,000 = 540,000
Profit tax expense = 540,000 * 16% = 86,400 lei.

This expense will be recorded as a profit tax expense in the company's accounting records.

One of the many cases where one can see a difference between the accounting principles and the fiscal principles relates to prudence principles. For accounting purposes, the company must recognise any impairment of its assets, even if the loss is not yet realised. For tax purposes, such an expense is not recognised, which means that the company has to add back this expense to compute the taxable profit.

**Example 5**: A company recognised a trade receivable of 100,000 lei. The debtor faced some financial problems; therefore, the expected recovered amount is only 50%. For tax purposes, the company is allowed to deduct a bad debt allowance in the limit of 30% a. The revenues of the year are 500,000 lei.

For accounting purposes, the company has to recognise a bad debt allowance of 50% of 100,000 lei (as an expense and an adjustment/impairment to the trade receivables). For tax purposes, only a part of this expense will be allowable.

The accounting profit = 500,000 − 100,000 * 50% = 450,000
The taxable profit = 500,000 − 100,000 * 30% = 470,000

Profit tax expense = 470,000 * 16% = 75,200 lei. This expense will be recorded as a profit tax expense in the company's accounting records.

As we have already established, accounting losses are recognised in the Profit and Loss Account. Once reported, losses can only be offset by another element of equity. However, the tax losses are not recorded in the accounting records, but usually in one of the registers which the company prepares for tax evidence. Moreover, usually tax losses expire, as opposed to the accounting losses.

**Example 6**: A company recognised a tax loss of 100,000 lei 8 years ago when it was a tax payer. The accounting loss reported for that year was 80,000 lei. Now the company is considered a microenterprise, so it pays income tax. Income tax is charged on the income (turnover), regardless of if the company reported a profit or not. Moreover, tax losses are not deductible for income tax payers. In the current year, the company reported revenues of 1,000,000 lei. In Romania, the tax losses are only allowed to be retained for 7 years, after which they expire. As the tax loss is already 8 years old and considering that the company is a microenterprise, it cannot deduct the loss; the income tax will be computed based on the revenues. The tax loss is lost forever. However, the accounting loss will still be kept in the retained earnings.

## 11.9 Conclusions

The following summary questions are providing conclusions of this chapter:

### Chapter summary questions:

| | |
|---|---|
| 1. What are the main factors which influence tax policies of Governments? | The main factors that influence tax policies of Governments are economic, social and environmental factors. |
| 2. Provide examples of direct taxes | Examples of direct taxes are income tax, taxes on property, or custom taxes. |
| 3. Provide examples of indirect taxes | Examples of indirect taxes are VAT and excises. |
| 4. What is tax avoidance? | Tax avoidance means any legal method of reducing your tax burden, e.g. taking advantage of tax shelter opportunities explicitly offered by tax legislation. |
| 5. What is tax evasion? | Tax evasion refers to the conduct of paying low tax or no tax at all, deliberately misleading the Tax Authority. |
| 6. What does the transfer prices refer to? | Transfer prices are prices used between related parties (i.e. entities that, directly or indirectly, are controlled by or could control others) |
| 7. Provide an example where the accounting effect is different from the tax one | The classical example is the difference between the taxable profit and the accounting profit. The taxable profit relates to taxable revenues minus expenses allowed from tax purposes, whereas the accounting profit relates to all revenues and expenses accrued within the business process. |

**Quizzes (only one correct answer)**

1. Identify in which of the following cases tax evasion is implied?
   a. Choosing the microenterprise regime instead of profit tax
   b. Selling a house and not declaring the full selling price
   c. Choosing the sole trader regime instead of being a company
   d. Using money instead of credit/debit cards
2. Which of the following could be considered to be tax avoidance?
   a. Paying the local tax by March 31st to benefit from a tax discount
   b. Not declaring nor taxing the rental agreement concluded with a tenant
   c. Choosing the profit tax payer regime instead of being a microenterprise
   d. Recording false expenses to lower the profit tax payable
3. Which of the following is an example of direct tax?
   a. Salary tax
   b. Social security contributions
   c. Excises
   d. VAT
4. Which of the following is an example of indirect tax?
   a. Salary tax
   b. Social security contributions
   c. Profit tax
   d. VAT
5. Which of the following is not a factor that impacts taxation?
   a. Human factors
   b. Social factors
   c. Environmental factors
   d. Economic factors
6. If the company reports non-taxable revenues, will the taxable base be different than the accounting profit?
   a. No
   b. Yes, taxable base will be higher
   c. Yes, taxable base will be lower
   d. It depends on the tax rate

7. If the company reports disallowed expenses (non-deductible), will the taxable base be different than the accounting profit?
   a. No
   b. Yes, taxable base will be higher
   c. Yes, taxable base will be lower
   d. It depends on the tax rate
8. For reporting purposes, the revenues and expenses are recognized based on:
   a. the accounting principles and the policies adopted by the company
   b. the tax principles
   c. the neutrality principle
   d. the predictability principle
9. If a gain from selling financial instruments valued at FVTOCI is recognised in the retained earnings and is taxable for tax purposes, will the taxable base be different than the accounting profit?
   a. No
   b. Yes, taxable base will be higher
   c. Yes, taxable base will be lower
   d. It depends on the tax rate

## Exercises

1. Name 3 reasons which could justify the interest of both corporations and individuals in taxes.
2. Name 3 tax principles and 3 accounting principles.
3. Name 3 examples of situations where the taxable base is different than the accounting profit.
4. For accounting purposes, a company recognises revenues of 500,000 lei, from which 100,000 lei dividend income is from a Romanian company (not-taxable, according to the law) and expenses of 300,000 lei from which 50,000 lei is a disallowed expense. The tax losses reported from the previous year are 20,000 lei.
   Compute the taxable profit and the profit tax.
5. For accounting purposes, a company recognises revenues of 1,500,000 lei, from which 400,000 lei dividend income is from a Romanian company (not-taxable, according to the law) and expenses of 800,000 lei from which 150,000 lei is not properly

documented as required by the tax law (a disallowed expenses). The tax losses reported from 10 years ago are 20,000 lei. The accounting loss reported for the previous year was 10,000 lei. During the year, the company sold financial instruments classified as FVTOCI and generated a loss of 40,000 lei (deductible). Half of the profit tax will be payable in 5 years as a result of a tax relief applicable to the company.

Compute the taxable profit and the profit tax.

# Appendix

**Class 1—Capital accounts**
**10 Capital and reserves**
101 Capital
*1011 Subscribed capital not paid*
*1012 Subscribed capital paid*
*1015 Patrimony (autonomous public sector entities)*
*1016 Public patrimony*
*1017 Private patrimony*
*1018 National institutes of research and development patrimony*
103 Other elements of the own capital
*1031 Benefits granted to employees in the form of own capital instruments*
*1033 Exchange rate differences related to net investment in a foreign entity*
*1038 Differences in fair value of financial assets available for sale and other own capital elements*
104 Premium related to capital
*1041 Share premium*
*1042 Merger /demerger premium*
*1043 Share premium contribution in kind*
*1044 Debenture conversion premium*
105 Revaluation reserve
106 Reserves
*1061 Legal reserve*
*1063 Statutory or contractual capital reserve*
*1068 Other reserves*

107 Exchange rate differences from conversion
108 Non-controlling interests
*1081 Non-controlling interests—profit (loss) for the period*
*1082 Non-controlling interests—other own capital*
109 Own shares
*1091 Short-term own shares*
*1092 Long-term own shares*
*1095 Shares of the absorbing entity owned by the entity absorbed*

**11 Retained earnings**
117 Retained earnings
*1171 Profit/loss carried forward*
*1172 Retained earnings due to the adoption of IAS for the first time, with the exception of IAS 29*
*1173 Retained earnings due to the changes in accounting policies*
*1174 Retained earnings resulting from the correction of accounting errors*
*1175 Retained earnings representing the surplus obtained from revaluation reserves*
*1176 Retained earnings resulting from the adoption of Accounting Regulations according to the European Directives*

**12 Profit/ Loss for the period**
121 Profit/ Loss for the period
129 Profit appropriation

**14 Gains or losses in respect of issuance, redemption, sale, free transfer or cancellation of own capital instruments**
141 Gains in respect of sales or cancellation of own capital instruments
*1411 Gains related to sale of own capital instruments*
*1412 Gains related to cancellation of own capital instruments*
149 Losses in respect of issuance, redemption, sale, free transfer or cancellation of own capital instruments
*1491 Losses related to sale of own capital instruments*
*1495 Losses arising from reorganizations, caused by cancellation of held capital instruments*
*1498 Other losses related to own capital instruments*

**15 Provisions**
151 Provisions
*1511 Provisions for litigation*
*1512 Provisions for guarantees to customers*
*1513 Provisions for the decommissioning of tangible non-current assets and other similar actions*
*1514 Provisions for restructuring costs*
*1515 Provisions for pensions and similar obligations*
*1516 Provisions for taxes*
*1517 Provisions for termination of employment*
*1518 Other provisions*

**16 Loans and similar debts**
161 Debenture loans
*1614 Foreign debenture loans guaranteed by the State*
*1615 Foreign debenture loans guaranteed by banks*
*1617 Domestic debenture loans guaranteed by the State*
*1618 Other debenture loans*
162 Long-term bank loans
*1621 Long-term bank loans*
*1622 Long-term bank loans in arrears*
*1623 Foreign Government loans*
*1624 Foreign loans guaranteed by the State*
*1625 Foreign loans guaranteed by banks*
*1626 State Treasury loans*
*1627 Domestic loans guaranteed by the State*
166 Debts relating to financial assets
*1661 Debts towards affiliated entities*
*1663 Debts towards associates and jointly controlled entities*
167 Other loans and similar debts
168 Accrued interest on loans and similar debts
*1681 Accrued interest on debenture loans*
*1682 Accrued interest on long-term bank loans*
*1685 Accrued interest on debts towards affiliated entities*
*1686 Accrued interest on debts towards associates and jointly controlled entities*
*1687 Accrued interest on other loans and similar debts*
169 Premium on redemption of bonds and other debts
*1691 Premium on redemption of bonds*
*1692 Premium on redemption of other debts*

**Class 2—Non-current assets**
**20 Intangible assets**
201 Set-up costs
203 Development costs
205 Concessions, patents, licences, trademarks and similar rights and assets
206 Intangible assets of exploration for and evaluation of mineral resources
207 Goodwill
*2071 Positive goodwill*
*2075 Negative goodwill*
208 Other intangible assets

**21 Tangible assets**
211 Freehold land and land improvements
*2111 Freehold land*
*2112 Land improvements*
212 Buildings

213 Plant and machinery and motor vehicles
*2131 Plant and machinery*
*2132 Measurement, control and adjustment devices*
*2133 Motor vehicles*
214 Fixtures and fittings
215 Investment property
216 Tangible assets of exploration for and evaluation of mineral resources
217 Biological assets

**22 Tangible assets in transit**
223 Plant and machinery and motor vehicles in transit
224 Fixtures and fittings in transit
227 Biological assets in transit

**23 Non-current assets in progress**
231 Tangible assets in progress
233 Investment property in progress

**26 Financial assets**
261 Shares in affiliated entities
262 Shares in associates
263 Shares in jointly controlled entities
264 Investments accounted for using the equity method
265 Other long term investments
266 Deferred green certificates
267 Long term receivables
*2671 Amounts to be received from affiliates*
*2672 Accrued interest on amounts to be received from affiliates*
*2673 Receivables related to associates and jointly controlled entities*
*2674 Accrued interest on receivables related to associates and jointly controlled entities*
*2675 Long term loans*
*2676 Accrued interest on long term loans*
*2677 Bonds acquired on third party issuances*
*2678 Other long term receivables*
*2679 Accrued interest on other long term receivables*
269 Amounts payable in relation with financial noncurrent assets
*2691 Amounts payable in relation with investments in affiliated entities*
*2692 Amounts payable in relation with associates*
*2693 Amounts payable in relation with jointly controlled entities*
*2695 Amounts payable in relation with other financial assets*

**28 Depreciation of non-current assets**
280 Amortization of intangible assets
*2801 Amortization of set-up costs*
*2803 Amortization of development costs*

*2805 Amortization of concessions, patents, licences, trademarks and similar rights and assets*
*2806 Amortization of intagible assets of exploration for and evaluation of mineral resources*
*2807 Amortization of goodwill*
*2808 Amortization of other intangible assets*
281 Depreciation of tangible assets
*2811 Depreciation of land improvements*
*2812 Depreciation of buildings*
*2813 Depreciation of plant and machinery and motor vehicles*
*2814 Depreciation of other tangible assets*
*2815 Depreciation of investment property*
*2816 Depreciation of tangible assets of exploration for and evaluation of mineral resources*
*2817 Depreciation of biological assets*

### 29 Impairment of non-current assets
290 Impairment of intangible assets
*2903 Impairment of development costs*
*2905 Impairment of concessions, patents, licences, trademarks and similar rights and assets*
*2906 Impairment of intangible assets of exploration for and evaluation of mineral resources*
*2908 Impairment of other intangible assets*
291 Impairment of tangible assets
*2911 Impairment of land and land improvements*
*2912 Impairment of buildings*
*2913 Impairment of plant and machinery and motor vehicles*
*2914 Impairment of other tangible assets*
*2915 Impairment of investment property*
*2916 Impairment of tangible assets of exploration for and evaluation of mineral resources*
*2917 Impairment of biological assets*
293 Impairment of non-current assets in progress
*2931 Impairment of tangible assets in progress*
*2935 Impairment of investment property in progress*
296 Impairment of financial assets
*2961 Impairment of investments in affiliated entities*
*2962 Impairment of investments in associates and jointly controlled entities*
*2963 Impairment of other long term investments*
*2964 Impairment of amounts to be received from affiliates*
*2965 Impairment of receivables related to associates and jointly controlled entities*
*2966 Impairment of long term loans*
*2968 Impairment of other receivables*

### Class 3—Inventories and work in progress
### 30 Raw materials and consumables
301 Raw materials
302 Consumables

*3021 Auxiliary materials*
*3022 Fuel*
*3023 Packaging materials*
*3024 Spare parts*
*3025 Seeds and sapling*
*3026 Fodder*
*3028 Other consumables*
303 Materials in the form of small inventory
308 Price differences on raw materials and consumables

**32 Inventories in transit**
321 Raw materials in transit
322 Consumables in transit
323 Materials in the form of small inventory in transit
326 Biological assets in the form of inventories in transit
327 Goods purchased for resale in transit
328 Packaging materials in transit

**33 Work in progress**
331 Work in progress
332 Services in progress

**34 Goods**
341 Semi-finished goods
345 Finished goods
346 Residual products
347 Agricultural products
348 Price differences on goods

**35 Inventories at third parties**
351 Raw materials and consumables at third parties
354 Goods at third parties
356 Biological assets in the form of inventories at third parties
357 Goods for resale at third parties
358 Packaging materials at third parties

**36 Biological assets in the form of inventories**
361 Biological assets in the form of inventories
368 Price differences on biological assets in the form of inventories

**37 Goods purchased for resale**
371 Goods purchased for resale
378 Price differences on goods purchased for resale

**38 Packaging**

381 Packaging materials
388 Price differences on packaging

**39 Write-down of inventories and work in progress**
391 Write-down of raw materials
392 Write-down of consumables
*3921 Write-down of consumables*
*3922 Write-down of materials in the form of small inventory*
393 Write-down of work in progress
394 Write-down of goods
*3941 Write-down of semi finished goods*
*3945 Write-down of finished goods*
*3946 Write-down of residual products*
*3947 Write-down of agricultural products*
395 Write-down of inventories held at third parties
*3951 Write-down of raw materials and consumables at third parties*
*3952 Write-down of semi finished goods at third parties*
*3953 Write-down of finished goods at third parties*
*3954 Write-down of residual products at third parties*
*3955 Write-down of agricultural products at third parties*
*3956 Write-down of biological assets in the form of inventories*
*3957 Write-down of goods for resale at third parties*
*3958 Write-down of packaging materials at third parties*
396 Write-down of animals
397 Write-down of goods purchased for resale
398 Write-down of packaging materials

**Class 4—Third party accounts**
**40 Suppliers and similar accounts**
401 Suppliers
403 Bills of exchange payable
404 Suppliers of non-current assets
405 Bills of exchange payable to suppliers of noncurrent assets
408 Suppliers—invoices to be received
409 Advance payments to suppliers
*4091 Advance payments to suppliers for the purchase of inventories*
*4092 Advance payments to suppliers for the purchase of services*
*4093 Advance payments for tangible assets*
*4094 Advance payments for intangible assets*

**41 Customers and similar accounts**
411 Customers
*4111 Customers*
*4118 Doubtful customers or customers involved in litigation*

413 Bills of exchange receivable
418 Customers—invoices to be issued
419 Advance payments from customers

**42 Payroll and similar accounts**
421 Employees—salaries payable
423 Other social benefits granted to employees
424 Profit share payable to employees
425 Advances to employees
426 Employees' rights not claimed
427 Retentions from salaries payable to third parties
428 Other employee-related debts and claims
*4281 Other employee-related debts*
*4282 Other employee-related claims*

**43 Social security and similar accounts**
431 Social security
*4311 Company's contribution to social security*
*4312 Employees' contribution to pension fund*
*4313 Company's contribution to health insurance*
*4314 Employees' contribution to health insurance*
437 Unemployment fund
*4371 Company's contribution to unemployment fund*
*4372 Employees' contribution to unemployment fund*
438 Other personnel-related debts and claims
*4381 Other personnel-related debts*
*4382 Other personnel-related claims*

**44 Amounts payable to the state budget, special funds and similar accounts**
441 Income tax
*4411 Tax on profit*
*4418 Income tax*
442 Value added tax
*4423 VAT payable*
*4424 VAT receivable*
*4426 Input VAT*
*4427 Output VAT*
*4428 VAT under settlement*
444 Tax on salaries
445 Subsidies
*4451 Government subsidies*
*4452 Non-repayable loans in the form of grants*
*4458 Other amounts received as subsidies*
446 Other taxes and similar liabilities

447 Special funds—taxes and similar liabilities
448 Other debts and claims with the Treasury
*4481 Other debts payable to the Treasury*
*4482 Other claims receivable from the Treasury*

### 45 Group and shareholders/associates
451 Settlement between affiliated entities
*4511 Settlement between affiliated entities*
*4518 Accrued interest for settlement between affiliated entities*
453 Transaction with associates and jointly controlled entities
*4531 Transactions with associates and jointly controlled entities*
*4538 Accrued interest on transactions with associates and jointly controlled entities*
455 Amounts owed to shareholders
*4551 Shareholders/associates—current accounts*
*4558 Accrued interest on shareholders'—current accounts*
456 Transactions with shareholders/associates related to capital
457 Dividends payable
458 Transactions related to joint operations
*4581 Transactions related to joint operations—liability*
*4582 Transactions related to joint operations—asset*

### 46 Sundry debtors and creditors
461 Sundry debtors
462 Sundry creditors

### 47 Accruals, subsidies and similar accounts
471 Deferred expenses
472 Deferred income
473 Suspense account
475 Investment subsidies
*4751 Governmental investment subsidies*
*4752 Non-repayable loans in the form of investment subsidies*
*4753 Investment donations*
*4754 Inventory surpluses in the form of non- current assets*
*4758 Other amounts received in the form of investment subsidies*
478 Deferred income related to assets received by transfer from customers

### 48 Internal transactions
481 Transactions between the entity and sub- units
482 Transactions between sub-units

### 49 Allowances for doubtful debts
491 Allowances for doubtful customers
495 Allowances for doubtful debts from group companies and shareholders / associates
496 Allowances for doubtful sundry debtors

**Class 5—Treasury accounts**

**50 Short term investments**
501 Shares in affiliated entities
505 Redeemed debentures
506 Debentures
507 Green certificates received
508 Other short term investments and related receivables
*5081 Other short term financial investments*
*5088 Accrued interest on debentures and short term investments*
509 Amounts payable for short term financial investments
*5091 Amounts payable for shares in affiliated entities*
*5092 Amounts payable for other short term financial investments*

**51 Bank accounts**
511 Outstanding lodgements
*5112 Cheques*
*5113 Bills of exchange held to maturity*
*5114 Bills of exchange forwarded for discount*
512 Cash at bank
*5121 Cash at bank in lei*
*5124 Cash at bank in foreign currencies*
*5125 Amounts under settlement*
518 Interest
*5186 Accrued interest payable*
*5187 Accrued interest receivable*
519 Short term bank loans
*5191 Short term bank loans*
*5192 Short term bank loans in arrears*
*5193 Foreign government loans*
*5194 Foreign loans guaranteed by the State*
*5195 Foreign loans guaranteed by banks*
*5196 State Treasury loans*
*5197 Domestic loans guaranteed by the State*
*5198 Accrued interest on short term loans*

**53 Petty cash**
531 Petty cash
*5311 Petty cash in lei*
*5314 Petty cash in foreign currencies*
532 Cash equivalents
*5321 Postage and fiscal stamps*
*5322 Holiday vouchers*
*5323 Transport tickets*
*5328 Other cash equivalents*

**54 Letters of credit**

541 Letters of credit
*5411 Letters of credit in lei*
*5414 Letters of credit in foreign currencies*
542 Cash advances

**58 Internal transfers**
581 Internal transfers

**59 Impairment of treasury accounts**
591 Impairment of shares in affiliated entities
595 Impairment of redeemed debentures
596 Impairment of debentures
598 Impairment of other short-term financial investments and related receivables

**Class 6—Expense accounts**
**60 Expenses related to inventories**
601 Raw materials
602 Consumables
*6021 Auxiliary materials*
*6022 Fuel*
*6023 Packaging materials*
*6024 Spare parts*
*6025 Seeds and sapling*
*6026 Fodder*
*6028 Other consumables*
603 Materials in the form of small inventory
604 Materials not stored
605 Electricity, heating and water
606 Biological assets in the form of inventories
607 Goods for resale
608 Packaging costs
609 Trade discounts received

**61 Third party services**
611 Maintenance and repair expenses
612 Royalties and rental expenses
613 Insurance premiums
614 Research expenses

**62 Other third party services**
621 Externally contracted manpower
622 Commissions and fees
623 Entertaining, promotion and advertising
624 Transport of goods and personnel
625 Travel
626 Postage and telecommunications

627 Bank commissions and similar charges
628 Other third party services

**63 Other taxes, duties and similar expenses**
635 Other taxes, duties and similar expenses

**64 Personnel expenses**
641 Salaries
642 Benefits in-kind and luncheon vouchers granted to employees
*6421 Benefits in-kind granted to employees*
*6422 Employees luncheon vouchers*
643 Expenses with remunerations in the form of own equity instruments
644 Expenses with bonuses for employees from profit
645 Social security contributions
*6451 Company's contribution to social security*
*6452 Company's contribution to unemployment fund*
*6453 Company's contribution to health insurance*
*6455 Company's contribution to life insurance*
*6456 Company's contribution to optional pension funds*
*6457 Company's contribution to voluntary health insurance premiums*
*6458 Other social security and welfare contributions*

**65 Other operating expenses**
652 Expenses with the environment protection
654 Bad debts written off
655 Expenses from revaluation of tangible assets
658 Other operating expenses
*6581 Compensations, fines and penalties*
*6582 Gifts and subsidies granted*
*6583 Net value of assets disposed of and other capital transactions*
*6586 Expenses representing transfers and contributions due under special acts*
*6587 Expenses related to natural disasters and other similar events*
*6588 Other operating expenses*

**66 Financial expenses**
663 Losses on amounts receivable in relation with long term financial investments
664 Losses on disposal of financial investments
*6641 Losses on disposal of long term financial investments*
*6642 Losses on disposal of short term financial investments*

**665 Foreign exchange losses**
*6651 Unfavorable foreign exchange differences related to monetary items denominated in foreign currency*
*6652 Unfavorable foreign exchange differences relating from evaluation of monetary items which belong to the net investment in a foreign entity*
666 Interest expense

667 Discounts granted
668 Other financial expenses

## 68 Depreciation and provisions; adjustments for impairment losses
681 Depreciation and provisions; adjustments for impairment losses—operating expenses
*6811 Depreciation of non current assets*
*6812 Provisions*
*6813 Impairment losses on non current assets*
*6814 Impairment of current assets*
*6817 Impairment losses on goodwill*
686 Impairment losses and write down of financial assets
*6861 Updating provisions*
*6863 Impairment losses on financial non-current assets*
*6864 Impairment of financial current assets*
*6868 Amortisation of premiums on redemption of debentures and other debts*

## 69 Income tax and other taxes
691 Income tax
698 Other taxes not included above

## Class 7—Revenue accounts
## 70 Net turnover
701 Sales of finished goods, agricultural products and biological assets in the form of inventories
*7015 Sales of finished goods*
*7017 Sales of agricultural products*
*7018 Sales of biological assets in the form of inventories*
702 Sales of semi-finished goods
703 Sales of residual products
704 Services rendered
705 Revenues from research studies
706 Rental and royalty income
707 Sale of goods purchased for resale
708 Revenues from sundry activities
709 Trade discounts offered

## 71 Revenues associated to the production cost of the work in progress
711 Revenues associated with the costs of inventories
712 Revenues associated with the cost of services in progress

## 72 Own work capitalised
721 Capitalised costs of intangible non-current assets
722 Capitalised costs of tangible non-current assets
725 Capitalised costs of investment property

## 74 Subsidies for operating activities

741 Subsidies for operating activities
*7411 Subsidies related to the turnover*
*7412 Subsidies for raw materials and consumables*
*7413 Subsidies for other external costs*
*7414 Subsidies for wages and salaries*
*7415 Subsidies for social security contributions*
*7416 Subsidies for other operating expenses*
*7417 Subsidies related to other income*
*7418 Subsidies related to interest payable*
*7419 Subsidies related to other income*

## 75 Other operating revenues
754 Bad debts written off and subsequently collected
755 Revaluation of tangible assets
758 Other operating revenues
*7581 Compensations, fines and penalties*
*7582 Gifts received*
*7583 Proceeds from disposal of assets and other capital transactions*
*7584 Amortisation of investment subsidies*
*7588 Other operating revenues*

## 76 Financial revenues
761 Revenues from long term financial investments
*7611 Revenues from shares in affiliated entities*
*7612 Revenues from shares in associates*
*7613 Revenues from shares in jointly controlled entities*
*7615 Revenues from other financial assets*
762 Revenues from short term financial investments
763 Revenues from long term receivables
764 Revenues on disposal of financial investments
*7641 Revenues from other financial investmets*
*7642 Gains on disposal of short term financial investments*
765 Foreign exchange gains
*7651 Favorable foreign exchange differences related to monetary items denominated in foreign currency*
*7652 Favorable foreign exchange differences relating from evaluation of monetary items which belong to the net investment in a foreign entity*
766 Interest income
767 Discounts received
768 Other financial revenues

## 78 Write back of provisions and adjustments for depreciation or impairment losses
781 Write back of provisions and adjustments for operating impairment losses
*7812 Write back of provisions*

7813 *Reversal of impairment losses on non-current assets*
7814 *Reversal of write-down of current assets*
7815 *Revenues from negative goodwill*
786 Reversal of adjustments for impairment losses
7863 *Reversal of impairment losses on financial non-current assets*
7864 *Reversal of write-down of financial current assets*

### Class 8—Special accounts
### 80 Off-balance sheet accounts
801 Commitments
*8011 Guarantees and endorsements*
*8018 Other commitments*
802 Commitments received
*8021 Guarantees and endorsements*
*8028 Other commitments received*
803 Other off-balance sheet accounts
*8031 Leased tangible assets*
*8032 Assets held for processing or repair*
*8033 Assets held in custody*
*8034 Receivables written off but still followed up*
*8035 Inventory under the form of used small inventory*
*8036 Royalties, rents and similar debts*
*8037 Bills of exchange discounted before maturity*
*8038 Goods received for administration, concession and rented*
8039 Other off-balance sheet items
805 Interest for the leasing and other assimilated contracts not held till maturity
*8051 Interest payable*
*8052 Interest receivable*
806 Certificates for green house gases emissions
807 Contingent assets
808 Contingent liabilities
809 Assignment of receivables

### 89 Balance sheet
891 Opening balance sheet
892 Closing balance sheet

### Class 9—Management accounts
### 90 Internal transactions
901 Internal transactions relating to expenses
902 Internal transactions related to costs of conversion
903 Internal transactions relating to price differences

### 92 Cost accounts

921 Costs related to the core business
922 Costs related to auxiliary activities
923 Production overheads
924 Administrative overheads
925 Distribution costs
93 Production cost
931 Cost of output
933 Cost of work in progress

# Bibliography

ACCA, Adjustments to financial statements, Financial Accounting (FA) Technical articles 2018, available at: https://www.accaglobal.com/sg/en/student/exam-support-resources/fundamentals-exams-study-resources/f3/technical-articles/adjustments-financial-statements.html (accessed 31 October 2018).

ACCA Complete Text—Taxation UK TX—Finance Act 2017, *Kaplan Publishing House*, 2018.

ACCA Complete Text P2 Advance Corporate Reporting, *Kaplan Publishing*, 2018.

ACCA Financial Reporting, Paper F7 (International), Course Notes, BPP Learning Media, 2011.

Alexander, D., Nobes, C., Financial Accounting: An International Introduction, *Pearson Education Limited*, first edition, Harlow, Great Britan, 2001.

BEPS Project Explanatory Statement, 2015 Final Reports, available online: https://www.oecd-ilibrary.org/taxation/beps-project-explanatory-statement_9789264263437-en (accessed 15 January 2019).

Deutsche Telekom Consolidated Annual Report for Financial Year 2017, Explanatory Note 6—Property, Plant and Equipment, available at: https://www.annualreport.telekom.com/site0218/notes/notes-to-the-consolidated-statement-of-financial-position/property-plant-and-equipment.html.

Dutescu, A., Ghid pentru întelegerea si aplicarea Standardelor Internationale de Contabilitate, *CECCAR Publishing House*, Bucuresti, 2002, ISBN 973-85640-8-5.

Dutescu, A., Olimid, L., Financial Accounting, *CECCAR Publishing House*, Bucuresti, 2004, ISBN 973-8478-56-1.

Dutescu, A., Popa, A.F., Ponoraca, A.G., Sustainability of the Turism Industry, Based on Financial Key Performance Indicators, *Amfiteatrul Economic*, vol. 16, special no. 8, pp. 1048–10, 2014.

European Patent Convention of 5 October 1973, as revised by the Act revising Article 63 EPC of 17 December 1991 and the Act revising the EPC of 29 November 2000, art. 52.

Gîrbină, M., Bunea, Ş., Sinteze, studii de caz şi teste grilă privind aplicarea IAS-IFRS revizuite, *CECCAR*, Bucureşti, 2008, România.

Harrison, W., Horngren, C., Thomas, W., Tietz, W., Financial Accounting, *Pearson Prentice Hall*, 11th Edition, 2016.

IASB, International Financial Reporting Standards, 2017 Edition.

Lien, D., The Use and Abuse of the Hedging Effectiveness Measure. *International Review of Financial Analysis*, No. 14, 2005.

Microsoft Corporation 2017 Annual Report, Note 9—Business Combinations, available at: https://www.microsoft.com/investor/reports/ar17/index.html.

OMV Petrom 2017 Annual Report, available at: https://www.omvpetrom.com/pbd_download/723/624/Annual_report_2017_print_en%20(1).pdf.

Paunescu, M., Romanian Taxation System; Editura ASE, 2014.

Paunescu, M. F 6 Taxation—Romanian Variant; Editura ASE, 2014.

Pugna, I.B, Dutescu, A., Stanila, G.O., Corporate Attitudes towards Big Data and Its Impact on Performance Management: A Qualitative Study, *Sustainability*, vol. 11 (3), 2019, available at: https://www.researchgate.net/publication/330706270_Corporate_Attitudes_towards_Big_Data_and_Its_Impact_on_Performance_Management_A_Qualitative_Study.

PWC, Derivative Instruments and Hedging Activities, second edition 2013, available at: https://www.pwc.com.cy/en/industries/assets/derivative-instruments-and-hedging-activities.pdf.

Stickney C.P., Weil, R., Schipper, K., Francis, J., Financial Accounting: An Introduction to Concepts, Methods and Uses, *Cengage Learning*, 2010.

## *Romanian Legislation*

Accounting Law no. 82/1991, as subsequently amended.

Law no. 84/1998 on Marks and Geographical Indications.

Ministry of Public Finance Order no. 1802/2014: Accounting Regulations on individual and consolidated annual financial statements, as subsequently amended and updated.

Patent Law no. 64/1991, as subsequently amended.

Romanian Company Law no.31/1990, as subsequently amended until 2009.

# Index

**A**
Accounting, 1–8, 10–12, 14, 18, 19, 21, 25, 29–32, 34, 36, 42, 44, 49, 52–54, 62–67, 69, 70, 72, 73, 79, 94, 98–100, 103, 105, 106, 109–111, 113–115, 117, 118, 120, 125–127, 131–133, 135, 139, 141, 143, 144, 146, 148, 151, 153, 158, 167, 170, 172, 175–178, 183–187, 191, 206, 207, 210, 217, 224, 228, 231, 232, 238, 239, 242, 244, 254, 262, 263, 265, 268–270, 276, 295, 302, 303, 305, 308, 311–316, 318, 319
Accounts, 1, 2, 7, 11, 36, 37, 67–71, 73, 74, 79–81, 83, 85, 86, 90, 92, 100, 111, 114, 117, 118, 129, 149, 160, 161, 186, 187, 195, 201, 232, 243, 248, 273, 297
Accruals, 18, 47, 81, 99, 114, 205, 248, 263, 265
Acquisition cost, 94, 95, 104, 112, 127, 140, 141, 147, 159, 173, 175, 182–184, 186, 187, 198, 201, 202, 230, 310
Adjustments, 2, 14, 48, 201, 218, 261, 263, 264, 289, 310, 313, 315
Amortised cost, 246, 247, 252
Assets, 4, 7, 8, 15, 19–21, 23, 24, 30–32, 34, 35, 37, 39, 40, 42, 48, 49, 52, 53, 62, 64–67, 69, 70, 86, 89, 93, 131, 132, 135, 136, 140, 143–148, 150–152, 157, 158, 161, 162, 166–168, 170, 178, 186, 187, 190, 192, 193, 195, 198, 206, 209, 222, 242, 243, 245, 254, 261, 262, 270, 273, 280–282, 288, 298, 300, 308, 312, 314, 315

**B**
Balance, 19, 52–54, 68–70, 72, 86, 100, 105–107, 111, 118, 120, 126, 152, 153, 158, 159, 161, 185, 224, 226, 228, 229, 231, 238, 267, 290, 312

Balance Sheet, 2, 6, 15, 17, 18, 20, 22–24, 29–32, 35, 37–40, 42, 46, 48–51, 53, 62, 64, 81, 86, 90–93, 100–102, 107–110, 126, 129, 140, 142, 145–147, 153, 156, 157, 162, 166–170, 178, 185, 187, 190, 192–194, 196, 197, 204, 206, 207, 218, 226, 230–232, 238, 246, 250, 262–265, 267, 280, 289, 291, 293
Bonds, 36, 38, 39, 192, 204, 205, 243—247, 249, 250, 253–255

## C

Capital, 4, 5, 8, 16, 19, 35, 36, 38–40, 48, 53, 65, 68, 89, 140, 143, 151, 174, 205, 221–231, 238, 241, 243, 244, 247, 251, 277, 282, 283, 292, 293, 298–300, 305–307
Carrying amount, 21, 23, 144, 146, 147, 152, 156–159, 162–164, 167–169, 173, 175–177, 184–186, 246, 247, 253, 265, 270
Cash, 6, 8, 14–16, 20–24, 30, 32, 35–38, 46–50, 52, 53, 64–66, 68, 74, 90–92, 127, 152, 167, 171, 190, 213, 222, 224–226, 238, 242, 246, 248, 253, 254, 262, 271, 273, 278, 291
Cash equivalents, 35, 37, 49–51
Closing procedures, 64, 261
Company, 2–4, 6, 8, 10, 11, 14, 15, 17–25, 34–36, 38–41, 45, 47, 52, 62, 64–67, 70, 73, 74, 90, 92, 94–96, 98–100, 102, 103, 107–109, 111, 112, 114, 118, 120, 125–129, 131, 133–135, 139, 141, 142, 146, 147, 149, 151, 152, 161, 166, 170–173, 175–178, 182–187, 189–191, 193–203, 206, 209–213, 217–219, 222–231, 233, 234, 238, 239, 242–244, 246, 247, 249, 252, 258, 259, 267–270, 273, 274, 278–283, 290–293, 296, 297, 302, 307, 308, 312–316, 318, 319
Company Law, 2, 5, 7, 143, 223
Cost, 2, 18, 19, 21–24, 31, 34, 43, 46, 52, 55, 62, 75, 94, 99–104, 106–110, 114, 116, 118, 135, 140–147, 151, 152, 156, 158, 161–163, 167, 168, 170, 172, 174, 176, 177, 183, 201, 205, 218, 234, 244, 247, 262, 264, 265, 270, 272, 282, 288, 290, 296, 298, 301, 309, 310
Cost of goods sold, 43, 99, 103, 112, 113, 117, 127
Credit, 46, 47, 68–70, 72–75, 78–81, 115, 120, 156, 195, 231, 252, 253, 279
Current assets, 2, 32, 35–37, 39–41, 51–53, 57, 59, 60, 107, 109, 124, 136, 139, 147, 160, 265, 266, 275, 277, 278
Current liabilities, 32, 37–40, 49, 191, 192, 203, 250, 265, 278

## D

Debit, 68–74, 78–81, 84, 109, 110, 120, 156, 201, 228, 229, 231, 289
Depreciation, 8, 34, 35, 42, 43, 45, 95, 98, 113, 114, 125, 127, 128, 132, 143, 145–147, 149–151, 153, 156–159, 161–163, 165, 168, 170, 172, 173, 175, 177, 178, 182–187, 207, 218, 234, 253, 263, 288, 290, 312, 313, 315

Depreciation methods, 14, 52, 151–153, 160–162, 179, 180, 182–185
Derivative, 241, 243, 245, 246, 253, 254
Diminishing balance methods, 158, 183
Direct tax, 302, 303, 306
Disclosure, 15, 17–19, 31, 49, 53–56, 108, 109, 167, 190, 199, 212, 230, 231
Disposal, 104–106, 112, 113, 129, 140, 167, 184, 185, 234, 239
Double-declining method, 158, 163, 168, 169, 185, 218
Duties, 94, 140, 298

### E
Equity, 2, 15, 16, 19–21, 30, 31, 37, 40, 46, 52, 53, 64, 65, 67–70, 79, 81, 84, 86, 89, 90, 166, 169, 193, 221, 223, 226, 231, 233, 238, 242–246, 249, 254, 258, 261, 262, 276, 279, 282, 315
Estimates, 108, 128, 151, 172, 183, 185, 187, 210–212, 252, 259, 267, 269, 291, 314
Expenses, 15, 18, 20, 21, 30, 34, 37, 41–47, 49, 104, 107

### F
Fair value, 3, 23, 24, 31, 143, 146, 162, 166–168, 174, 175, 184, 185, 187, 206, 218, 233, 234, 239, 246, 249, 252–255, 258, 259, 262
Financial accounting, 6, 9, 10, 29, 149
Financial Accounting Standards Board (FASB), 2

Financial instruments, 39, 195, 242–247, 249, 251–253, 319
Financial ratios, 273, 276
Financial statements, 4–6, 8, 11–20, 22, 23, 25, 27, 29–31, 43, 53–56, 62, 63, 79, 80, 93, 100, 107, 110, 136, 141, 142, 145, 146, 148, 152, 157, 163, 164, 168–170, 185, 187, 196, 199, 207, 210, 211, 213, 218, 219, 222, 231, 238, 244, 258, 259, 261, 263, 268, 270–274, 276, 288, 291, 292, 295, 312
First-in-first-out (FIFO), 100–104, 107–109, 112, 113, 118, 120, 129
Foreign currency, 171, 172, 198, 224, 245, 253

### H
Hedge, 241, 242, 253–255

### I
Impairment adjustment, 109, 110, 177, 178
Income, 8, 21, 33, 37, 53, 163, 170, 187, 252, 297–305, 307, 309, 315, 318
Income statement, 6, 15, 30, 41, 43, 44, 46–50, 64, 79, 85, 90, 92, 109, 129, 139, 218, 265–269, 271, 272, 274, 291
Income tax, 37, 38, 43, 49, 134, 136, 191, 192, 207, 263, 296, 297, 299–304, 309, 310, 315, 316
Indirect tax, 8, 95, 141, 201, 203, 302, 303
Initial recognition, 94, 140, 141, 143, 174, 175, 246, 249

Intangible assets, 32, 34, 48, 131–133, 135, 136, 139, 146, 149, 156, 158, 161, 179
International Accounting Standards Board (IASB), 2, 12, 13, 16, 18, 22, 30, 132, 241
International Financial Reporting Standards (IFRS), 2, 12, 13, 19, 56, 98, 100, 103, 109, 110, 113, 139, 148, 149, 167, 190, 195, 205, 223, 241–243, 246, 251, 252, 265
Inventories valuation/measurement, 14, 22–24, 132, 137, 167, 174, 190, 191, 228, 246, 247
Inventory, 13, 15, 23, 24, 27, 32, 34–36, 38, 41, 51, 62, 64, 73, 76, 90, 93–95, 99–112, 115–120, 125, 127, 129, 176, 189, 191, 193, 201, 261–265, 275, 277–279, 288–290, 293

## J
Journal entry, 63, 73–79, 85, 111, 116, 120, 142, 145, 147, 148, 157, 160–162, 168, 169, 194, 196, 202, 203, 205, 210, 217, 218, 224, 225, 227–230, 233, 238, 239, 247, 250, 255, 263–268, 271, 272, 289

## L
Last-In-First-Out (LIFO), 100, 102, 103, 106, 107
Leasing, 20, 191, 193, 205, 206, 208, 218
Liabilities, 4, 8, 15, 17, 19–25, 27, 30–32, 36–38, 40, 64, 66–71, 73–75, 77, 79, 81, 84, 86, 87, 89, 90, 111, 136, 142, 167, 174, 189–193, 196, 198, 201, 203–207, 209, 210, 212, 213, 222, 224, 225, 231, 242–244, 246–250, 254, 258, 261, 262, 265, 270, 271, 275, 299, 307
Liquidity, 14–16, 32, 39, 40, 84, 253, 277, 292, 293
Loss, 21, 39, 41–46, 49, 53, 62, 72, 116, 117, 142, 147, 174, 195, 196, 198, 221, 223, 225, 229, 231, 233, 238, 249, 252–254, 262, 263, 302, 315, 316, 319

## M
Managerial accounting, 6, 7, 9, 10

## N
Net realisable value, 23, 24, 62, 103, 108, 109, 127, 129, 262, 264, 265, 288, 290
Non-current assets valuation, 151
Non-current liabilities, 32, 37, 190, 192, 203, 204, 250

## P
Performance, 6, 7, 14–16, 18–20, 29, 30, 53, 54, 65, 73, 134, 144, 167, 273, 283, 292, 293
Periodic inventory, 108, 117–119
Perpetual inventory, 118, 119
Production cost, 94–96, 98–100, 108, 117, 126, 127, 129, 143, 149, 184
Profit, 3, 10, 14, 15, 21, 30, 39, 41–46, 52, 53, 62, 72, 100, 103, 107, 113, 166, 174, 201–203, 219, 221, 223, 225, 227–232, 249, 254, 262, 263, 272, 273, 280–283, 291, 296, 299, 301, 302, 309–316, 318, 319

Profit and Loss Account, 6, 10, 13, 15, 16, 21, 29, 30, 41, 42, 45, 47, 53, 72, 79, 81, 83, 85, 86, 100, 113, 114, 116, 144, 148, 153, 156, 162, 170, 172, 231, 254, 255, 265, 292, 315

Property, plant and equipment, 32–34, 48, 132, 144, 153, 154, 174, 233, 234

Provisions, 54–56, 81, 110, 192, 195, 203, 207, 209–213, 230, 246, 268, 269, 296, 305–307

## R

Receivables, 27, 32, 34–36, 49, 92, 110, 111, 186, 190, 191, 193–196, 198, 203, 210, 212, 215, 226, 228, 243, 262, 263, 267, 268, 270, 271, 278, 289, 315

Recoverable value, 24, 176, 178, 187, 288, 289

Reserves, 53, 163, 164, 179, 221, 225–231, 233, 235, 238, 239, 263

Residual value, 145, 151, 152, 156, 158, 159, 163, 168, 183, 185–187, 206, 218, 239

Retained earnings, 39, 42, 45, 52, 225–227, 229, 231, 233–235, 238, 263, 316

Revaluation, 24, 27, 42, 53, 143, 146, 153, 162–164, 166, 184, 186, 198, 221, 233–235, 239

Revenues, 15, 18, 21, 30, 36, 38, 41–44, 47, 49, 62, 67, 68, 70, 72, 79, 81, 85, 99, 107, 112–115, 117, 135, 144, 148, 169, 194, 210–212, 231, 249, 261–263, 265, 273, 302, 305, 307, 312–316, 318

Revenue tax, 302

## S

Salary, 38, 42, 191, 193, 201, 217, 301, 303, 306

Shares, 4, 5, 34–36, 39, 47, 52, 53, 92, 133, 222, 223, 225–230, 233, 238, 243–246, 249, 250, 253, 258, 259, 283

Solvency, 15, 40

Statement of cash-flow (Cash-Flow Statement), 6, 10, 29, 47, 52, 122, 201, 205, 218

Statement of Changes in Equity, 6, 16, 29, 30, 52–54

Statement of the Financial Position, 6, 30, 33

Straight-line method, 145, 153, 156, 182–187, 239, 288, 290, 312, 314

Subsequent expenditure, 140, 144

Subsequent measurement, 174

## T

Tangible assets, 34, 48, 131, 132, 136, 146, 149–151, 179

Taxable profit, 8, 10, 263, 302, 312–315, 318

Taxation system, 297, 301

Tax avoidance, 296, 307–309, 311

Taxes, 8, 38, 43, 45, 140, 168, 191, 200, 296–308, 311, 312, 318

Tax evasion, 296, 307–309

Trial balance, 64, 79–82, 84, 87, 90, 127, 186, 261–263, 267, 283, 289, 291

True and fair view, 6, 18, 29, 54, 107

## U

Useful life, 8, 132, 144, 145, 150–152, 156, 158–161, 163, 170, 172, 173, 176, 182–187, 234, 239, 290, 314

US Generally Accepted Accounting Principles (US GAAP), 2, 12, 37, 103, 190

## V
Value-Added-Tax (VAT), 43, 92, 94, 95, 103, 110–113, 115, 118, 125, 126, 128, 141, 142, 145, 147, 156, 163, 168, 171, 183, 184, 186, 201–203, 212, 218, 300, 303, 306–308
Value in use, 167, 168, 185, 187, 262

## W
Weighted-Average-Cost (WAC), 103–106

# Financial Accounting